THE BRITI

THE BRITISH OFFICER
Leading the Army from 1660 to the Present

ANTHONY CLAYTON

Routledge
Taylor & Francis Group

LONDON AND NEW YORK

First published 2006 by Pearson Education Limited
Hardback edition published in 2006
This paperback edition published 2007

Published 2013 by Routledge
2 Park Square, Milton Park, Abingdon, Oxon OX14 4RN
711 Third Avenue, New York, NY 10017, USA

Routledge is an imprint of the Taylor & Francis Group, an informa business

ISBN 13: 978-1-4058-5901-1 (pbk)

British Library Cataloguing in Publication Data
A CIP catalogue record for this book can be obtained from the British Library

Set by 35

In memory of my wife
Judith,
who devotedly supported my writing this work,
but did not live to see its publication

CONTENTS

FOREWORD

This work sets out to chronicle the origins, development and roles of the Regular officers of the British Army from the Restoration to the present. It is not a history of the Army, still less studies of generalship or campaigns. My subject has been the combat arms regimental officer from officer cadet and Lieutenant to Major and Lieutenant-Colonel. Generals may plan operations but it falls to regimental officers to convert those plans into action on the ground and actually lead soldiers in accordance with the plans; a study of the regimental officer is therefore a valid theme. In particular, the physical conditions in which regimental officers have to make life and death decisions may be very severe, circumstances not always understood either by political leaders who have not served in any of the Armed Services, or by a general public reared in the age of the Health and Safety Executive. But almost always, from Tangier in the 1660s to Iraq in 2003–04, some knowledge of the very different ranges of conditions is essential to any understanding of the work of an officer.

For obvious reasons of producing a book of readable length this work has to be generally limited to the study of career Regular officers, though the Army's massive expansion in the two 20th century World Wars needed some extension. Also, in conflicts from the 18th century onwards, the Army has often been engaged in fighting in several parts of the world simultaneously, yet space has again perforce limited study to conditions in the principal theatre or theatres where the greatest number of officers were involved.

Setting out as it does to be a history of the evolution of the role of the military officer, this work is not offering social behavioural analyses of command and cohesion loyalties, though material concerning officers' relationships with the rank and file may be common to both the discipline of history and that of social anthropology.

A further very important point needs to be made at this outset. The work of officers in leading, training and administering a military unit is only one side of the coin, the work of the unit's Non-Commissioned Officers, Warrant Officers, Sergeants and Corporals, being of equal importance. This point is made again in the chapters that follow. This work's study must, however, limit itself to the one group, commissioned officers.

Officers have, of course, always been paid, in the early years sometimes more in theory than in practice. Often the pay has been meagre, officers being expected to recoup from a variety of practices which would now be considered corrupt, or to have private incomes or an expectation of wealth to inherit. These factors limit the value of attempts, until the 20th century, to equate officers' pay to their needs, the salaries of other professions, or standards of living. Rates of pay at different times are recorded in the chronological chapters, and in Appendix 3 some guidance on needs and living costs are set out.

A very rich source for any study of Army officers is regimental history. Almost all regiments or corps in the Army have produced their histories, some of outstanding quality. The recently produced history of the Devonshire Regiment, for example, provides a wealth of material on regimental life and the part played by the regiment in the history of the county. One is of course aware that regimental histories will dwell on the work of good officers while remaining discreet about those found to be less satisfactory, and even more aware that the sources selected for this work as representative are only a fraction of the total available, a total that would require a lifetime's study.

Many people have helped me with advice and criticism, but I have several especial debts of gratitude. The first is to my old friend and colleague of Territorial Army days, Charles Carlton; he suggested that I should write this work. A second is to Andrew Orgill and all his staff at the Central Library of the Royal Military Academy Sandhurst for all the help they always provide and, as important, the welcome that I always receive on my working days in the library. Without this help and encouragement, this book could never have been written. Other especial helpers include senior officers, serving and retired, who found time to read and give me immensely valuable comments on the manuscript, or sections of it. A few of these were in very responsible active appointments, my debt to them all the greater.

Friends and colleagues who have also helped include Lieutenant-Colonel Michael Broadway, John Card, Jock Haswell, Julian James, Dr Tony Heathcote, Matthew Midlane, Professor Michael Mott, Michael Orr, Penelope Hatfield, Lieutenant-Colonel Roger Robinson, Dr John Sweetman and Professor H.P. Willmott. A third and very large group who have contributed, often simply by personal example, are the many Regular officers with whom I have worked during my years on the Academic Staff at Sandhurst, and also during my service in the Territorial Army. So many of them have enriched my understanding of their profession.

For work, at times very arduous indeed, in turning my handwritten manuscript chapters and footnotes into a readable typescript I am, as I have been for many years and for other books, greatly indebted to Monica Alexander for all her patience and care.

For so many of the illustrations I am very grateful to the number of regiments that have allowed me to use photographs or drawings in their regimental histories.

I would like finally to thank the staff of Pearson Higher and Professional Education for all their support in completing this manuscript. I appreciated it particularly at a difficult time in my own life.

Anthony Clayton
University of Surrey

ACKNOWLEDGEMENTS

We are grateful to the following for permission to reproduce copyright material:

Plates 1 and 17 reproduced by kind permission of The Princess of Wales's Royal Regiment and its forbear Queen's Royal (West Surrey) Regiment; Plates 2 and 22 reproduced by kind permission of the Regimental Lieutenant Colonel Coldstream Guards; Plate 3 reproduced by permission of The Royal Scots (The Royal Regiment); Plate 4 reproduced by permission of The Black Watch (Royal Highland Regiment); Plates 5 and 32 reproduced by permission of The Royal Welch Fusiliers; Plate 6 reproduced by permission of The Royal Artillery Institution; Plate 7 reproduced by permission of The Museum of the King's Royal Hussars; Plate 8 reproduced by permission of The Royal Norfolk Regiment Association and The Royal Anglian Regiment Association (Norfolk); Plate 9 reproduced by permission of The Institution of the Royal Army Service Corps and the Royal Corps of Transport; Plate 10 reproduced by permission of The Royal Green Jackets; Plates 11 and 33 reproduced by permission of the Scots Guards; Plate 12 reproduced by permission of the Royal Tigers' Association, The Royal Leicestershire Regiment and Leicestershire Branch, The Royal Anglian Regiment; Plate 14 reproduced by permission of The Royal Dragoon Guards; Plate 15 reproduced by permission of The Worcestershire

Regiment Museum Trust; Plate 16 reproduced by permission of The Regimental Museum, The Duke of Cornwall's Light Infantry; Plates 18 and 24 reproduced by permission of The Trustees of the Imperial War Museum, London; Plate 19 reproduced by permission of Queen Alexandra's Royal Army Nursing Corps; Plates 20 and 23 reproduced by permission of Regimental Museum 1st The Queen's Dragoon Guards; Plate 21 reproduced by permission of the Irish Guards; Plate 25 reproduced courtesy of the Trustees of the Army Medical Services Museum; Plate 30 reproduced by permission of Sir John Baynes and the Old Comrades of the Cameronians Association; Plates 31 and 34 reproduced by permission of The Institution of Royal Engineers; Plate 35 © Crown Copyright/MOD, reproduced with the permission of the Controller of Her Majesty's Stationery Office.

In some instances we have been unable to trace the owners of copyright material, and we would appreciate any information that would enable us to do so.

CHAPTER I

INTRODUCTION – THE HISTORY
OF A PROFESSION

The British Army Regimental Officer of the early 21st century, on training or in action, will appear almost indistinguishable from the rank and file; only a small drab tag bearing the badge of rank hanging on his or her chest will show that the wearer holds the Sovereign's Commission. The uniform, a camouflage combat kit, will bear no medal ribbons; even rank badge shoulder epaulettes, too easy for a sniper marksman to discern, have gone. Nevertheless the simple tag carries an authority and a status that has a long historical tradition.

This work concerns the regimental officer of the Regular Army, the man and, from the 20th century on, the woman inside the uniform. Successive chapters will seek to show who the officers of the Army, from the days of King Charles II to the present, have been and are, from where they came, what ideals or traditions have motivated them and their own perceptions of themselves. Also discussed are officers' relationships with the men they command, their training, initial and continuous, for their role, the linkages between the military and the nation's royal, political and social establishments and, by no means least, the personal family issues facing officers in their careers. These all have to be seen amid evolving national history, developments in military technology and changing concepts within leadership practice and theory. All contribute to the mystique behind the drab tag, but the wearer is still an individual with a personal mix of values, virtues and weaknesses. Chapters 15 and 16 will be concerned with the Indian Army and colonial regiments, and with specialist professional officers such as doctors and chaplains.

Military combat has, from Old Testament times, always required the services of a small number of individuals who will provide the leadership required for, and by, large bodies of men, the followships. These men need, firstly, the purely professional skills required for the type of combat in which they are engaged, the skills of weaponry and tactics. However, equally important, good officers have increasingly needed and developed group dynamics, the ability to lead people to perform deeds of which they never believed they could be capable, to endure hardship, ceaseless toil and monotony, to subordinate their own individual interests to that of the team, to face fear and, if so required, the unlimited commitment of injury and death. Two such men, within recent memory, were Colonel James Carne of the Gloucestershire Regiment in Korea in 1951 and Colonel 'H' Jones of the Parachute Regiment in the Falklands in 1982. Without such abilities the ablest field tactician may not succeed in motivating his soldiers sufficiently to secure a victory. The abilities imply inner personal qualities much less easy to define or describe, an empathy with the followship, the ability to understand the needs of the soldier, to appreciate the qualities and recognise the anxieties in each individual, and an intuition that can sense the state of morale within a group even if it is not expressed in words. These qualities have roots in ancient Greek concepts of obligation, Roman stoicism, Christian concern for fellow humans and a romantic sense of purpose higher than self-interest. With many honourable exceptions, however, they were not greatly evident in the mass of officers of the 17th and early 18th centuries where the officer–soldier relationship was too often one of institutional corruption, indifference and social class superiority on the part of the officer, with fear of punishment among the soldiers. Change was to develop slowly throughout the 18th and 19th centuries, in part occasioned by the military needs of weapons and tactics and in part by the changing nature of both society and the followership. Soldiers became increasingly recruited from restless urban societies no longer possessing the hierarchic cohesion of the countryside, and in the mid-20th century expecting to be told very clearly why they were being asked to risk their lives. At the same time, officers' perceptions of their responsibilities progressively widened.

The qualities do not replace management, they extend it. Management can deploy a soldier to the front line, furnish him with clothing, equipment and weaponry that he will need, and train him for the conditions of battle. But something more is needed to provide the *élan* for an attack or for a dogged defence under great pressure, involving the risking of life; the challenge of the battlefield, whether the Northern Ireland border or Iraq, is of a very different order to that of the market or the production line and one requiring a much greater sense of purpose. Unit command certainly requires an element of management as well as leadership, but within a regiment, at sub-unit levels, company, squadron, battery, platoon, troop, personal leadership is all-important. The army, the regiment, needs to be seen by the soldier as an institution they admire, in which they are proud to serve, and not an occupational job to do in order to move on to the next, more profitable, appointment.[1]

And here it becomes possible to extrapolate and summarise that within the institution, army or regiment, the leader – the officer – has to operate in a triangular relationship of which he or she is one point, the second being their rank and file, and the third the society and political direction that recruit, pay and deploy them. The styles of command from officer to soldier have varied and evolved clearly according to the changing social backgrounds, education and psychology of the soldier. Much more opaque has been the third, the attitudes of the British public and society as a whole towards the Army and its officers.

A conditioning factor for the relationship between the first two points of the triangle, the officer and the soldier, is the tradition, with origins derived from the insular situation of the country and its common law tradition, that service in the Army should generally be voluntary and not obligatory. Of course push factors such as poverty, unemployment and a tiff with either a lover or the law have led men throughout the ages to volunteer where in happier economic or social circumstances they might have chosen a less demanding profession. Nevertheless, the ethos has, except for the last years of the First World War and the years 1939 to 1960, generally been one of voluntary engagement, free men from a free society of their own will accepting discipline and the responsibility of bearing arms. The British soldier is a 'private' and has never been an automaton; on parade he looks the inspecting officer in the eye as he stands in front of him, he does not swivel his gaze around before and after the officer passes. Drill and division into small units and sub-units, both essential for military duties, have over the last 200 years been designed for officers and soldiers alike to remould the individual as a soldier, not to destroy his individuality as a person. Perhaps the most famous of all the British Army marches, Kenneth Alford's *Colonel Bogey* – especially the traditional barrack room words attached to the tune – illustrates best the paradoxical mix of respect and readiness to accept discipline with at the same time a good humoured, almost two-fingered, gesture towards authority.

It can also be argued that the antecedents of the British Army in the Middle Ages and Early Modern periods left other specifically English marks on the concept of a military officer that survive to this day. In the Middle Ages no standing army was thought necessary except, from 1486, the purely palace force of the Yeomen of the Guard. When men were needed, the monarchs, from Saxons to Tudors, turned to landowners, many of whom at one time or another had received gifts of land from the monarch, and expected all landowners, aristocrat or squire, to furnish men for the *fyrd* (the Saxon armed force) and later the Militia. For this they were given a Colonelcy commission and some money – insufficient for the costs involved. Later, individuals were given indentures to raise bodies of mercenaries for operations outside England as the Militia were not liable unless they volunteered – or were coerced. A rudimentary draft system for the Militia, providing for some very basic military training, was created in the reign of Queen Elizabeth I. Throughout, however, for its commanders, the Militia process involved concepts, later inherited by the Army, of an element of financial 'sacrifice', of *noblesse oblige*. This element included a linkage binding local notables in any particular county or region with the monarchy, together with a leadership based on the local notables, gentlemen.[2] Until 1939 officer cadets at both the Royal Military Academy Woolwich and the Royal Military College Sandhurst were styled 'Gentleman Cadet', a style abolished by the post-1945 Labour Government.

The units of volunteers and Militia sent to fight, not always very satisfactorily, in the Netherlands in the last fifteen years of the 16th century were formed of between 700 and 900 men with a Colonel in command and the men divided into companies commanded by a Captain. Above unit level were a number of 'Colonel-Generals', with at the summit a Master General of the Ordnance, a Master Gunner and a Forage Master, and at Commander-in-Chief level a Serjeant-Major General. The term 'Colonel' derived from the Italian word *colonnal*, a little column, i.e. the officer leading the little column at the head of a regiment; 'General' became the term attached to an officer whose command was general, i.e. not limited to one or a very small group of units. But, in sum, the style, one to last for a long time, was that of the amateur rather than the professional and Queen Elizabeth I's military units were far from being a standing army.

The Civil War armies, those of both the King and the Parliamentarians, and especially Cromwell's New Model Army, provided even more distinctive and long-lasting marks. The Royalists' tradition reaffirmed a personal loyalty to the person of the Sovereign; at the battle of Naseby the field word of the Royalists was 'Queen Mary'. Cadets at Sandhurst are to this day commissioned following a 'Sovereign's Parade'. From the Parliamentarian armies came the concept of military service in a just moral cause, both the cause and the role of the officer being execution of the Will of Almighty God. At the battle of Dunbar Cromwell's Army's word was 'The Lord of Hosts'!

In 1644, in the *Souldiers Catechisme*, the troops of the Parliamentary Army were instructed that the Word of God assured them that their profession was a noble one; that their cause, a religious one, was just, as their adversaries had persecuted justice, liberty and true religion; that they owed it to posterity and to themselves to stand up for the good; that those who did not share these beliefs were at best cowards if not actual enemies with whom God would deal; that their cause being good would prevail and that of the enemy being bad would fail because God was on the side of the righteous; and that if soldiers were good and God-fearing they would be blessed by God.[3] This catechism could have been written by Field-Marshal Montgomery in 1944, the wording in his Orders of the Day was but little different.[4]

The demands of the wars forced both sides into organising armies and units into much more clearly defined structures and military hierarchies for the sake of efficient command and control. Cromwell's New Model Army of 1645, which by 1649 had incorporated most of the units of the other Parliamentarian forces, already shows a familiar officer rank structure. At the top was the Commander-in-Chief, the Lord General (one, briefly, was even given an honorific role as Field-Marshal), the General's deputy a Lieutenant-General, a number of staff Generals for particular purposes, such as pay, transport, victuals and intelligence, Serjeant-Major Generals (Serjeant being soon dropped from the title) commanding formations, Colonels in command of infantry, cavalry or dragoon regiments assisted by a Lieutenant-Colonel and a Major, together with Captains, Lieutenants and Ensigns for the infantry companies or Cornets for the cavalry troops, and Quartermasters. Surgeons and Chaplains were also provided for regiments.[5] The officers of both the Royalist and Parliamentarian armies were mostly landed gentry and squirearchy, though the Parliamentarians did also include a number from trades and crafts. Equally important from the Civil War period, more from the red-coated Parliamentarian units than those of the King, was inherited the vital and distinctive British component of the relationship between the officer and his soldiers, the regiment itself, with binding personal and psychological linkages. With the possible exception perhaps of the French Army's *Troupes de Marine*, no other 21st century army has a military unit system in which the unit is so much a mutual-obligation extended family in which the officers develop a paternal concern for the welfare of their men. In time this came to extend to assistance in times of trouble not only during but also after military service. Regiments and regimental *esprit de corps* also create both a determination not to let the regiment and fellow members down and, in addition, a competitive spirit in rivalry with other units, all of enormous value for military efficiency.[6] Both sides sought, with varying degrees of success, to discipline their armies with a strongly developed regimental system. From medieval times army commanders had issued codes, laws, articles or orders for the disciplining of soldiers – and officers. In both the Civil War armies these were modelled on Swedish or Dutch codes. In the Parliamentarian armies, officers commanding units were required to have a copy and read it aloud regularly to the men under their command. Regimental courts tried minor offences, courts-martial the more serious. The New Model Army was the better disciplined, punishments ranged from shooting or hanging for mutiny; whipping (up to sixty lashes) for plundering, violence or fraud; or for minor offences running the gauntlet, sitting for periods of time on an uncomfortably angled wooden horse stand with hands tied and weights attached to legs, mutilation and branding, or an open humiliation. Marriage without leave was severely punished. Officers convicted of offences were usually cashiered; pay fraud and drunkenness were the commonest officer offences.

The Cromwell Protectorate era also saw the first example of a commitment to be undertaken by the British Army in centuries to follow: colonial warfare and the maintenance of order in tropical territories. In 1655 General Monck sent four companies of foot soldiers to take Jamaica. The expedition, like many others subsequently, was poorly prepared in every way, the soldiers suffering and dying from disease; it was, however, eventually successful. A final but less fortunate mark left by the political armies of the Civil War, in particular the Parliamentarians, was a public distaste for the military, a consequence of the bloodshed and destruction caused by the war, high taxation, billeting, the depredations of unpaid soldiers and the arbitrary rule of ambitious generals. Other factors, among them the peripheral but dominant social class from which the majority of officers were drawn in the three centuries that followed, the occasional use of the military for repressive purposes, military incompetence and the on-going looting and raping by drunken soldiers, all served to perpetuate this distaste and, for the Army and its officers, contributed to their sense of distance from wider society. Change in public attitudes really only became effective during and after the Second World War, with, firstly, the popular image of Field-Marshal Montgomery, 'Monty', at last bringing both military success and a remarkable common touch when addressing soldiers or the general public and, secondly, the increasing skill shown by the Army in operations since 1945.

Other formative features are considered in detail in the chapters that follow, commencing with the three Restoration armies, English, Scottish and Irish, forming the first non-political permanent standing force, a British Army, albeit federal, raised to fight for the British Sovereign against the Sovereign's foreign foes. These features include the long-lasting effects on the officer of the system of purchasing commissions and, on-going until the Second World War, an anti-intellectual self-confidence, too often to prove disastrous, and belief that the innate abilities of the gentleman amateur would always triumph over the professional or the native tribesman. The regimental system developed a clan-like loyalty binding officers, NCOs and soldiers with, for the officers also, a gentleman's club. A view held until the 1960s and even the 1970s was that young eighteen- or nineteen-year-old officers would show dash in the field and be most easily moulded into the pattern of their regiments. Empire entailed the social consequences for officers of much military service being outside Britain. An identity of values – moral, social and sporting – was shared with the ruling establishment with on-going legitimisation of military service by its links, the King's (or Queen's) Commission and the Oath of Allegiance, to the Sovereign and therefore believed to be free of political partisanship. Existing to this day also, despite the temptations of consumer society, remains the belief that the army officer's calling is something special, a vocation for which not all men or women can meet the required standard, and for which voluntary personal sacrifices have to be made for the common good, even if the commercially minded and the general public may show little or no appreciation or gratitude.

In sum, the centuries of gentlemanly amateurism came eventually to blend with military professionalism, together with an institutional classical and later Victorian sense of obligation and service. Combat would be only in good cause. The military profession would be a vocation, not 'just a job'.[7] This philosophy of life remained unquestioned until the end of the 20th century. It was also the keystone of the third point of the triangle, the improvement over time in the relationship between the Army's officers and the public, a keystone carefully nurtured at times to a point of mystique by the Army in defence against charges that it was not fulfilling a productive role. The professionalism and courage of officers and the opening of opportunities for men and women from all socio-economic groups to become officers revived public respect, even if at times a little grudging, for most of the second half of the 20th century.

The turn of the century, however, was to see both profound social change and an enormous increase in media attention on the Army, in particular its officers, with significant consequences for regimental officers, responsibilities and the attitude of the public towards them. Chapter 14 and the conclusion of this work in Chapter 17 seek to set out some of these consequences.

NOTES

1 A useful study of this subject appears in Charles G. Moskos and Frank R. Wood (Editors), *The Military: More than Just a Job?* (London and Washington, Pergamon and Brasseys, 1988).

2 The services of the *fyrd* and Militia are well summarised in John Pimlott, *The Guinness History of the British Army* (London, Guinness, 1993), i.

3 A summary appears in Norman Copeland, *Psychology and the Soldier: The Art of Leadership* (London, Allen and Unwin, 1944), 94–95.

4 '... Let us pray that the Lord Mighty in Battle will go forth with our armies and that His special providence will give us strength...' Personal Message from the C-in-C. To be read to all troops. Signed B. L. Montgomery, General, 5 June 1944.

5 C.H. firth, *Cromwell's Army: A History of the English Soldier from 1642 to 1660* (London, Methuen, 1902), iii.

6 A useful social anthropologist's view of the British Army's social structure is advanced in C.M.StG. Kirke, 'Social Structures in the Regular Combat Arms of the British Army: A Model', unpublished Ph.D. thesis, Cranfield University, 2002. Lieutenant-Colonel Kirke sets out four components: a top-down formal hierarchy, informal structures of

friendship and association, a loyalty/identity component of a unit or sub-unit, and a functional component, the common task. All are present in a regiment.

7 Moskos and Wood, *Military*, x, 'Great Britain' by Cathy Downes discusses some of the particular features of the British tradition.

CHAPTER 2

THE OFFICER IN THE
RESTORATION ARMY

The first standing Army for Britain, a force of some 5,000 men on the English establishment, was formed at the Restoration in 1660–61. Separate forces were maintained on the Scottish and Irish establishments. Its formation was regarded with much suspicion, a standing force not being thought necessary and, following the excesses of the Cromwell period, not desirable. Parliamentary preference was for any military expenditure to be confined to the part-time Militia under the control of county Lord Lieutenants – generally large land-owning aristocrats, with Deputy Lieutenants drawn from the gentry – as a check on any Royalist excesses. A number of Militia Acts to strengthen the Militia were passed in the first years of Charles II's reign. The King had, in exile, been impressed by the military strength of the French monarch and desired to have a permanent military force to secure his own status. Parliamentary reluctance to grant the necessary credits, however, obliged him to meet most of the costs out of his own revenue, or from the loan of units raised in Britain to foreign monarchs willing to pay the bills. In 1661, though, he was assisted by the threat of a militant republican movement, giving him justification for the small forces, a useful start.

The small Army created, given the bland title of 'His Majesty's Guards and Garrisons', was intended also to reflect both a continuity and a reconciliation. Most of Cromwell's New Model

Army was paid off and disbanded, including by 1662 the garrison of Dunkirk from which, though, a few regiments were sent to Tangier. The Restoration Army comprised initially a regiment of Foot (later the Coldstream Guards) and a regiment of Horse (later part of the Life Guards) from the Commonwealth Army, and two regiments of Foot (later combined to form the Grenadier Guards) and two troops of Horse (later another part of the Life Guards) which had served the King in exile, together with a small number of dockyard and other fortress garrisons. In the course of the year a further Horse unit (later the Royal Horse Guards) of Cromwellian origin was included. In 1661 a troop of Horse and a Foot regiment (later the Royal Dragoons and the Queen's Royal Regiment respectively) were raised specifically to garrison Tangier, part of the dowry of Queen Catharine of Braganza.[1] Finally in 1661 a Scottish regiment that had been in the service of the King of France, later the Royal Scots, were recalled briefly for internal security duties in England; this unit returned to France and except for a few months in 1666–67 served abroad on loan until 1678 when it came back to Britain and was incorporated in the standing army.

This force was only little expanded in Charles II's reign as opposition to a standing army was continuous and vocal. In 1662 a third Guards regiment (later the Scots Guards) was formed from companies already serving in Scotland. In 1664 for service in ships a further regiment was raised, the antecedent of the Royal Marines with, formed in the following year and also on the payroll of the Admiralty, the Holland Regiment (later the Royal East Kent Regiment, the Buffs) from the small number of volunteers, mostly English, from four English and three Scottish regiments in the service of the Netherlands.[2] An offshoot of the Holland Regiment, including it appears a number of Irishmen, formed a further regiment of Foot in the Netherlands service from 1674.[3]

The garrison of Scotland for most of Charles II's reign was the Guards regiment already noted, a troop of Horse, a few garrison companies and a militia. However, internal unrest in Scotland increased progressively to a state approaching anarchy, the sense of Scottish independence being fuelled by the English attempt to outlaw the assemblies of conventicles, private groups gathered for worship, and impose episcopacy. In 1678 three troops of dragoons, sword-carrying mounted infantry, were raised to impose law and order; to them were added three more troops in 1681, the whole constituting the Royal Regiment of Scots Dragoons.[4]

There was also a standing force, of a very poor sort, in Ireland. In 1676 this totalled six regiments of Horse and six of Foot. At the Restoration the officers were mostly Cromwellian veterans; these were progressively replaced by gentlemen, mainly English and all Protestant. The force barely deserved such a title, its senior officers being absentees and the juniors defrauding their soldiers' pay, indulging in heavy drinking and duelling.

In 1680 for the defence of Tangier an additional infantry regiment was raised (the future King's Own Royal Regiment); a number of its officers had served previously in a 'Royal English Regiment' under the French crown.[5]

These units formed, or were to form, components of the first standing army. A very large number of other regiments composed of English, Scottish and Irish officers and soldiers served abroad, and were paid abroad, so escaping parliamentary and public criticism. Some served for long periods; others were raised in England or Ireland for a particular war or campaign, in particular the Dutch Wars, and were later disbanded, with units already noted incorporated in the standing army. This work must necessarily be concerned only with the officers of the standing army.

The establishments for the different regiments varied only slightly. All were commanded by a Colonel, with a Lieutenant-Colonel as a Deputy, and a Major (originally Sergeant Major), as a link between the Colonel and the main body of the regiment. Later, the Major came to be assisted by an Adjutant (originally *Aide-Majeure*). At sub-unit level, in 1661 the King's Troop of the Household Cavalry was commanded by a Captain, with four Lieutenants, a Cornet (the term deriving from the horn shape of a broad pennant, Spanish *corneta*), a Quartermaster, four Sub-Brigadiers, later restyled Corporals, a Chaplain and a Chirurgeon (surgeon), and 200 'Private Gentlemen', a pattern generally followed with some minor variations at different times in the 1660s by other troops.[6] There were no proper NCOs until 1756 in the Household Cavalry. The Sub-Brigadiers held commissions as Lieutenants of Horse and were assisted by Lance-Corporals who were not commissioned. At drill 'right hand men' controlled the evolutions. The Quartermasters ceased to hold commissions in 1667 so as to be 'observant to their captains'. The Chaplains to the Guards troops were directed to read from the Book of Common Prayer daily to the morning parade.

The Foot Guards regiments were also headed by a Colonel, a Lieutenant-Colonel, a Major, a Chaplain and a Surgeon (with a Surgeon's Mate). Their 1,200 soldiers were divided into twelve companies, four of 120 men and eight of ninety each, with as officers a Captain, a Lieutenant and an Ensign. The Foot Guards had NCOs, two Serjeants and three Corporals per company.[7] The troop of Horse raised for Tangier comprised a 'Captain and Colonel', a 'Captain-Lieutenant' and a Cornet together with a Quartermaster, four Corporals and 100 privates. By 1684 when the unit had expanded to regimental size the establishment provided for a Colonel, a Lieutenant-Colonel, a Major, a Chaplain, a Chirurgeon, an Adjutant, a Quartermaster and a gunsmith, with six troops each of fifty men officered by a Lieutenant, a Cornet and a Quartermaster together with two Serjeants and three Corporals. The Foot regiment's establishment was a ten-company equivalent of the Guards regiments with only the addition of a gunsmith.[8]

Companies and troops clearly operated as one sub-unit, not dividing into platoons, so a small number of officers was therefore sufficient. The Horse unit sent to Tangier was armed with long swords and pistols, the soldiers protected by a cuirass and an iron head-piece. The Foot soldiers were armed with pikes, hangers (short swords), grenades and muskets. A specific grenadier company, to be armed with arquebusiers, an early form of grenade launcher, was added to all the Foot regiments in 1678–82, though for some time the grenades were still simply lit and thrown by hand. Grenadiers also carried hatchets to hack away at enemy field defences. At the end of Charles II's reign the bayonet was beginning to replace the pike and flintlock muskets the former matchlock variety, both processes to last decades.

Artillery was the responsibility of the Master-General of the Ordnance, an office with origins dating back to the 15th century. After the Restoration he came to be assisted by a Chief Firemaster and a Surveyor-General. In Charles II's reign there were very few permanently employed artillerymen, though at the end of his reign a small number of 'Gentlemen of the Ordnance' together with a few Engineers under a Chief Engineer for fortifications were appointed. Generally, in the Restoration years, the forts were adequately garrisoned.[9]

The Horse Guards units included, as Brigadiers, Lance-Corporals and gentlemen privates many who had served as Colonels or junior officers in the Royalist Army. This was a congenial lifestyle reward for loyalty, and the Life Guards officer's nominal rank was always equated to grades much higher in recognition of this. Their duties, in common with the Foot Guards regiments, were parades and ceremonial, escorting the conveyance of specie (money in coin), escorting prisoners, the closing down of brothels, internal security work against republican and other conspiracies in London and different areas of the country, and guard mounting in Whitehall. There were no barracks (except in Ireland) until the 1680s; soldiers lived either in garrison forts or in lodgings and ale-houses. It can be assumed that much of their officers' time must have been spent in turning the men out, on time and in a fit condition for their duties.

Outside London, and also for some within the capital in billets, senior officers occupied the best rooms in a tavern, more junior officers the second best, while soldiers slept in the cellar or attic. In 1681 Somerset House, the Royal Mews and the Savoy were used as barracks for the Guards. Some officers volunteered to serve aboard ships in the Dutch Wars, and detachments of Horse and Foot Guards were sent to serve in France in the 1672–74 Dutch War. The Foot Guards regiments stiffened the Militia bands in face of Dutch invasion threats, on one occasion in 1667 at Upnor Castle actually repelling a Dutch landing. In 1676 detachments of Foot Guards and other regiments were sent to Virginia and in 1680 four Guards companies were sent to Tangier. In 1681 at the height of the political crises caused by the desire of Whig parliamentarians to exclude the King's brother, James, Duke of York, from the succession as he was a Roman Catholic, Charles used the Guards units to parade in Oxford, where Parliament was meeting, to prevent any uprising.

The Tangier garrison regiments saw almost continuous small-scale but real action against Moroccan assaults. To withstand these a system of rudimentary blockhouses linked by trenches was constructed, but this frequently proved unreliable in face of Moroccan attacks and mining, particularly when combined with poor command and control by incompetent garrison commanders. The regimental officers, nevertheless, came to show considerable professional skill and bravery. Nineteen officers were killed when a force including the General, the Earl of Teviot, were ambushed in 1664; the force, all Foot soldiers, fought to the death. All in the garrison had to learn lessons of thoroughness and attention to detail. The Foot regiments' officers gave fire orders to direct their pikemen and their musket firepower, ordered the formation of squares and displayed tactical skill in feints and withdrawals. A notable achievement in 1678 was that of a small force led by Captain Leslie that reoccupied perimeter forts that had been taken by the Moroccans. The Horse regiment officers led useful reconnaissance patrols and spirited sword charges. The day-to-day problems centred more on soldiers' morale, strained at times to mutinous mutterings and on a few occasions to open protest, the overall result of reverses at the hands of the Moroccans, unhealthy climate and conditions, unpaid pay, homesickness, poor food and either drunkenness or anger at interruptions in the supply of wine. The Moroccan terror practice of killing and mutilating their prisoners further sapped morale and in 1680 led to reprisals by the garrisons' soldiers which their officers were unable to restrain.

In the other colonies, Bombay briefly, the West Indies and North America, conditions were even worse, heat, humidity and disease exacting a heavy toll on the British troops who served there. As a result military organisation patterns emerged which would last nearly 300 years – in Bombay indigenous men being recruited to serve under British officers occasionally stiffened by a British unit or units, elsewhere the raising of local militias from colonial settlers.

The routine of regimental life began to form in Charles II's reign. In Tangier, after reveille sounded by drummers, an Ensign or Lieutenant would parade and exercise the regiment daily. Three days a week the Adjutant of the Governor's regiment visited these parades and detach men for guard duties; on the other three weekdays after regimental prayers a garrison parade commanded by a Field Officer was held. Soldiers were then exercised by two Captains; drill movements included marching, counter-marching and doubling of ranks and files, together with the special movements needed by pikemen, musketeers and grenadiers. Ensigns carrying the Colours were guarded by pikemen. Regiments 'stood to' at dawn and dusk, and patrols moved around the boundaries every two hours. In 1680 regulations ordered that men march in step. On Sundays all regiments paraded for divine service. Other arrangements to last to this day provided for duty Field Officers and Orderly Officers; day-to-day administration lay with the Major and the Adjutant.

They ultimately were responsible for parading the regiment and specifically with preparing a rota for guards, provision and issue of bullets, powder and match and the instruction of the company officers in their duties. A system of special flag, bell or drum signals for different eventualities was set up. Officers were granted home leave during which they were supposed to recruit. Many, however, arranged for their leave to be prolonged while they looked for a home posting, with the result that the garrison regiments were often very short of officers. Others remained on duty for as long as sixteen years without leave. Officers, like their soldiers, were often unpaid for long periods, as much as two and a half years at a time, monies either not having been sent or having been embezzled along the route. Some officers were accompanied by their wives, and children were born in the garrison area; a few bought small houses.

A social and sporting life was established in Tangier, officers hunting wild boar or shooting a variety of wildfowl. The garrison officers socialised at White Hall Fort where dinners and dances with wives, local notables and merchants, could be enjoyed – the forerunner of the club, so important a feature of later colonial society. An Anglican Garrison church was built. Less fortunate was the predilection among officers for violent quarrelling carried, although strictly forbidden, to the point of duelling, any unfortunate results being accounted for as accident or disease. Two Guards officers fought a duel at a time when the garrison was under attack in 1680; the survivor was convicted of manslaughter and sentenced to have his hand branded by burning. One officer convicted of drunkenness was made to apologise at the head of his regiment. Others were cashiered (dismissed from service) or sent to work, a few in chains, on the harbour mole, a particularly dangerous area. One or two regained commissions by fighting in the ranks with great bravery.[10] Another frequent cause of the duelling was the different origins of the officers, royalists, republicans, Irish and others.

Uniform distinctions appeared. The troop of Horse for Tangier paraded in their cuirasses and iron headpieces together with long scarlet vests and high boots reaching to the middle thigh. Officers wore hats decorated with feathers.[11] In 1678 the King ordered that every soldier was to be issued with a long red coat and a shirt, but their shape and other garments were left to fashion and each individual colonel's preference. Breeches were bulky, usually red with, below them, red worsted stockings. Officer rank was indicated by corselets, light body armour: the Captain's corselet was gilt, the Lieutenant's steel studded with gold, the Ensign's silver. In Tangier officers wore a long grey undress coat, with a waist or shoulder sash fringed with gold or silver.

The Life Guards had gold-laced scarlet coats, gauntlets, cloaks, capes, leather breeches and boots for ceremony, with buff jackets and cuirasses for active service. Officers wore sashes. The Foot Guards wore long red tunics with different colour facings and different headgear for musketeers and pikemen; again officers were distinguished by gold embroidery on their tunics, corselets and sashes.

In 1684 gorgets became the officially authorised mark of rank for Foot regiment officers, a Captain's gorget being gold coloured, a Lieutenant's black studded with gold and an Ensign's silver. Officers were generally clean shaven, but with long sideburns and hair (a wig) worn shoulder length. Some sported a small moustache but none grew beards. The awarding of medals, which Cromwell had authorised, was not continued and was not to be resumed for 100 years.

As already noted, pay due was not always forthcoming. For most of Charles II's reign a regiment's Colonel drew a basic twelve shillings per day (c. £219 per annum), a Lieutenant-Colonel seven shillings per day (c. £127), and a Major five shillings per day (c. £91); each also received an additional eight shillings (£146) as company commanders. Captains, Lieutenants and Ensigns were paid a basic eight shillings (£146), four shillings (£73) and three shillings (£54) respectively per day. By 1684 these rates had all been increased by a shilling or two. Many officers, particularly in the Guards regiments, had other sources of income in trade, business, urban property or land. Living on pay in the lifestyle they sought was out of the question. A small number were involved in crime, extending to robbery, the arranging of the murder or beating up of personal enemies, or other shady practices, with many more involved in pay frauds, often massive, from falsified muster lists. A Lieutenant-Colonel, Pinchbeck, was actually cashiered in 1673 for falsifying lists, though generally such offences were covered over.

Officers were entitled to a maximum of two months' leave per year; in practice many took much longer periods despite a regulation that no more than one-third of the officers of a unit could be away at any one time. Those officers who were members of either House of Parliament were entitled to extra leave when Parliament was sitting.

The custom of officers taking meals together in a billet or a tavern appears to have originated in this period. One or two regiments still possess silver tableware dating from Charles II's reign. When the Duke of Grafton was installed as Colonel of the King's Guards the regiment was paraded in a square and the King delivered his Commission in person. Dinners for the senior officers at Whitehall and the subalterns at a restaurant followed.

There was no system of training for officers, nor even any simple test of physical fitness. Regiments drilled and paraded regularly, but field exercises were apparently very much less frequent. Regimental officers were responsible for the training and drilling of recruits, two months being thought necessary. The best officers in the early 1660s were those with combat experience gained under Charles I or under Charles II when in exile, together with a very few from the New Model Army. As time passed the most professional officers came to be those who had gained experience abroad and returned to England at times of emergency – these then held command and Field Officer appointments. These men were generally from impoverished upper-class families (some ruined as a consequence of the Civil War), with a very small number from the New Model Army and others who were pure mercenaries.

The standing regiments in England were officered by gentlemen officers, in the early 1660s loyalist aristocrats with a smaller number of career soldiers and younger sons. In time these came to be replaced by untitled gentry in increasing numbers. All commissions, including those of the Chaplain and the Surgeon, had to be paid for, often twice over, firstly to the Secretary for War on a set table of charges, but often also to an officer already holding a position but moving on or retiring. The costs were considerable, a Guards Captaincy averaging £1,000. This system ensured, firstly, that the standing army officers were men of property and therefore likely to be politically safe, and, secondly, that an officer's sale of his final commission served as his pension. Promotion was, in consequence, slow but it was nevertheless possible to pursue a military career.

In normal times all officers were appointed by the Crown, the appointment often the result of political influence – most notably support from Monck, by now the Duke of Albemarle, or from the King's brother the Duke of York. At times of emergency such as a Dutch War, Colonels of the regiments raised temporarily could select their own junior officers, who paid only a small fee. The garrison officers, whose duties were often at best part-time, were drawn from or in the gift of local notables and landowners, some appointments being in effect hereditary. There was virtually no interchange between officers serving in England with those in Scotland or Ireland, and no officers were commissioned from the ranks. A few families began to acquire a tradition of army service.

The day-to-day personal behaviour of officers was often drunken and arrogant, slights or affronts leading to quarrels and duels, especially over petty issues of social status. By the standards of the time, however, this was not regarded as particularly objectionable and, except in very serious cases, the social connections of officers served to shield offenders. The example set to soldiers by many of their officers was deplorable.

A number of officers were members of either the House of Commons or the House of Lords, and in reverse, a few members of the House of Commons were given commissions as a form of pension to ensure political reliability. From all, loyalty was expected and to ensure this against what was perceived as the most dangerous threat, that of Roman Catholicism, all officers were required to swear Oaths of Allegiance and Supremacy. A number of Roman Catholic officers were thereby forced to leave the Army in 1667, while others were posted to Tangier, or Bombay, or to regiments at sea. Such measures of royal protection for Roman Catholics lasted until 1678 when Test Act requirements were applied in full and a further number of officers dismissed.

Discipline at regimental level appears to have been based largely on fear and the shock effect of harsh punishment. The legalities were the subject of much controversy. Martial Law had been so unpopular in the Cromwell era that it could not be applied in England, and the Articles of War, which set out a variety of disciplinary offences, lacked any enforcement procedure. Offenders had, in theory, except in cases of treason, desertion or felony, to be sent to the local magistrates' court when it next sat, to be tried under Common Law. To try to circumvent this a system of military law was improvised for offences other than desertion, murder, robbery or treason. In this virtually useless system courts-martial sat, their composition being dependent on the rank of the accused – thirteen officers for a soldier or a subaltern, or five officers for a regimental court-martial for minor offences. The courts heard charges, listened to a defence and called witnesses. At the end of the day, if the court found the defendant legally guilty, he would be sentenced according to the Articles of War, but the only sentences that could be awarded and carried out were suspension from command or dismissal.[12] One can assume, however, that local regimental punishments perhaps involved unauthorised whipping or simply the imposition of fatigue duties. Overseas, more effective courts-martial were accepted as necessary, and were permissible under the Articles of War. In the case of the Tangier garrison, for example, by 1683 a court-martial was composed of three officers, one from each of the garrison regiments. The court could impose any punishment that did not result in loss of life or limb. There was no 'prisoner's friend' to help an accused soldier. Sentences recorded included imprisonment, continuous whipping by an executioner of a soldier obliged to march backwards and forwards through the regiment on parade for falling asleep while on sentry duty, a sergeant reduced to the ranks for not being present at commanding officers' rounds, long periods for a private on the crude wooden horse with heavy weights about his neck and feet for selling his shoes, and for another private found drunk on duty to be tied neck and heels weighted by two muskets for an hour until the blood flowed out of his mouth and nose.[13] The penalty for cowardice or mutiny was death by hanging or firing squad. Much depended on the kindness or severity of the court officers, severity being more common than kindness.

While duty Orderly Officers carried out daily rounds of inspection of feeding arrangements and, when overseas, hospitals, their concern appears to have been primarily to ensure the efficiency of the soldiers rather than their welfare as individuals. In sum, the reign of Charles II saw the foundation blocks of a Regular Army with a corps of Regular officers. At the top, by 1684 a War Office was in existence with authority over movement, quartering and the raising of regiments. Articles of War and military law codes differing slightly to meet particular local conditions had been prepared, and delicate questions of regimental precedence and seniority of officers resolved. At the War Office were to be found an exceedingly efficient official 'Secretary at War' and officials concerned with the different branches of staff work. At regimental level, manuals laying down a common system for words of command, drill and unit level tactics appeared in the late 1670s.[14] Uniform, of a sort but with clear rank insignia for officers, had been laid down, even if not universally observed. Some regiments had their own badge. Drums, and in England fifes or trumpets and in Scotland pipes, enriched Foot or Horse unit life. Even if the conduct of officers was indifferent, regiments with their own identities had been formed and were starting to gain sufficient reputation to make the Army acceptable.

NOTES

1 In the Army of 2004 the Royal Dragoons are now part of the Blues and Royals, (Royal Horse Guards and 1st Dragoons), and the Queen's Royal Regiment (2nd Foot) is a part of the Princess of Wales's Royal Regiment. A troop of Horse at this time was equivalent to a squadron later.

2 The Buffs, 3rd Foot, now forms part of the Princess of Wales's Royal Regiment.

3 This regiment, later the Royal Northumberland Fusiliers, now forms part of the Royal Regiment of Fusiliers.

4 The Royal Regiment of Scots Dragoons, later the Royal Scots Greys, now forms part of the Royal Scots Dragoon Guards (Carabiniers and Greys).

5 The King's Own Royal Regiment, 4th Foot, now forms part of the King's Own Royal Border Regiment.

6 Captain Sir George Arthur, *The Story of the Household Cavalry* (London, Constable, 1909), 32–37; R.J.T. Hills, *The Life Guards* (London, Leo Cooper, 1971), 5.

7 Lieutenant-General Sir F.W. Hamilton, *The Origin and History of the First or Grenadier Guards*, (London, John Murray, 1874), 45–46.

8 General de Ainslie, *Historical Record of the First or the Royal Regiment of Dragoons* (London, Chapman and Hall, 1887), 9, 17; Lt. Col. John Davis, *The History of the Second, Queen's Royal Regiment*, (London, Richard Bentley, 1887), 20.

9   Captain Francis Duncan, *History of the Royal Regiment of Artillery* (London, John Murray, 1872), 48.

10 A.J. Smithers, *The Tangier Campaign: The Birth of the British Army*, (Stroud, Tempus, 2003), *passim*, and Colonel L.L. Cowper (Editor), *The King's Own: The Story of a Royal Regiment* (Oxford University Press, 1939), 13–20, provide interesting accounts of Tangier garrison life.

11 Cowper, *King's Own*, 11. The illustration (Plate 1) of the officers of the Tangiers Regiment, drawn in 1669, includes an element of artistic licence.

12 John Childs, *The Army of Charles II* (London, Routledge, 1976), iv.

13 Cowper, *King's Own*, 21–22.

14 The most important of these, published first in 1675, reprinted later and extended to the Scottish and Irish armies in 1679, was the *Abridgement of English Military Discipline*.

CHAPTER 3

THE OFFICER IN THE ARMIES
OF THE LATER STUARTS

Charles II was succeeded by his younger brother, the Duke of York, as King James II. James was a very much more energetic and military person than his easy-going elder brother and held certain clear and determined views on the roles of monarch, Army and religion. He sought to establish his own personal authority over the country by means of improved, centralised government, with tolerance and favour for Roman Catholics, together with, as an eventual aim, the return of the country to the Roman faith. As part of this grand design, the Army was to play an important lead role.[1]

He was fortunate in that, partly as a result of an attempted uprising by an illegitimate son of Charles II, the Duke of Monmouth, he was not faced with the same opposition from Parliament as his brother had been in his plans for a substantial increase in the size of the Army; he had little time for the Militia. His reign, almost four years, saw the raising in England of five (later six) new regiments of Horse, two of Dragoons and nine of Foot, together with a reinvigoration of the fortress garrisons.[2] The Scottish Army's establishment was not increased.

In terms of formal battlefield commitments, the Army was little used in James II's reign; the only really significant battle was that of Sedgemoor in late 1685 where Monmouth was defeated, and this battle occurred before the new regiments had been raised, trained and equipped. Its chief longer-term importance lay in the skill shown by James's first field commander, John Churchill, created Earl of Marlborough as a reward for his work. Drafts of men from the Foot regiments were later sent to New England and to the service of the East India Company, but the main role of the Army, distributed all over England, was to impose the royal authority. The paradox of James's reign lies in some strengthening of the Army's professionalism but at the same time in corruption becoming institutionalised.

Officers were encouraged to think and learn about their profession. Observers were sent to study and report on operations in Europe, in particular the Turkish–Hungarian fighting, fortifications and artillery. When some 10,000 men of the Army camped on Hounslow Heath for six weeks in the summer, the opportunity of large formation training was taken; in one year a fort was built and besieged. Drill was taught by numbers. The normal length of a day's march was eight miles, billeting difficulties and the state of roads making longer marches impracticable. The march of one regiment of Foot from Hounslow to Plymouth took from 9th to 31st August in 1688. Field officers rarely marched with the men, leaving this to Captains and Subalterns, who in any case usually rode on horseback. In Foot regiments two additional Subalterns, for the grenadier companies, were added to the establishment.[3] As yet no body of artillery officers was formed; when guns were fired it appears that anyone available with the necessary expertise, such as metal workers or garrison personnel, were used. Among these at Sedgemoor was the 66-year-old Bishop of Winchester, Peter Mews, who directed the fire of the royal cannon drawn by his own horses, at the same time adding one more wound to the several he had suffered in the Royalist Civil War army.[4]

The routine duties of military life were similar to those of the previous reign – escort of bullion, highway patrolling, fire-fighting, much ceremonial and the suppression of protest demonstrations and riots, particularly Nonconformist and Roman Catholic. Leave was granted generously, sometimes just taken without sanction and often more than the entitlement. The worst offenders were often the Chaplains, many giving more time to work as parish priests. Officers in London were absent less often, the boredom of provincial life being a major cause.[5] The expenses of being an officer started to rise; for example, officers were expected to provide their own tents, and rivalry over elaborate tent decoration added to the costs. At the Hounslow Heath camps a space of some 20 feet, known as 'the street', separated the officers' tents from those of their companies.

Maintaining discipline presented a variety of problems. As James II's reign progressed, religious tensions mounted, and duelling and violence against civilians continued. Junior officers of high social status objected to or disobeyed the orders of officers they considered socially inferior. Punishments, however, remained very light, as it was held that an officer's commission was his life's investment and it would be too severe to take this from him; officers were dismissed only for disloyalty or opposition to the government in Parliament.

The discipline of soldiers was even worse. An increased number were Irish, drafted into English regiments; they and the Scots soldiers appear to have been the worst, with the English only slightly better. Soldiers swore, blasphemed, killed, robbed and injured civilians wherever they were posted and billeted. Many officers did not investigate thefts by soldiers, a major reason no doubt being that there was little that they could do about it – until the last year of James's reign all such cases had to go to the civil courts, to the contempt of regimental officers. In March 1688 a standing court-martial was established but the law was to remain confused until the reign of William and Mary. But as a result of soldiers' behaviour the Army once again drew the hatred of the civilian population on its head.

As part of his design to extend his authority James II in 1688 directed over thirty officers to stand for Parliament. He made plans for more to do so, plans overtaken by events. He also appointed a small number to county deputy lieutenancies and commissions of peace. Regiments were posted to cities, in particular in Lancashire, where James suspected disloyalty.

It was, however, not only his growing authoritarian ambitions but his Roman Catholic policies that were to prove his undoing. From the start of his reign Catholic officers were favoured and a slow replacement of Protestant officers by Catholics was begun. The policy in England remained slow as there was no steady supply of suitable Catholic replacements, a number of those selected by James proving to be of poor quality. The worst consequences were to be felt in the Army in Ireland where replacement was wholesale; the Test Act did not apply and James instituted an oath of allegiance to him personally. The new Catholic officers were of poor backgrounds, corrupt and uneducated. They rendered the force valueless and James's hopes that Ireland could be a secure Catholic base for the reconversion of England were only too soon to prove vain.

The divisive policies of James II, highlighted by the annual camps on Hounslow Heath to overawe the capital and Parliament, led to informal groups such as the Treason Club and the Association of Protestant Officers, with some defections as early as 1687. Conspicuous among these were officers of the former but now abandoned Tangier garrison. Wider national discontent led to an invitation signed by a number of political heavyweights to William of Orange, ruler of the Netherlands, and his wife Mary, the Protestant daughter of James II, to replace him. Although William landed in Devon with a relatively small force of Dutch, German and Danish soldiers, James's army fell apart, defections being led now by the Earl of Marlborough. James fled and the event known in English history as 'The Glorious Revolution' followed as the English, Scottish and Irish armies all disintegrated into leaderless confusion. Soldiers deserted *en masse*; the officers were divided. Many, including a number of Protestants holding reservations about regime changes by force and not accepting William's claim to legitimacy, resigned or deserted, the Catholics joining James's army in Ireland. Many of those who remained in service had no liking for William and sharply resented the presence of the Dutch officers.

The Revolution in practice simply meant the triumph of Parliament over the monarchy. An important part of that triumph was the assertion of a Parliamentary consent for the existence of the Army. This control was set out unmistakably in the 1689 Declaration of Rights which stated that any standing army without Parliamentary consent was illegal – but at the same time conversely accepting that the Army should exist, its funding to be provided by Parliament. Thereby the practices to be followed in all the years to come were established, that of hasty expansion in times of need or crisis with reductions and cuts when peace dividends seemed possible. In practice, power was now shared between Monarch and Parliament, the Monarch still retaining powers in the actual raising of regiments and the commissioning of officers. In this field William was never tempted to use the Army for personal absolutist ambitions, though he did initiate a purge of Catholic officers and men.[6]

A step was also made towards some system of military law. A Scots regiment of Foot stationed at Ipswich mutinied when ordered to move to Flanders, so bringing urgency to the question. An Army Act was passed by Parliament authorising the convening of courts-martial by the Crown or General officers to try cases of desertion, sedition or mutiny, with powers to award death sentences for the most serious offences. The Act was to be renewed annually. At the time it was intended simply to impose tight limits on the powers of military officers, but in practice mutiny and sedition came to be interpreted very widely for the enforcement of discipline. Battlefield conditions and necessities also led to wider interpretations of the system. In Flanders, outside the remit of Common Law, the wood horse, flogging and other physical punishments were fairly generally imposed by regimental courts-martial, usually formed of a president and twelve officers. The cruel physical and mental inhumanity of these punishments imposed by officers on their own soldiers only represented a military version of the total absence of social concern in society as a whole where courts awarded similar punishments. Also at the same time, billeting and any obligation to provide free quartering for regiments, which under James II had even extended to private houses, was made illegal, so beginning to end one cause of the Army's unpopularity. Friction between the military and inn-keepers over behaviour and payments nevertheless continued in the absence of barracks. The measure also aroused resentment – and indiscipline – among soldiers who now had to meet the costs of accommodation from their pay.

Although at the outset of his reign William was obliged to garrison London with his Dutch soldiers and despatch all the English regiments, including the Guards, to the provinces, he too soon found he had need of the Army. A number of hurried and improvised measures to restore some measure of unity were put in hand after the disintegration of 1688. The best and most professional of Charles II's and James II's officers were retained and helped in the rebuilding of the regiments, many of which had lost or were to lose a quarter or more of their officers from resignation or in the purges. William's overriding aim was to use British manpower and resources to safeguard the Netherlands against the ambitions of the French King, Louis XIV, with also an immediate need to suppress a Highlander uprising in Scotland and reverse a landing of James II and French troops in Ireland, a landing supported by Catholic rebels. After an initial success at Killiecrankie the Highlander revolt was suppressed, the officers of an English regiment and a Lowland Scots regiment holding their men steady in the face of ferocious

Highlander sword charges. Operations in Ireland, despite the early and in the long run decisive victory of the Boyne, were to last until 1691. Conditions for officers and men were at first very testing. The sea crossing in filthy, insanitary and overcrowded transport ships, with mouldy food and polluted drinking water, was followed by campaigning often in rain so heavy that any pitching of tents was impossible and officers ordered their men to build wooden shacks with straw roofs. Sickness and lice followed; many men apparently had no footwear. Some of the bodies of the large number of soldiers who died had to be used as windshields.[7] Camps on Hounslow Heath in summer were no preparation for all-weather campaigning in Ireland. The supply system failed totally and soldiers took to plundering for food. Many officers found these conditions, for which they had had no proper field training and were not physically fit, totally beyond them, remaining indifferent to the disease and suffering of their men.[8] Later, conditions improved, with supplies and pay arriving when due. Fighting, however, did not stop for the winter and to the end terrain conditions were treacherous. In the final stages, at Aghrim, officers had to lead their men wading waist deep in bog. In England itself regiments on home service were only slightly better placed, many living in insanitary and squalid forts, tasked to respond to threats of invasion which never materialised.

The British Army, in Ireland, in contrast to the Dutch, Germans and Danes of William's forces, had showed up as second rate. Reputation was, however, to be redeemed after a shaky start marked with officers still unfit and amateurish, and soldiers poorly uniformed and shod, by a steadily improving performance in the 40,000 strong multi-national force assembled by William to defend the Netherlands, the war becoming known as the War of the League of Augsburg.

Despite some serious reverses, most notably an attempt to take Brest, the British contingent under Marlborough came to be reckoned a battleworthy force, although the British regiments were not in one formation but interspersed with units of allied forces. The Low Countries campaign itself was one of protracted and indecisive manoeuvre marches and sieges to acquire towns and territory for political bargaining with pauses in the winter months. At its height William's armies totalled some 80,000 of which 17,000 were British. In some of the major engagements, at Walcourt in 1689, at Steenkerk in 1692 and the siege and recapture of Namur in 1695, British regiments and their officers fought with valour and skill in both attack and withdrawal. A number of officers were killed along with the men they were leading. As early as 1689 a Foot regiment (later numbered the 16th) fought so skilful a rearguard action after an attack by a much superior French force that it gained the praise of the Allied force commander.[9] Thirty-two Guards officers were killed in 1695 in the recapture of Namur where three Guards battalions, the Royal Scots and the 7th Fusiliers formed the vanguard of the attack, the officers fearlessly leading the Guardsmen, under heavy French fire, up to the French palisades before firing their first volley.[10]

One regiment was sent to the Mediterranean for several months on board warships where conditions were once again insanitary and filthy; ambitious plans for landings in the south of France were, however, abandoned and only one local attack on a Spanish port was made. Detachments sent to the West Indies were decimated by disease; those serving in New England or Canada were more fortunate, providing they survived the wretched conditions on their sea journeys, which many did not.

The skills expected of officers multiplied in the changing conditions of the battlefield where drilling, control of fire, ability to live in the field and discipline were necessary. The flintlock musket could almost double the rate of fire, a little later to increase again when paper cartridges replaced powder horns. The plug-bayonet, taking time to fix, time in which, as at Killiecrankie during the Highlanders' uprising, an opponent could take advantage, was replaced by a bayonet fixed to the musket, so immediately making the pike obsolescent and very soon obsolete. Muskets were repaired and spares retained by the artillery train artificers. The traditional six-man-deep line was now under Marlborough replaced by a three-man-deep line, the front rank kneeling. Volleys were ordered no longer for ranks but by first, second and third firings, controlled by the subdivision of companies into platoons, with the enemy distant at 100 paces being considered the best moment to open fire. Battalions were formed up with only a yard or so between them in a continuous line. The grenadier companies of several battalions might be brigaded together to form the first wave of an attack. Officers carried swords and pistols. The cavalry were given only limited ammunition with instruction to use it only for the protection of their horses while feeding, but also to ensure maximum momentum in the attack. Cavalry at this time usually operated in one or two troop (i.e. squadron) deployments rather than full regimental charges and operations, and the pace of the charge increased from trot to gallop. A lesson learnt, the need for proper artillery, led to the raising of a special regiment of artillery in 1697. The period of the withdrawal of regiments to winter quarters in earthwork-protected camps was used for training and the collection of supplies of food and ammunition for the next year, together with some patrolling, occasional raids and the levying of impositions on the local civilian population. One-third of the officers of each regiment in Flanders were sent back to Britain for recruiting each winter. Officers were given quotas which they were expected to fill; some regiments left junior officers behind to recruit throughout the year. Sometimes a bounty would be paid to a successful recruiter. All these activities had to be the subjects of orders from senior and, now increasingly, subaltern officers.

Despite the turbulence caused by the events of 1688, the reigns of James II and William III institutionalised and developed the systems of patronage and corruption initiated under Charles II, systems that were to last for a very long time. At the top the Government might withhold pay from a regiment for months or years and then pay out in paper promise money, or a small proportion of the money due. Colonels continued to raise regiments (these were still known by the name of the Colonel) and were expected to pay for their clothing, all of their equipment except tents and muskets but including side-arms, and the replacement of lost equipment, and if so minded make some provision for men wounded in action or war widows. In return Colonels received a grant, inadequate and usually belated. A variety of practices developed to ensure that Colonels, assisted by their agents, and their officers were not out of pocket. Muster returns were increasingly falsified, often including names of men dead, or with dummies or labourers brought in for the occasion appearing on muster parades. Excessive charges might be made for clothing, or unauthorised and excessive deductions made from a soldier's pay for food or bread in the field (where rations were supposed to be provided), medicines and medical treatment, uniform embellishments and regimental or agents' charges. Clothing and quartering accounts were the subject of negotiations with tradesmen. Even when supplemented by deductions from soldiers' pay or other funds available, officers might have to dip into their pockets if the regiment was to look smart. Some clothiers specialised in officers' uniforms, and that well-known feature of officers' lives, the regimental tailor, first appeared. Soldiers' pay would be withheld even if it reached a regiment, or soldiers would be offered interest-bearing loans. A Colonel might levy an additional charge for acceptance in his regiment even if the aspirant officer had already purchased a commission. Others arranged for their sons, on occasions even infants, to be given commissions.[11]

The system was accepted, with almost everyone being involved in it, because it only reflected practices in civilian society of the time. William III made efforts to reform it but these were not pursued and all failed. Officers were supposed to take an oath that they had not bribed anyone or bought their commissions, but the measure was a complete dead letter. On one occasion a show trial of one Colonel, Hastings, in 1695 led to the Colonel being cashiered on conviction of embezzling pay, excessive deductions, improper sale of clothing and accepting money for facilitating promotion, but this was simply the case of a man who took *too* much and was found out.[12]

The actual annual rates of pay for officers were slightly increased. A Colonel of a Foot regiment was paid £410, with an allowance of £140 for servants, a Guards Colonel's rate was higher, £681, and a Cavalry Colonel's £600. Each could probably add to this considerably, perhaps several hundred pounds, by dubious practices. A Captain of Foot earned £170, an Ensign £60. These officers, too, would be able to supplement their pay. The seamless web of corruption in fact suited everyone. Purchase of commissions ensured that officers continued to come from the ruling establishment; the financial stake was so considerable that it acted as some – if not a great – restraint on officers' behaviour. Also, being a system based on property (except at the top) it served as a protection against political interference. However, men of ability and ambition but no money were left disadvantaged. In the corruption and absence of any real accountability lay the main causes of the generally poor quality of much of the officering of the period, mostly characterised by drunkenness and increased duelling over trifles but in which a number of officers were killed (on one occasion a Captain severely wounding a Major-General), arbitrary arrogance and contempt for the law. Losing money on cards, gaming, riding, banquets and balls occupied more time than military duties – except in action when officers' aggressive energies were put to proper use, a paradox to last for over 150 years.

Officers, aristocracy, squirearchy, with now a few from trade and a very few from the ranks but with also a small number of

Huguenot exiles from France, were all as much preoccupied with the business side of their lives as with the professional, to the disadvantage of the latter. Within regiments officers' business interests meant that much power went to sergeants, little attention being paid by either amateurish officers or sergeants to the livelihood of ordinary soldiers. Further, the conditions of the time, the absence of barracks with companies of a regiment scattered over several villages in a rural area, meant that with the regiment under-officered, many also being on leave, only sergeants could exercise control. The system of purchase had also an overall effect of keeping the Army as a collection of regiments rather than a unified force.

In practice the system came to operate on a whole-career basis. An officer on first being commissioned paid the price of that commission to the officer whose departure from the regiment had created the vacancy. On promotion he paid the cash value difference between the rank he held and the rank to which he was now advancing, again to the officer who was leaving. Other officers who moved up a rank also paid on the same basis. These sums of money made up the value of the retiring officer's commission which when he left he would sell, so providing him with a useful gratuity. The number of officers now required had also risen sharply, from 973 for all three armies of Charles II to its peak of 5,000 in William's reign.

Although there were always sufficient or more aspirants for the Guards, other regiments, especially those thought to have been raised for one particular need, were often short of officers. Although all commissions had to be purchased, the price in such short-lived regiments was very low. Sometimes, also, officers cashiered would be re-engaged in another regiment at a lower rank.

Except at times of epidemic, or unseemly rushes for promotion after battle, promotion was slow. For Subalterns and Captains it was by seniority within the regiment, senior Ensigns to Lieutenants, senior Lieutenant to Captain. Colonels, subject to later approval by the

Secretary of State for War, had the right to appoint Subalterns. For Field Officers, Majors and Lieutenant-Colonels, Colonels suggested names to the Commander-in-Chief for William III's approval. This approval was not always given, William looking for professional competence and Whig political reliability; he might also have officers on half-pay to consider; an ability to recruit men also counted. In practice, as already noted, members of the aristocracy or squirearchy were preferred. Influence and favouritism also continued to play their part, but experience and ability generally counted most for promotion to senior rank. Most officers' ambitions were limited to command of their regiment, a limited aim to last until the mid 20th century. There remained resentment against William's liking for Dutch or German officers, and their being placed in command of British troops. Fewer officers were now Members of Parliament. And as yet there was still no system of training for officers, though a number acquired useful experience serving initially as a 'private gentleman' in the aristocratic ranks of the Life Guards and, despite all the temptations on offer, many developed in time and with experience into capable battle Field Officers.

The whole inefficient, amateurish, class-based system inevitably affected not only the life but also the quality of individual soldiers attracted to serve in the ranks. Recruitment produced men from the dregs of society, from prisons and workhouses, others being 'recruited' while heavily drunk or by some other specious ruse. A number were unfit or elderly. Regiments formed from men of such poor quality and given such poor reward led to rowdy, often violent behaviour in public places, so returning a popular dislike of the Army and creating problems of discipline for the officers. Many soldiers, not for the first or the last time in British military history, took on part-time work as after the deductions from their pay they were left penniless or exceedingly poor. Desertion, despite the severe punishments, was common; sometimes bodies of men deserting in the group were, when apprehended, formed into companies and despatched to the West Indies. There were a number of cases of minor mutinies in units serving in England, and it is possible that a few of the worst officers were, in the confusion of battle, killed off by their own men.

By the time the nine-years-long League of Augsburg war ended in 1697, however, the officers of the regiments who had fought in Marlborough's contingent of William's armies had gained, in many cases the hard way, much valuable experience and sense of responsibility. Those who had remained in Britain could claim no such credit. The newly formed artillery regiment was disbanded. The rewards presented by an ungrateful Parliament were an initial reduction of the Army to 10,000 followed by a further reduction to 7,000 (excluding the Army in Ireland and elsewhere overseas). Sharp competition for survival resulted, the best officers being retained and the losers opting to serve in Continental armies, or, in a few cases, turning to crime. The problems were exacerbated by the considerable arrears of pay due to many, for which funds could not be found. The solution of half-pay until full funding was available was devised. In practice the disbandment was mainly one of men, regiments being retained but companies reduced to half-strength; both officers and men were in any case to be required again very soon.

There was, nevertheless, to follow within three years one of the great periods of British military history, the reign of Queen Anne and the victories of Marlborough – Blenheim, Oudenarde, Ramillies, Malplaquet and the forcing of the Ne Plus Ultra lines – in the War of the Spanish Succession. The military genius of Marlborough has been the subject of much study; this work, however, is concerned with the execution of his operations by subordinate officers. The brilliance of his plans and his choice of battles rather than leisurely sieges imposed severe demands on regimental officers; two examples provide vivid illustration. The long march of his army to the battle of Blenheim in 1704 required march discipline, as well as immensely careful forward planning, and the surprise needed to force the Ne Plus Ultra lines in 1711 necessitated a march of forty miles in eighteen hours. The victories of Marlborough do, however, have to be offset by the relative failure of the performance of Allied armies, including a large British contingent, in Spain.

At the top was the Secretary to the Force, a senior functionary, in the period when Marlborough was Commander-in-Chief. His power, already considerable, was the greater as Marlborough was out of the country for long periods of time. Another senior functionary was the Master-General of the Ordnance responsible for the artillery. For a while Marlborough was both Commander-in-Chief and Master-General; at other times the post was held by a civilian. There was no General Staff, civilian commissioners handling pay and personnel issues. A Board of General Officers existed from 1708, but it soon limited its deliberations to matters of regimental precedence and detail of uniforms.

In the field Marlborough's staff included a Quartermaster-General as a chief staff officer, a Provost-Marshal, a Chaplain-General, a Surgeon-General, a Waggon-Master-General and a number of liaison officers, *aides-de-camp*, usually relatives or well connected, who provided combat intelligence as well as coordination of command. The Act of Union with Scotland put the Scottish regiments on a common establishment. Marlborough's Army, expanded by sixty-nine new regiments of Horse and Foot units, a total of 10,000 British officers and men in his coalition force, was not organised into Army Corps or Divisions, though Lieutenant-Generals might command right or left sectors of the front, with the right being the senior and point of honour. Three, four or five regiments might be brigaded together with a Brigade Major to coordinate.[13] At regimental level officers' duties might begin with the control of a march to contact. A day's march was now generally some ten miles, being the maximum distance bread could be carried; every fourth day was to be a halt for the baking of fresh bread. Marlborough when nearing contact with his enemy often preferred a night or early morning advance. Ahead of the marching column would be the Quartermaster-General's reconnaissance party; these would look for suitable locations for halts and gather intelligence. Contemporary maps were of limited value only, as they contained no contours to show hill or valley features. At an overnight halt officers would have to supervise the billeting if a regiment was in a town, or if in the field the layout of the encampment for its own protection, the raising of tents, watering of horses, posting of picquet (picket) lines and sentries, gate guards, roving patrols and stand-to instructions. When the troops arrived arms would be piled adjacent to each company's tents and, with good fortune, tea would be provided. Officers messed by company, in each company one officer would be tasked with regimental duties, another with messing and food supplies. If the halt was to be for a few days a defensive ditch might be dug. Foraging parties, sometimes of over 2,000 soldiers, might be sent out with officers on the watch for pillaging or desertion.

On an advance-to-contact march officers had to ensure regiments were correctly aligned to face a threat from an enemy either in front or on a flank. Cavalry rode on the flanks and provided a forward warning screen; infantry units were in the centre and further back to protect the vital logistic, pontoon and artillery trains. Companies within battalions in most regiments still remained under strength, generally fifty men, and sometimes less. Contact made, tactics varied according to circumstances but officers were usually directed to deploy, with guns, $1\frac{1}{2}$ pdr. (pounder) field pieces, forming a first line with, behind them in depth, supporting cavalry, second-line infantry and, at the rear, reserve cavalry. For sieges three lines of trenches for the besieging units would be prepared, out of range of the defenders' guns, by conscripted labour or by parties of fifty men under a Captain.[14]

Engineers would commence mining and infantry commanders would plan a variety of assaults to test defences and deceive the besieged as to their real attack plan. En route to a siege, regiments might have to be provided to protect the long convoys of heavy siege guns and mortars, convoys that could stretch for fifteen miles. The most feared task for which officers had to lead their soldiers was that of entering tunnels that had been mined, perhaps to meet the enemy in pitch darkness or to be blown up by an enemy bomb.[15]

In these years the respective duties of officers and NCOs became set. The officers were responsible for the regiment's following the Commander-in-Chief's operational plans, set out for the regimental officers by the Lieutenant-Colonel or Major, and were responsible for the general training and efficiency of the regiment. The NCOs' duties were to ensure the rank and file soldiers were prepared for their roles, competent with their weapons and well turned out. NCOs would also be in charge of picquets, the posting of vedettes and sentries, and cleanliness and order in barracks or camps.

Logistics were largely in the hands of a wide variety of 'private finance initiative' civilian contractors; these also were responsible for the movement of the artillery train. Marlborough's successful management of supply, pre-stocked arsenals and light two-wheeled 'bread waggon' carts for transportation, was a major factor in his triumphs. Such successful management had important morale effects: soldiers had total confidence in their Commander-in-Chief, in turn making the duties of regimental officers easier. But the potential morale problems – in some cases not overcome with, in consequence, discipline problems – were nevertheless very real. On some occasions, if for one reason or another, food supplies failed to arrive, Colonels and officers might have to pay for local purchase of food for their men. Casualty rates in battle could be over 20 per cent, to which had to be added illness arising from bad food or insanitary barracks. The medical services were exceedingly poor, crude field hospitals with ill-trained or untrained doctors, and one bread-waggon cart per regiment for the movement of the wounded.[16] It was, however, possible for officers to nominate the most deserving for admission to the Royal Hospital, Chelsea. But in these circumstances, and bearing in mind the very rough quality of the soldiers, discipline and punishments had, of necessity, to be severe.

To fill vacancies caused by the death of Field Officers in battle, brevet (unpaid) ranks were granted. The effects of officers killed would be auctioned and the proceeds passed on to relatives; some fortunate relatives might also receive contributions from a whip-round or the price of the dead officer's rank.

After major victories, a bounty might be paid to all ranks. After Blenheim, a Colonel received £72, a Lieutenant-Colonel £51, a Major £45, a Captain £20, Lieutenants and Quartermasters £14, Surgeons £12 and Ensigns £11. The widow of an Adjutant killed received £40 and the widow of a Lieutenant £28.[17] Privates received £1.

No account of the Marlborough campaigns would be complete without provision of some examples of the personal bravery characteristic of officers and the casualties they sustained. At the 1711 siege of Bouchair an Ensign of the 23rd Foot, short in stature and unable to wade through watery mud, jumped on to the shoulders of his grenadiers to be one of the first to charge into the fortress.[18] The Lieutenant-Colonel and the Major of one infantry unit, the 16th Foot, were both killed leading their men in the assault on French palisade defences at Blenheim, other officers vainly trying to thrust swords at the enemy through gaps in the palisade while under heavy fire.[19] In Spain all four of the British cavalry regiments lost their commanding officers in the fighting at Almanza in 1707.[20] At Malplaquet in 1709 the 3rd Foot lost four Captains and two Lieutenants killed with three Captains, four Lieutenants and two Ensigns wounded.[21] Numerous accounts record the spirit with which both cavalry and infantry regiments went in to the big battles and maintained morale and enthusiasm in difficult conditions; soldiers would not have done so without good leadership at regimental as well as at command level. Officers were beginning to foster a family regimental *esprit de corps* from men of very rough origins; example must have played a major part.[22] Being an officer in an army even as early as that of Marlborough was already far from being just a job and, in the officer paradox, combat efficiency took place over corruption and the easy life in the great campaigns.

The War of the Spanish Succession ended with the 1713 Treaty of Utrecht. The fall from royal favour of Marlborough and his replacement by the Duke of Ormonde once again brought high politics at the top back down into regimental life. Officers known to favour the succession to the throne of George of Hanover were asked to resign or sell their commissions. Seventeen officers of the First Guards were so pressured, two being replaced by known Jacobite Roman Catholics.[23] Fortunately for all, shortly afterwards, Queen Anne died and George I succeeded peacefully.

NOTES

1 For a detailed examination of the Army in James II's reign see John Childs, *The Army, James II and the Glorious Revolution* (Manchester University Press, 1980).

2 The present day (2004) British Army's antecedents whose traditions are carried on, despite amalgamations, are set out in Appendix 2. The successors of the founder Restoration regiments have already been noted in Chapter 2.

3 Albert Lee, *The History of the Tenth Foot (The Lincolnshire Regiment)* (Aldershot, Gale and Polden, 1911), 28, notes the 1687 strength of the regiment as one Colonel, one Lieutenant-Colonel, one Major, one Adjutant, eight Captains, twelve Lieutenants, ten Ensigns, a Surgeon, a Chaplain and a Quartermaster.

4 Sidney Lee (Editor), *Dictionary of National Biography* (London, Smith Elder, 1894), 315.

5 'Life for the officers [of the 11th Foot] was deemed dull. There were few chances to pursue the normal interests of a gentleman. Nor was it possible, at such a distance from the capital to keep a finger on the pulse of patronage with a view to promotion.' R.E.R. Robinson, *The Bloody Eleventh: History of the Devonshire Regiment* (Exeter, The Devonshire and Dorset Regiment, n.d.), I, 7.

6 For an excellent detailed study of William III's army see John Childs, *The British Army of William III, 1698–1702* (Manchester University Press, 1987), and Corelli Barnett, *Britain and Her Army 1509–1970* (Harmondsworth, Penguin, 1970), vi.

7 Robinson, *Bloody Eleventh*, 17.

8 F. Loraine Petre, *The History of the Norfolk Regiment* (Norwich, Jarrold, n.d.), 14.

9 Brigadier Peter Young and Lt. Col. J.P. Lawford, *History of the British Army* (London, Arthur Barker, 1970), 17.

10 The Hon. J.W. Fortescue, *A History of the British Army* (London, Macmillan, 1899), I, 378–379.

11 This practice was ended in 1711.

12 Sir Henry Everett, *The History of the Somerset Light Infantry (Prince Albert's), 1685–1914* (London, Methuen, 1934), 34–36, describes the case.

13 David Chandler, *Marlborough as Military Commander* (London, Batsford, 1973), v, provides a detailed account of Marlborough's operational art. Major R.E. Scouller, *The Armies of Queen Anne* (Oxford, Clarendon, 1966), supplements this with an organisation account.

14 Robinson, *Bloody Eleventh*, 55.

15 Albert Lee, *Tenth Foot*, 158–159, provides a clear account of this type of operation.

16 John Fortescue, *The Royal Army Service Corps* (Cambridge University Press, 1930), I, 22.

17 C.T. Atkinson, *Regimental History of the Royal Hampshire Regiment* (Glasgow University Press, 1950), 19–20.

18 Chandler, *Marlborough*, 296, quoting from M. Bishop's *Life and Adventure of Matthew Bishop 1701–1711*, published in 1744.

19 T.J.B. and others, *The Story of the Bedfordshire and Hertfordshire Regiment (the 16th Regiment of Foot)*, (privately published, n.d.), 57.

20 Fortescue, *British Army*, II, 486.

21 Captain C.R.B. Knight, *Historical Records of the Buffs East Kent Regiment* (London, Medici Society, 1935), I, 66.

22 The point is well made in Field Marshal Lord Carver, *Seven Ages of the British Army* (London, Grafton, 1986), 78–79.

23 Lieutenant-General Sir F.W. Hamilton, *The Origin and History of the First or Grenadier Guards* (London, John Murray, 1874), II, 60.

CHAPTER 4

THE OFFICERS OF THE
GEORGIAN ARMY TO 1793

For the first half of the 18th century, the Army changed but little. The second half of the century saw some developments in weaponry, organisation and command, to bear fruit in the Seven Years War, but with a return to organisational incompetence in the War of American Independence, much of this to continue for almost a century. The ending of the War of the Spanish Succession had, not surprisingly, resulted in another Parliamentary demand for a peace dividend, with the almost immediate disbandment of thirteen cavalry and twenty-two infantry units. Others were only saved by transfer to the Irish establishment. After various modifications in the eight years 1714–22, Parliament, reluctantly accepting the need for the Army, eventually settled upon a strength of 18,000, with an additional 12,000 on the Irish establishment.[1] But many in Parliament still favoured and pressed for a return to the primacy of the Militia, controlled as it was by Whig landowners, in preference to the Army.

The military commitments in the early and mid-18th century included three further Jacobite risings within Britain in 1715, 1719 and 1745, and from 1742 involvement in the War of the Austrian Succession fought in Germany and Belgium. In addition the officers of the Army had domestic commitments similar to those of the late Stuart period: ceremonial, highway patrolling, prevention of smuggling, escorting of prisoners and bullion, fire-fighting, frictions over billeting, road-building in Scotland, and the maintenance of civil law and order. At its most routine this latter could be simply the presence of a regiment in a restless region, city or county, in particular Scotland, Cornwall and Devon. More serious were the Glasgow troubles of 1725 when, following assaults on soldiers and violent rioting, the 16th Foot opened fire on a crowd, killing eight people and wounding nineteen.[2] In 1757 regiments had to be turned out to suppress riots of Militia men protesting against a project to send drafts from the Militia to serve overseas. At times of threatened French invasion, regiments would be sent to coastal areas. The 1715 Jacobite rebellion was checked at Preston and then again at Sheriffmuir, after which a relatively mild repression followed, with a small number of executions and deportations but with a larger number of estates being confiscated. The 1719 uprising was largely thwarted by the destruction of the main Jacobite force in a storm at sea; a diversionary landing was easily disposed of. The 1745 rebellion was much more serious, having much French support and necessitating the withdrawal of British forces from operations in Flanders. The rebels, after a spectacular victory at Prestonpans, reached Derby but were forced back into Scotland to be defeated at Culloden, a battle in which no quarter was given, murder squads even being sent out after the battle to kill all Jacobite wounded and also the many civilians who came to their aid. There followed a much more serious repression which brought no credit on the English and Scottish officers involved. Executions, most in England for reasons of security, deportations, burning of houses and destruction of crops and stock were all thought to administer a salutary lesson.[3]

The War of the Austrian Succession saw a convincing British and coalition victory at Dettingen in 1743, but had later serious reverses at Fontenoy in 1745, at Roncoux in 1746 and at Luffeldt in 1747. For the war an expeditionary force, eventually to total over 16,000, had to be prepared in haste.[4] The hurried preparations meant that at the outset officers and soldiers were very inadequately trained, though with experience regiments became more efficient. The annual campaigns differed little in their operational art from those fought in the time of Marlborough. Although in George I's reign uniform arms drill was laid down, in practice, and despite instructions issued in 1727, there were still no proper common procedures either in the movements of regiments on the march or in much of the tactics on the field of battle. These all depended on the choices of individual Colonels, a distinct weakness of overall efficiency.

In general, tactics centred on the improved fire-power of the 0.75 inch flintlock musket, introduced in the 1720s, the first long hand versions of the famous Brown Bess. Firepower was now properly controlled in rolling volleys, a unit's front rank kneeling if attacked with fire only being ordered by officers when it was certain every shot would hit and hurt. Musket fire having halted the enemy's attack, sabre cavalry and infantry bayonet counter-attacks would follow. The bayonet was to be used to stab an opponent on the left breast so that it might go through to the arm and prevent the opponent from drawing a sword. Well controlled by officers, withdrawals and retreats as at Fontenoy would be effectively covered by companies turning about and firing volleys. Attacks were led by the officers and men of the grenadier companies of several regiments grouped together. The task of keeping the ranks of advancing infantry, two or three deep, dressed in line when under fire was far from easy.[5] The need for an advance screening force for intelligence gathering (both topographical and operational), to harass and, in defence, to delay an approaching enemy, was becoming very clear by the late 1740s with important later consequences.

In 1716 two companies of artillery were formed at Woolwich leading, with the addition of two more companies from Minorca and Gibraltar, to the formation of the Royal Regiment of Artillery in 1722; a number of the rank and file gunners were, or had been, sailors. Field guns were now interspersed with the front line of the infantry to fire into enemy assaults. In the campaigns officers also had numerous less spectacular routine but essential tasks to carry out: foraging, march discipline, prevention of pillage, reconnaissance, the organisation of camps, tentage, camp security with quarter-guards, sentries, outposts and patrols, food supplies, care of the sick and wounded, and the administration of prisoners (officer prisoners were generally treated civilly, soldier prisoners roughly). A Field Officer of the camp picquet would have to make a round between 11 p.m. and 3 a.m. with a company roll call at evening tattoo (recall to quarters), after which candle lighting was to be extinguished. Officers had to ensure that all soldiers were issued with eighteen rounds of musket ammunition and two flints, that cooking pots were kept clean, and that wood was cut only for proper purposes such as the building of latrine 'houses' in the rear of the camp.

There were also training tasks for officers in regiments hurriedly raised: drill, marching, deployment and the most efficient use of the Brown Bess. Drill consisted of Manual Exercise (loading, firing, bayonet drill and saluting, all taught by numbers), Platoon Exercise (volley firing), Evolutions (movement at the halt), Firings (fire control by platoon volleys) and Manoeuvres (tactical movements). The first three could be taught by companies, the last two had to be by regiment, particularly as platoons were sometimes grouped together in six platoon 'Grand Division' fronts. Such Grand Divisions would have a Captain in command with a Lieutenant and an Ensign. The remaining officers would be posted to the rear to prevent desertion and be available as replacements for casualties. Within a firing platoon the officer would be at one end of the front rank. The actual battlefield orders were firstly 'Make Ready', at which the front rank knelt while the centre rank took a half pace to the right and the rear rank a full pace. This was followed by 'Present' when muskets were raised at the advancing enemy. The fire orders that followed were intended to ensure that one rank was firing while the other two were reloading but the orders still varied by regiment.

Drums and trumpets were used for signalling commands by both cavalry and infantry. Marching became divided into quick and 'soft', i.e. slow; from 1747 marching in step to drum and fife began. In tactical movements, the manoeuvres included advancing in line, deploying to a flank and forming a square; in the latter, men from the grenadier company covered the corners, platoon officers stood in the small intervals between companies, and other officers were in reserve in the centre of the square.[6]

Cavalry drills were more complex with both mounted and dismounted drills. These included closing and doubling files either on the centre or on the flanks, with changes of direction to be made on the wheeling of small units on the ground where they stood, so preserving compactness and control. Officers would have had to issue their orders while in addition, perhaps under fire, controlling their own mounts.

Further preparatory orders for cavalry and infantry covered firing on foot when arms were loaded, fixing and unfixing bayonets, and repriming, reloading and laying down arms. In one regiment these required thirteen, eight, five and nineteen words of command respectively. A further four words of command were needed to draw swords, six more for the drawing of pistols, five more for unslinging carbines and two more for returning swords. Finally, eight commands were needed to order dismounted action and the leading of horses to the rear.[7] The Regiment of Artillery, after its formation in 1722, provided a battery for a camp in Hyde Park in the following year. A Colonel of the Regiment had been appointed earlier, the twenty-gun battery had a Captain and a Lieutenant, seven NCOs, forty 'matrosses' (limber personnel), two drummers and seventy-six horses.[8]

A small separate artillery regiment for Ireland was formed a little later. The artillery officers had to command a very mixed collection of men indeed – engineers and pioneers responsible for planning and necessary earthworks, fireworkers in charge of the ammunition, kettle drummers, civilian carpenters and metal and rope tradesmen, and the commissariat personnel. A corps of Engineers was formed in 1717, but their command was civilian labour only.

The War of the Austrian Succession also saw, while on the march and in embryonic form, the first appearance of Divisions, though at the time these would be little more than two or three regiments. One division on the march would take over the billets of the division in front. In practice the Army still remained a very loose confederation of regiments, so much independence remaining in the hands of Colonels. Some of these had achieved General's rank but in the absence of an appointment given a regimental Colonelcy as a reward. Some of these, and others also, became in actual practice non-executive directors, deputing regimental work to their Lieutenant-Colonels. A few regiments had two battalions, the First Guards three. Within infantry units the establishment changed only very slightly, a Lieutenant being added to the grenadier company and a 'Second Lieutenant' to each company in 1742. Companies varied in strength from fifty to seventy private soldiers. In 1747 (possibly as early as 1743) instructions to refer to infantry units by their number of seniority rather than by the name of their Colonels were issued, but they and others issued later were ignored for many years.[9]

There is some evidence that officers of a unit were developing a corporate loyalty; the officers of the 11th Foot, for example, erected a memorial to one of their number who died in 1750.[10] Family ties and traditions also began to form: five brothers served as officers in the 30th Foot. Some were now commissioned from the ranks, and a very few were awarded battlefield commissions. Otherwise the social background of officers remained unchanged, but aristocracy and gentry were now becoming better educated and cultured with a new emphasis on civility and manners, together with a certain stylish nonchalance. A need for adventure and escape from English provincial life seems to have been the attraction for military service. King George I tried to end the purchase of commissions and other corrupt practices but with only limited success, over two-thirds of Commissions still being purchased. The prices of commissions had remained fairly static, a Colonelcy at £6,000, a Majority £1,800, a Captaincy £1,000 with Lieutenants and Ensigns £300 and £200 respectively.

Discipline among the officers remained poor. Advancement was to be secured not by conscientious performance of duties but by gaining, by whatever means, the goodwill of the Secretary at War. Professional zeal was not respected or fashionable, though several officers were cashiered for poor performance in the 1745 fighting.

Foot regiment officers' uniforms became more standardised. If an officer was a little thin on top he had to wear a wig below his laced hat. He was expected to have two sets of uniform – a long frock coat opened to show his gorget rank badge, a cravat of rich lace, a waistcoat in the regiment's chosen colour, a scarf or a sash over his shoulder, silver buttons, gloves and silk stockings, together with boots, garters, sword and belt, cloak and bed linen. The expenses of uniform, camping equipment, perhaps a tent of the correct regimental pattern and horse furniture were now quite considerable. To them had to be added costs of messing, food, alcohol, laundry, soap and hair powder, stationery and a supplement to the allowance paid for servants. On the march, when silk stockings were replaced by boots or gaiters, if passing a General, an officer would dismount, fall in with his company and take his spontoon – a half pike or halberd – from his servant. Colonels were entitled to six servants, Lieutenant-Colonels and Majors three, Lieutenants, Ensigns and Quartermasters one. An allowance of six pence per day was, in theory, payable for each servant.[11]

Officers either provided themselves with carriages or were allowed 'bat-horses' from one to eight according to rank.[12] When a regiment took to the field on operations cash allowances, baggage money and forage money were paid to cover the costs of local purchases of horses and food. Some officers' pay was slightly increased, a Major's by a shilling a day and a Colonel's by two shillings. Colonels also now received a daily allowance of one shilling and four pence for 'widows', one shilling and two pence for clothing lost by deserters and one shilling for recruiting. A few allowances for special duties were also payable. Subaltern officers on duty road building in Scotland received an extra two shillings and six pence per day, part of which was intended to defray the costs of building shelters for their men. Officers serving in India received two shillings per day for a Captain, one shilling for a Lieutenant. Prize money was also payable.

The essential corruption of the whole system continued to enable officers both at home and overseas to supplement their income in dubious ways, 'managing' regimental funds and falsifying muster rolls. Nevertheless, a Subaltern's outgoings exceeded his pay and allowances and only when an officer became a Captain could he begin to show some legitimate profit.[13]

The relationship between officers and their men, however, remained generally cold and harsh, at least until the Seven Years War. The general view of soldiers early in the century was that of Lieutenant-Colonel Blackader of the 26th Foot, '. . . mercenary fawning, lewd dissipated creatures, the dregs and scum of mankind'.[14] The Duke of Cumberland, at first as a Guards officer and later as Captain-General, tried to urge officers to concern themselves more with their men's welfare, but with little real success. The only alleviating feature was that, although there was fairly frequent cross-posting, the longer periods of time officers were now serving in regiments did begin to make the better officers a little more concerned with their men's well-being.[15]

A curious feature of life in many regiments first appeared in the first half of the 18th century, the formation of regimental Masonic Lodges. These were in most regiments open to all ranks to join; senior NCOs appear to have been the leading supporters but many officers were also members. Later, in the Wellington era, admission was refused to anyone who had not been a Mason before joining the Army. The Lodges no doubt contributed to mutual understanding across the ranks barrier, and also appear to have eased the problems of movement and postings when a regiment with a Lodge was posted to a station overseas with a Lodge.[16]

In respect of formal discipline, for both officers and men, a recast version of the *Articles of War* was printed in 1718.[17] Offences and regulation were listed in forty-six articles. Blasphemy was to be dealt with by civil courts, profaning a church or assaulting a Chaplain by court-martial. Treachery, disobedience or mutiny were court-martial offences, liable for the death penalty. Officers were to obey regulations concerning pay. For soldiers desertion, persuasion to desert, breaking out of prison, abandoning their post or plundering could incur the death penalty. Officers enlisting a deserter or a man escaping from confinement were to be cashiered. Officers who duelled were to be cashiered, NCOs and soldiers to be whipped. Regimental courts-martial were to consist of five officers and a President; they could order corporal punishment subject to approval by the Commanding Officer. Officers drunk on duty were to be cashiered, NCOs and soldiers to be punished by the wood horse or other corporal punishment, and sentries quitting their post to run the gauntlet. Any offence incurring the death penalty was reserved for General Court-Martial – thirteen officers with at least a Field Officer as President. The military need for the speedy administration of discipline and justice was recognised by an Article requiring speedy trials. Other regulations covered sutling (petty trading), false alarms, making known the watchword, theft, embezzlement or sale of stores, and damage to quarters. The Articles were to be read out to all troops, including the artillery train, every two months. The Articles noted that any other offences not covered were to go before Justices of the Peace. These arrangements, formally giving much greater power to officers within a regimental or General court-martial system, represented the legal basis for discipline in the Georgian army. The now authorised punishments included stoppages of pay; lashes; 'picquet' where a man might have to hang by one hand tied to a post with feet poorly supported, perhaps also at the same time being whipped; the wood horse; running the gauntlet; being broken slowly on the wheel; the 'strupado' where a man with his arms and legs tied behind his back was hoisted up by a pulley and then dropped to be stopped with a jerk; or the whirligig, a wooden cage in which the victim was spun round at speed.

After the end of the War of the Austrian Succession, Cumberland pursued his quest for reform with regulations covering dress, incorporating different regiments' distinctive features; regimental administration, requiring company commanders to keep proper accounts, hear and investigate complaints and cease from imposing illegal stoppages; annual inspections of regiments by general officers, though how effective this was in establishing 'fitness for role' is doubtful; and finally a revision of instructions on drill and tactics.[18] Perhaps more important for the future of the British officer, though, had been the earlier (1741) opening of the first officer training college, the Royal Academy at Woolwich, for officers, NCOs and cadets of the Royal Artillery and practitioner engineer officers. From the middle 1720s a very small number of cadet gunners had been receiving some tuition at Woolwich in mathematics under Royal Artillery arrangements; the founding of a proper academy was a very significant advance. Admission to the Academy was by a nomination from the Master-General of the Ordnance; cadets aged from their teens to thirty were organised into companies, treated as officers and gentlemen and paid sixteen pence a day for gunners and twelve pence for mattrosses. Reports on their work were made each month but discipline was at first very lax indeed, with brawls in town and taunting of instructors in class. Cadets lived out until 1752 when barracks of a sort were completed, providing rooms for eight cadets with two in a bed, and the cadets all grouped into one company. Mathematics, physics and chemistry were taught (no text books were used) for theory three days a week, and three further days were spent in practical instruction in gunnery, organising the artillery train, mining, engineering and bridge building. However, any final examination was limited to a few questions before a board of officers. All Commissions were given to the Artillery until the formation of the Corps of Royal Engineers in 1757.[19] By the 1750s there were forty-eight cadets under instruction with more firm discipline. In 1764 further reforms provided for a Lower Division for boys aged twelve to fifteen, an increase of pay for gentlemen cadets to two shillings and six-pence a day from which, however, deductions for messing, servants, a surgeon and dancing instruction were made, and an increase in instructing staff to cover a wider syllabus, now extending to French and the art of warfare. The college was now renamed the Royal Military Academy and abuses such as entering the names of infants and ten-year old boys as cadets ended; discipline, however, still remained something of a problem. Examinations slowly became more rigorous with a number of failures.

Except in Ireland and in London there were still no barracks for soldiers. While officers now clearly dined together and participated in social events there were no officers' messes. Overall, the standard of efficiency in the Army had fallen since the days of Marlborough, the institutionalised corruption of the system being the main cause. But the second half of the 18th century was again to provide further contrasts in the officer paradox of an often louche lifestyle in Britain to set against undoubted bravery and often some real skill on the field of battle. The Seven Years War showed what the Army and its officers could do, but the War of American Independence was once more to highlight many of the Army's weaknesses.

The Seven Years War (1754–63) involved the Army in operations against the French in Canada, in Western Germany and in India. In Canada, after an initial reverse, success followed at Louisburg in 1758, at Québec in 1759 and at Montréal in 1760. In Western Germany British regiments achieved fame at Minden in 1759 and at Warburg in 1757 and in India with Eyre Coote's victory at Wandewash in 1760. The war can justifiably be called the first truly world war, and also one that called for drastic rethinking of the formal tactics of earlier years. The Army had to be expanded for its worldwide operations; including German units the total strength climbed to a little over 200,000, with 100 units on the British establishment. Infantry regiments received second battalions; the artillery increased to twenty-four companies.[20]

The opening reverse in the war in Canada, General Braddock's defeat at Monongahela River, was a consequence of attempting to use the traditional column advance-to-contact drills against a more mobile enemy, part regular and part irregular, well acquainted with the forest terrain and able to mount ambushes. The need for a new type of infantry to reinforce the British regiments and locally raised colonist militia was again evident. The Army was experiencing for the first time what is now called asymmetric warfare, combat with informally organised indigenous guerrillas prepared to use terror tactics such as scalping and mutilation. The answer was seen initially as light infantry corps marksmen to harass the enemy and scouts with, very soon afterwards, the formation of a special regiment.[21] This regiment, officers and men, was formed from both British and local colonial personnel, and sought to combine the role of traditional infantry with that of hunter and skirmisher. Red coats were rejected in favour of dark green with no lace, and men's hair was ordered to be cut short. As initially the Royal American Regiment, 60th Foot, later the King's Royal Rifle Corps, the four battalions of this regiment played lead roles in the very difficult virgin forest conditions of the campaign. The battalion establishments and pay were the same as for British battalions, though land grants were offered to officers as incentives and commissions were not purchased.

Action was very different from Flanders and officers had to have even steadier nerves and control. At Ticonderoga, for example, attacking battalions were ambushed from both flanks, with soldiers shouting and cursing, caught in the entanglement of fallen trees, tripped by briars and logs and unable to reach their enemy or even see him clearly enough to return fire. Nevertheless six successive attacks by seven battalions were made before the attempt to take the fort was abandoned. Twenty-three officers were killed in the attack, the 42nd Highlanders alone losing eight with seventeen more wounded. Forage was scarce, the weather often very wet, and fevers not checked by the mixture of ginger, sugar and the water of America ordered to be used as a prophylactic. Fortified stores and magazines had to be built along forest tracks.

A copy of the 1757 general orders of the British commander, the Earl of Loudoun, provides detail on the routine duties of officers in Canada at this time.[22] A summary of the matters covered is of interest: the provision of camp quarter guards of a Subaltern, three NCOs and forty men to be relieved every two hours; drums to beat reveille at 4.30 a.m. with all companies to be on parade and inspected for dress and cleanliness; training from 10.00 to 12.00 a.m. and from 4.00 to 6.00 p.m.; tattoo for all at 7.00 p.m., officers to be punctual and with soldiers 'by no means to get into a loose way of doing duty'. Company commanders were to examine each soldier's cartridges every Monday morning, and ensure that all men had good flints; warning order procedures to march out, at as little as an hour's notice, for the escorting of stores were set out. In wet weather arms were to be grounded on sticks. NCOs were to be instructed to check that all men had twenty-four rounds of powder and ball. General alarm and admission to the camp procedures were also set out, and musket firing exercise arrangements issued.

One apprehensive set of orders directed preparations prior to a General's inspection: camp lines to be clean, on beat of a drum guards of honour to turn out with rested arms until a further beat when all men were to turn out with their side arms. Other orders governed permission to leave camp for hunting, fishing or swimming, court-martial for soldiers who failed to attend roll call, the illicit sale of rum, preservation of buildings, food supplies for scouts on patrol, camp and tent pitching and cleanliness, strength returns, fresh sanitation 'houses' to be dug each week and the old ones filled in, unauthorised discharge of firearms and soldier punishments ranging from death sentences, drumming out or lashes (1,000 or 500) to a General's reprimand for an officer absent from duty.

The operations in Western Germany followed more familiar patterns. At the battle of Minden in 1759, for example, the Hanoverian and British force advanced to contact in eight columns, setting out with bands playing and colours flying – the right column comprising six cavalry regiments, a column of guns and two brigades of infantry; in the centre artillery; on the left three columns of infantry and one of cavalry. Infantry attacked French cavalry and repulsed cavalry attacks with precise drill movements and fire control. At Warburg in 1760 British cavalry carried the day.[23] Once again regimental officers were leading their men with valour and professionalism. In the campaign desertion appears to have been a serious problem, the necessity for frequent roll calls adding to the duties of officers.

The campaigning in India was fought mainly by regiments of Europeans recruited locally and by regiments of indigenous people led by British officers. Only one metropolitan British regiment, the 39th Foot, was involved. The regiment served alongside local units in the stiffest fighting but, both on the journey out and in India, officers and men alike suffered severely from disease. Four companies of artillery were sent to Bombay in 1755.

Service in other colonies posed different hazards for officers. The 39th Foot serving in Minorca lost, from disease, two Captains, five Lieutenants and an Ensign in the two years 1716 and 1717, these places being taken by officers on half-pay from disbanded regiments.[24]

Worse was to follow when the regiment, having shared in the privations caused by the Spanish siege of Gibraltar in 1727, was posted to Jamaica, seen by officers as 'the most expensive, disagreeable place under the sun'. The 38th Foot served for fifty-seven years in the West Indies, some officers acquiring property in the islands, others absenting themselves; the Chaplain was not seen at all in the years 1755 to 1769.[25] A system of rotation of units was instituted in 1749 but some regimental officers still faced long tours in unhealthy climates.

There is no doubt the Seven Years War enhanced the bonding of officers amongst themselves and with their men in regiments, sharing common dangers, suffering hardships and disease in common and with awareness of responsibilities for each other's lives.[26] The general indifference of the national government to the welfare of ordinary soldiers also led many officers to feel that they had a personal responsibility. At the same time, however, the system remained essentially corrupt; at the top there was division of control between the royal prerogative, the power of Parliament and the senior political figures, and the wishes of senior officers. The amateurish nature of the system was evident in the frequent breakdown of supply, there being no permanent supply system and transport depending on private commissariat arrangements and the requisitioning of horses and waggons when available. At the end of the Seven Years War the Army was reduced to 45,000 and the number of infantry battalions to seventy, most light companies being disbanded.

The long war of American Independence, 1773–83, saw developments in the asymmetrical warfare that had earlier so confused the British in North America. In addition to the difficulties of the almost roadless and sparsely cultivated terrain and the vast areas in revolt, of climate and disease, and of supply still in civilian hands, the British Army now found itself for the first time in history fighting a whole people, four million in total. Pioneers and frontiersmen were grouped into militias, one day warriors, the next apparently peaceful farmers, using ground with local knowledge and the natural skill of the frontiersmen. Towns could be occupied, set-piece battles could be won, but afterwards the colonists disappeared into forests to reappear later. Command was divided, strategy flawed, communications were inevitably slow and there were no clear battle-winning political or military objectives. The rebels saw their best course of action lay in avoiding battle and wearing the British down. After the battle of Bunker Hill in 1775 the British cause was lost, although the war was to last another eight years.

In contrast, when the French entered the war, fighting became more familiar in style. In St Lucia, at the battle of Vigie Point, the use of light infantry, well led by their officers and NCOs, was of key importance in advance as skirmishers fired on French columns from behind cover; when the French attempted to extend they threatened a bayonet charge, when the French closed up they were extended and fired in fusillade, and when the French advanced they fell back to prepare for further skirmishing and ambushes from all directions.[27]

For the war an initial three, and later a further five, infantry regiments were formed; two cavalry regiments became Light Dragoons. Light companies were revived; German regiments again also served. A number of officers, particularly in the new regiments, were Scots, Irish or Welsh, and there was much trafficking of commissions.

For the regimental officer the war in America was a very severe experience. Men with equipment weighing sixty pounds had to be encouraged and led to fight in terrain of bush, rocks, ravines and sometimes swamps. Roads, if there were any, might be blocked by fallen trees, bridges blown up. Rain, fog, heat and fatigue added to the difficulties. Officers waving swords would strive to keep their men in line. Moving the heavy field pieces of the artillery was especially difficult. There were numerous examples of officers' personal bravery and of their success in leading their men. But the American tactics of harassment by day and night led to erosions of unit strengths that could badly affect morale; American sharpshooters and snipers would also specifically target officers and NCOs. The rank and file would be tempted to plunder – or desert, for which leaflet inducements were offered by the Americans.

The Royal American Regiment had been reduced to two battalions after the end of the Seven Years War. Their officers' loyalties being divided, these units were now sent to the West Indies and the 3rd and 4th Battalions reformed from men from England and Germany.[28]

The hardships of the campaign, perhaps even more than in the Seven Years War, brought officers and soldiers together, each again recognising their responsibilities towards each other. Both suffered miserably from sicknesses – dysentery and fever in particular. Officers sympathetic to the plight of their soldiers became resigned to their pillaging, and they took care of the wounded, ensuring that deserving cases were declared invalids.

The elusive and partisan nature of the enemy also occasioned frustration and strain. While some senior and regimental officers were restrained and chivalrous in their behaviour towards captives or a newly occupied area, others were not, with some examples of arrogance and brutal excesses and the killing of wounded and civilians.[29]

When not in action officers, with the exception of a few who could not afford to do so or preferred other company, dined and messed together, with often very heavy drinking with numerous toasts, sometimes followed by cards. Great attention came to be paid to ceremonial with parades and gun salutes on royal and national anniversaries and on special regimental days, commemorating a previous battle or, for regiments of Welsh, Scots or Irish soldiers, St David's, St Andrew's or St Patrick's Day, all serving to link officers and men for the common purpose. Sometimes fancy dress displays were held. Well-respected NCOs felt able to speak freely to senior officers, on occasions by-passing those more junior. Conventions of cross-rank social behaviour were established and the ethos of pride and loyalty to the regiment firmly founded. finally, it merits recording that at the Saratoga surrender, officers appeared in full ceremonial dress – amongst their soldiers in uniforms worn and torn. The soldiers taken prisoner were often treated very badly despite all the representations made on their behalf by their officers, a number of whom were also initially maltreated but later were allowed log huts with stove chimneys, a coffee house and a theatre, though basic food was scaled down to Indian meal rather than wheaten flour.[30]

Some regiments served at sea on board warships. Some officers were accompanied by their wives, others had local mistresses. In winter in the cities, officers would have rooms for social gatherings and perhaps produce a play – usually a farce but sometimes Shakespeare – to raise money for soldiers' widows or families. In New York a Garrison Dramatic Club was formed by young officers supported by the daughters of merchants.[31] America also offered a range of sports opportunities – riding, horse racing, hunting, walking and golf.[32] In 1772 a booklet, *Military Guide for Young Officers*, set out principles for organising an Officers' Mess in the field, with set money contributions from officers and advice on dining tents, transport, kitchens and table linen. Wigs were generally discarded on active service and hair either cut short or tied in a pony tail. Officers off duty addressed each other as 'Mr' rather than by rank.

The Treaty of Paris ended the war, one in which the paradoxical virtues and faults of the Army had once again been shown up; they were to be further highlighted in the next thirty years. A nine-year period of benign neglect was to follow in which the general efficiency of the Army, despite some improvement in financial management, declined. Although numerous military publications and in 1778 new drill regulations were produced, the absence of many regiments abroad meant that standardisation was not achieved. All the old vices predominated: promotion by favouritism, especially in confidential reports, cronyism, purchase or success in recruiting, absenteeism and endless 'bumpers on' drunkenness, and the neglect of any professional training or education. The only instruction many officers received was that of very elementary paradeground words of command given by experienced sergeants. Although the establishment of the Army was not reduced, in practice rigid undermanning economy measures depleted many regiments. The officer in the now customary paradox of eagerness in action but high living at home became something of the subject of ridicule.[33]

NOTES

1 Specific newly raised units for this establishment included six cavalry regiments and one infantry battalion.

2 T.J.B., *Bedfordshire and Hertfordshire*, 130–131.

3 Christopher Duffy, *The '45* (London, Cassell, 2003), xxi.

4 Eight infantry battalions were raised for the war.

5 T.J.B., *Bedfordshire and Hertfordshire*, 135.

6 Robinson, *Bloody Eleventh*, 104–105, provides this clear account of infantry regimental procedures and the role of officers within them.

7 Major E.W. Sheppard, *The Ninth Queen's Royal Lancers* (Aldershot, Gale and Polden, 1939), 21–22. This regiment was one of dragoons at the time of these orders. The very difficult wheeling of a small unit on the ground where it stands is still performed by the massed Guards bands during the Trooping of the Colour parade.

8 Captain Francis Duncan, *History of the Royal Regiment of Artillery* (London, John Murray, 1872), I, 102.

9 Rex Whitworth, *William Augustus, Duke of Cumberland* (London, Leo Cooper, 1992), 152.

10 Robinson, *Bloody Eleventh*, 120.

11 Atkinson, *Hampshire Regiment*, 79.

12 Lieutenant-Colonel Neil Bannatyne, *History of the Thirtieth Regiment now the First Battalion East Lancashire Regiment 1689–1881* (Liverpool, Littlebury, 1923), 98–99.

13   C.T. Atkinson, *The Dorsetshire Regiment* (Oxford University Press, 1947), 55; for a detailed examination of several individual cases, Alan J. Guy, *Economy and Discipline: Officership and Administration in the British Army 1714–63*, (Manchester University Press, 1985), 94–110.

14   Scouller, *The Armies of Queen Anne*, 235.

15   For example, in the 39th Foot in 1740, the Lieutenant-Colonel, two Lieutenants and four Ensigns all had fifteen years or more of service in the regiment, the Lieutenant-Colonel himself having had thirty-eight years, Atkinson, *Dorsetshire Regiment*, 43–44, 47.

16   Masonry was described in the 1840s by one enthusiast, Dr J. Burnes, '. . . as a sort of rosy wreath that might be entwined round the iron pillar of military discipline imparting a grace and beauty to its form without impairing its integrity or strength . . . encouraging an attachment to the officer, and even devotion should he be a Brother, at the same time that it enhances the self respect of the soldier by making him feel . . . there is a point at which he and his military superior may be on the level where the good qualities of both may become prominently known to each . . .', R.F. Gould, *Military Lodges 1732–1899* (London, Gale and Polden, 1899), 196. The work is full of examples of Masonic folk history. Lodges survived Queen Victoria's strong disapproval. Some exist to this day, but friction arose in the post-1945 years when regiments with Lodges had to amalgamate with other regiments.

17   The text had earlier been laid before the House of Commons in 1717. A useful note on the 1717 and 1718 texts appears in Scouller, *The Armies of Queen Anne*, Appendix J.

18   Whitworth, *Cumberland*, 153. The drill regulations included Trooping the Colour.

19   F.G. Guggisberg, '*The Shop': The Story of the Royal Military Academy* (London, Cassell, 1900), 2–6; Alan Shepperd, *Sandhurst: The Royal Military Academy* (London, Country Life, 1980), 9–15. Guggisberg later became a distinguished colonial governor, Shepperd the virtual creator of the excellent Central Library at Sandhurst.

20   In the period 1755–59 three cavalry regiments and twenty-one infantry battalions were raised.

21 Lieutenant-Colonel Russell Gurney, *History of the Northamptonshire Regiment 1742–1934*, (Aldershot, Gale and Polden, 1975), I, 31; Lewis Butler, *The Annals of the King's Royal Rifle Corps* (London, Smith Elder, 1913), I, Introduction, i.

22 *General Orders of 1757 Issued by the Earl of Loudoun and Phineas Lyman in the Campaign Against the French* (Books for Libraries Press, Freepost, New York, 1970).

23 A valuable account of the West German campaign appears in Young and Lawford, *History of the British Army*, vii; 'The Seven Years War' by Sir Reginald Savory.

24 Atkinson, *Dorsetshire Regiment*, 29.

25 Colonel W.L. Vale, *History of the South Staffordshire Regiment* (Aldershot, Gale and Polden, 1969), 18.

26 Archibald Forbes, *The 'Black Watch': The Record of an Historic Regiment* (London, Cassell, 1896), 90–91. Forbes notes with pride how few officers of the 1759 regiment became Generals, the vast majority choosing to remain in regimental duty rather than seek staff or other 'votaries of non-regimental service'.

27 Fortescue, *British Army*, III, 265.

28 Butler, *Annals of the KRRC*, I, 207–208.

29 Christopher Hibbert, *Redcoats and Rebels: The War for America, 1770–1781* (London, Grafton, 1990); page 271 notes a particularly brutal massacre.

30 C.T. Atkinson, *The South Wales Borderers, 24th Foot, 1689–1937* (Cambridge University Press, 1937), 171.

31 Duncan, *Royal Artillery*, 330.

32 A rewarding account of an officer's life appears in Igor D. Gruber, *John Peebles American War 1776–1782* (Sutton, Army Records Society, 1998).

33 Corelli Barnett, *Britain and Her Army* (London, Penguin, 1970), 226, provides an example of the satire of the time. William Cobbett observed that heavy punishments were imposed on soldiers for drunkenness, but officers were only rarely punished.

CHAPTER 5

THE OFFICER IN THE ERA
OF WELLINGTON

The last years of the reign of George III saw the Army involved in two major wars, separated by a peace lasting a few months only. The first war was a consequence of post-Revolution French expansionism into the Low Countries and lasted – for Britain – from 1793 to 1802. The second was against the ambitions of Napoleon and lasted from 1803 to 1815. In the first war the Army performed poorly. At home this was a result of the post-1783 neglect and return to the louche life, together with the inexperience of ministers. In the field there was a general under-estimation of the vigour of the French ideology – driven revolutionary armies, with their vast *levée en masse* regimental attacks preceded by ferocious artillery bombardments and accompanied by awe-inspiring thunder of drums. Reforms were, however, initiated; these in time assisted the Army, under the military genius of the Duke of Wellington, to direct and motivate the British Army to withstand French attacks and go on to win spectacular victories culminating in that at Waterloo.

For the 1793 to 1802 war, fifteen new battalions of infantry and thirteen Light Dragoon regiments were raised in the years 1793–94, the sale of commissions proving very profitable for the government; two further units followed in 1799 and 1801. The first two troops of Horse Artillery (artillery to work with the cavalry) were formed in 1793, and in the course of the war three further field artillery units were raised. But in the first years of the war the Army was seriously short of men, with regiments often badly under-manned.

The main British effort at the outset was in Flanders. Individual regiments on occasions fought very well, but the inexperience and lack of professional motivation of officers was all too evident. There was widespread pillaging by British soldiers, apparently unchecked by their officers. The Adjutant-General commented that of the fifteen cavalry and twenty-six infantry regiments committed '. . . twenty-one are commanded literally by boys or idiots . . . ignorant of the simplest basic military knowledge and concerned only with their career advancement to be achieved by judicious purchase'.[1] At the top, command and strategy were poor and indecisive, often simply following patterns of the first half of the century and using firelock exercises and parade ground movements. The campaign was predictably a failure, and withdrawal followed at the end of 1794. Attacks and raids on mainland France brought only short-lived success. Four years of fighting in the West Indies was successful in strategic terms in that French trade was brought to a halt and French colonial acquisition ambitions frustrated, but a heavy price was paid in both casualties and disease. A French-supported uprising in Ireland in 1798 was put down; severe repression followed and an Irish dragoon regiment in which nationalists had been conspiring in favour of the uprising was disbanded. The rebellion was particularly worrying as so many soldiers in other regiments were Irish. A commando-style raid in the same year to block a sea lock at Ostend ended disastrously. In 1799 a major expedition was sent to occupy the Helder in Holland but the expedition had to be withdrawn, failure to cooperate with the allied Russian force being a major cause. Landings at Ferrol and Cadiz in Spain again provided only brief success. Several battalions had to be sent to India to support the regiments of the East India Company against the local ruler of Mysore who was receiving French support. The operations concluded with the capture and sacking of

Seringapatam, officers being unable to control their men. The year 1801 saw the first British Army force, 16,000 strong, arrive in Egypt, sent to destroy the French army that had been left there by Napoleon, the only really successful campaign of the war.

Transport by sea remained protracted, uncomfortable and unhealthy, men being crammed into rat-infested mess decks or coal holds in such numbers that on some ships only a third of the soldiers could rest asleep under cover at a time. Often the ships were old and leaking, and officers and men had to remain in damp uniforms for weeks on end, officers sharing the men's diet of salt horse and weevily biscuits. Weather could cause long delays before or during a voyage, sometimes as long as six months. Friction occasionally occurred between naval and military officers. On several occasions, either by intent or through necessity, officers and soldiers again had to fight as marines. Sometimes men, or whole companies of men, were lost when their transport sank.

Disease exacted a terrible toll in the West Indies operations and was no respecter of rank. In the period 1794–96 the 32nd Foot lost thirty-two officers, the 41st seventeen, the 66th nine, other regiments only a small number less, the main causes being malaria and yellow fever.[2] The overall poor performance led to reforms initiated by the Duke of York as Commander-in-Chief, appointed 'Field Marshal on the Staff' in 1795. Gross abuses of the purchasing of commissions system, including the gazetting of children, even infants as Lieutenant-Colonels, were ended. Though the system as a whole remained, no one could now purchase a commission under the age of sixteen. An officer wishing to purchase a Captaincy was now required to have two years' service; for a Major or a Lieutenant-Colonel's commission six years' service was made a condition. York also increased the number of unpaid promotions and the pay of Subalterns was increased.

In 1799 the absence of any training for staff officers was at last recognised with the opening of a military school in a back room of the *Antelope*, a rented public house at High Wycombe. The students, in their early twenties, were much younger than later staff officers. An émigré French royalist General, Jarry, a soldier of considerable field experience, was engaged to be Director of Instruction under the school's founder, Colonel Le Marchant.

Le Marchant's wide visionary plans provided for a three-department staged education programme for cavalry and infantry officers. These were to be an initial Junior Department preparatory stage for boys between thirteen and sixteen followed by a commissioning course, and a staff course for officers of at least four years' service in a Senior Department. The plans were not universally welcomed, many Commanding Officers believing that young officers were best trained in regiments, but the need for uniformity was recognised by York. In 1802 the Junior Department opened in a rented house in Great Marlow with an intake of sixteen fee-paying 'gentlemen cadets'. The High Wycombe school received the title of Royal Military College, three of its earliest products distinguishing themselves in the Egyptian campaign with well-prepared staff work preparing the beach landings.[3]

At the top York appointed a Military Secretary, as a channel for communication free from political interference for officers with grievances or worries, and gave extra authority to the Adjutant-General and the Quartermaster-General. The Army for the first time now had an effective headquarters staff. Standing Orders for the Army were revised and published together with a number of training pamphlets.

In respect of field training, after a special exercise of light infantry and cavalry and horse artillery, York in 1799 authorised the formation of the Experimental Rifle Corps, 'Corps of Riflemen', that later became the 95th Foot, the Rifle Brigade. In 1800 it comprised eight companies with two Lieutenant-Colonels and two Majors; the men were issued with the Baker high-precision rifle for which many officers had argued in the American war rather than the Brown Bess, and wore uniforms of dark green. Training carried the principles of the Royal American Regiment several stages further, and was of the greatest significance as much was in time to be taken from these principles by other infantry regiments. They represent the first serious British Army attempt at an Army core-values doctrine, particularly in leadership–followship, of which much is as valuable now as in 1800.[4]

Regimental life was to be based on mutual two-way trust and friendship between ranks, forming a family spirit, though respect for rank was to be marked by correct saluting procedures. Personal responsibility, initiative and flexibility were to motivate all ranks; if any superior fell, the next in rank must assume command and responsibility. All orders were to be given in moderate language with no blows or abuse. Bugle, horn or whistle were to be for commands on the field of battle. All ranks should serve in a spirit of cheerful volunteering. Riflemen were always to appear smartly turned out; specific instructions on care of arms and shooting standards were set out. Each individual rifleman was to select a fellow as a personal help-mate and companion. For the rank and file in general, a small library was opened and basic literacy and arithmetic instruction were to be provided for men seeking promotion to Corporal or Sergeant. A Sergeant's Mess was to be established and guidance given on the role and duties of junior NCOs. Regimental medals for Good Conduct, Long Service and Special Merit (a practice already in existence in some line regiments) were to be awarded, and soldiers were enjoined always to be humane in the treatment of prisoners and in behaviour in foreign lands.

Officers were to serve with their companies and not be cross-posted unless this was unavoidable, so providing continuity and trust. They were expected to know each of their own men as individuals and be concerned with their needs. Officers were also enjoined to encourage sports – for their own sake and not for any prize money; the sports set out included cricket, handball, football, athletics (running and vaulting), leapfrog and quoits. Especial importance, for its military value, was attached to group swimming instruction which with dancing, were seen as keeping men out of ale-houses in the evening. Above all, for officers, the greatest importance was attached to personal example. 'From the Officers of the Regiment the Colonel expects every example of what is good and great in a Soldier's and Gentleman's character.' The success of these principles when applied in training is well exemplified in the account of his service with the 95th written by Edward Costello.[5] The whole system was extended to Sir John Moore's Light Brigade (14th Light Dragoons and the 43rd and 52nd Foot), but could not at the time be applied to other line regiments whose soldiers were still drawn from some of the worst elements in society – criminals, drunkards and wild Irishmen – for whom more severe and less humane discipline still had to be enforced.

For the rest of the infantry a new booklet, *Principles of Military Movements*, by Colonel David Dundas, formed the basis of a 1792 official booklet, *Rules and Regulations for the Movement of His Majesty's Army*. This text, developed to a manual in 1803, represented a major step towards standardisation of infantry operational art and set out the steadiness necessary to repulse mass attacks, but it took time before the teaching became sufficiently absorbed and put into practice by Wellington. Also important was General Jarry's *Instructions Concerning the Duties of Light Infantry in the Field*. Within the cavalry, sword drill was standardised thanks to Le Marchant's *Rules and Regulations for the Sword Exercises of Cavalry*, published in 1796. Le Marchant himself, accompanied by a cadre of training officers, followed his publication up with visits to cavalry regiments. For the artillery, reforms introduced by the Master-General of the Ordnance provided for a special corps of artillery drivers who replaced the civilian gun teams, and, for engineering, a Royal Corps of Artificers to specialise in building. Studies of fortifications were produced and reading of them encouraged for all officers.

Plate 1 An Officer of the Tangiers Regiment, 1669. Courtesy of The Princess of Wales's Royal Regiment.

Plate 2 An Officer of the Coldstream Guards in the reign of James II.
Photo by kind permission of the Regimental Lieutenant-Colonel
Coldstream Guards.

Plate 4 The Surgeon-Major of the Black Watch, 1780. Courtesy of The Black Watch.

Plate 3 An Officer of the Royals (Royal Scots) c.1739. Courtesy of The Royal Scots.

Plate 5 An Officer of the 23rd Foot, 1800. Courtesy of The Royal Welch Fusiliers.

Plate 6 I Troop Royal Horse Artillery, Capt. Norman Ramsay at Fuentes de Onoro by G.D. Giles. Courtesy of The Royal Artillery Institution.

Plate 7 (a) and (b) Cavalry Officers, 1803 and 1812. Courtesy of The King's Royal Hussars.

Plate 8 Ensign and Colours, IXth East Norfolk Regiment in the Age of Wellington. Courtesy of The Royal Norfolk Regiment Association.

Plate 9 The Royal Waggon Train in the Peninsula War (note carrying of the wounded soldier). Courtesy of the Institution of the Royal Army Service Corps and the Royal Corps of Transport.

Plate 10 Rifle Regiment Officers at Shooting Practice, 1828. Courtesy of the Regimental Museum Archives, The Royal Green Jackets.

Plate 11 A 3rd Guards Officer on Court Guard Duty. Courtesy of The Scots Guards.

Plate 12 Officers of the 17th Foot in the Crimea. Courtesy of The Royal Tigers' Association, The Royal Leicestershire Regiment.

Plate 13 Academic study of the art of war: a lecture after lunch at the Staff College in the 1880s. (The instructor is the author's grandfather.)

Plate 14 Inniskilling Dragoon Guards Officers' Mess in the field, Boer War. Courtesy of The Royal Dragoon Guards.

Plate 15 Lieutenant Bennett of the Worcestershire Regiment, Transloi Ridge, 1916. Although wounded and armed only with a spade, Bennett rallied the men of his company to restore the momentum of the attack. He was awarded the Victoria Cross. Courtesy of the Trustees of The Worcestershire Regiment Museum.

Plate 16 Ypres: A Front Line Company Headquarters, 1915. Courtesy of the DCLI Museum Committee.

Plate 17 Group of Officers of the 1st Royal West Kent Regiment taken the day before the attack on Hill 60, 1915 and recording their fate in the battle. Courtesy of The Princess of Wales's Royal Regiment.

Changes were also made in officering. In 1793 Colonels of regiments who held a General's rank were released from the duty of long periods of service with their regiments. An additional Lieutenant-Colonel and an additional Major were authorised for regiments.[6] These additional officers were not to command companies and their initial purpose appears to have been that of casualty replacement, though later, if the battalion's companies had to be divided into groups of four, a Major might command each group. From 1803 no Field Officers were to command companies in addition to their other duties, a military gain but a financial loss to the officers concerned who lost their company command pay increment. The duties of the Adjutant, as the Lieutenant-Colonel's personal staff officer and expert on drill, were more clearly developed, as were those of the Quartermaster, promoted from the ranks, concerned with stores and generally not meant to participate in combat. In 1783 the first known purpose-built Officers' Mess was opened in the Royal Artillery barracks at Woolwich, an example to be followed as other barracks were built and opened.[7] In 1793 a more general barracks building programme for infantry and cavalry regiments was initiated, at last removing the rank and file from billets and ale-houses. Orderly officers of the day became tasked with mounting inspection of guards in the barracks.

In 1803, after the few months of uneasy peace, France declared war on Britain. The twelve years of fighting that followed saw the major British land effort in Portugal, Spain and later southern France and the Low Countries, with other lesser and generally unsuccessful campaigns in Italy, South America and North America, and also in the first years of the war, a major military commitment in India with a smaller one in South Africa, and finally a small but successful campaign in Java. A number of cavalry regiments were kept in Britain for internal security duties.

By 1803, nevertheless, the learning journey was advancing. It was now realised that French superiority in numbers and their attacks by successive columns could be countered. Success could be gained, firstly, by skilled skirmishing by light troops harassing the French columns' flanks and the use of ground wherever possible to conceal defending troops until, secondly, the correct moment arrived for men in square or lying down, now in two-deep lines rather than three, to rise and pour volley into the ranks of their attackers. The effect of the volleys would be increased by supporting artillery fire. Finally, to follow up the volleys, there were to be charges by infantry and pursuit by cavalry. These tactics, however, required more intelligent officering than the simplistic parade ground movements of previous wars and above all an offensive spirit, the development of which was largely the work of Wellington. Officers came increasingly to think out new ways of harassing and surprising the enemy.

Army numbers rose spectacularly. The Army's strength in May 1803 was 105,000, by 1805 it was 160,000, by 1807 200,000, eventually peaking at 230,000. Several regiments raised a second and sometimes a third battalion. However, in the Peninsula campaign Wellington never had more than 40,000 British troops under his command; the rest of his force were the King's German Legion or allies. Structuring became much more defined: in 1808 the British units were grouped into six brigades; by 1809 there were one cavalry and four infantry divisions.[8] A Light Division was formed in 1810. The force led by Wellington into the south of France in 1813 reached a total of eight divisions. The 1st Division gained the sobriquet of 'The Gentlemen's Sons' as it contained two Guards brigades, and the Light Division the simple but very clear elite 'The Division'.

The cavalry officers, reared in fox-hunting, habitually displayed more dash and courage than common sense, leading Wellington to order few large-scale cavalry charges, two notable exceptions being those of the charges of four regiments at Fuentes de Onoro in 1811 and of three regiments at Salamanca in 1812. In charges, officers led from the front. In the Peninsula, though, cavalry was mostly used on outpost duty, protection of foraging parties, escort of prisoners, covering withdrawals, small harassing attacks on the advance guards or flanks of French columns, occasional pursuits and, most importantly, reconnaissance where two or three officers would roam across country gathering intelligence – perhaps from concealment – counting the number of French regiments crossing a bridge or entering a valley. Cavalry, however, could never hold ground after a charge.

To the infantry officers fell the most testing roles, to which some played with brilliance, a number played adequately but a number, also, failed to meet all the exacting standards of their Army Commander.[9] A dismal few still adhered to old parade ground attention to drill and minutiae of uniform regulations. In battle the quality most needed was steadiness, ensuring that their platoon 'division' or company was well sited to discharge volleys to maximum effect at the best opportunity. Courage, in leading a bayonet charge, attempting to storm a fortress or holding together a group of frightened men as French cavalry swirled around them was essential. In a pitched battle noise, apart from being very frightening, could also make command exceedingly difficult with a cacophony from artillery, muskets, shouts, cries of the wounded men and horses, martial music; smoke was often thick and vision was blocked by trees, crops and buildings which could add to confusion. Fortitude was required to tolerate the severe weather and terrain conditions which were made worse when soldiers had to face the appalling evidence of French devastation, scorched earth and often scorched human beings. The setting of an example of good humour to men was perhaps the third most important quality needed. It would seem here that an important component of British Army officer man-management made its first appearance, gentle chaff and repartee across divisions of rank.

In addition to these obvious battlefield and line of march duties the infantry officer might have others. Light companies from battalions were sent forward to skirmish. Some officers had to super-vise the digging of zigzag trenches to provide concealed cover from an assembly area to a start line or other minor engineering duties, as so few engineer officers were available. Some had to lead men from boats in beach landings under fire or, less dangerously, super-vise disembarkation or unloading of stores. Assaults on a fort where a breach in fortifications had been made might have to be led by a 'Forlorn hope' party, which could vary in size from a Lieutenant, two Sergeants and twenty-five men to two Captains, two Lieutenants and 100 men. Watch had to be kept for the most serious disciplinary problems, alcohol and attempts at desertion, the latter not uncommon in particularly miserable weather. A watch had also to be kept on fraternisation with the enemy. Wellington strongly disapproved of this, but the incidence of fraternisation in quiet periods, exchanging alcoholic drinks and singing together, was quite common. Sometimes even officers fraternised, on occasions even with a sports competition of some variety against their French opponents. If the Commissariat supply system, still in private finance initiative civilian hands, failed to bring the foods purchased from Morocco, Turkey or even North America across mountain tracks, and failure was not infrequent, officers had some-how to maintain morale. Commands and orders, in camp or in battle, were conveyed by trumpet or bugle; regiments and even com-panies had their own individual calls for contingencies and duties. Captains and Subalterns were expected to march with their men but many officers preferred horseback. Some also preferred a musket rather than a sword in battle.

Artillery, Royal Field Artillery and Royal Horse Artillery were organised for battle into companies and troops respectively. The basic field piece was the 6 pdr. gun, though a few companies had the heavier 9 pdr. gun. Companies and troops were commanded by a Captain, assisted by a second Captain and three Lieutenants. For administration and movement, companies and troops were brigaded under the command of a Major or Lieutenant-Colonel. Ammunition included the newly invented shrapnel shell.

Engineer Officers, all too few, had particular responsibility when lines of fortifications, the most important being the 1810 thirty-mile-long line at Torres Vidras, had to be constructed. They had also to play a lead role in sieges, advising on the most suitable area to attempt a breach and assisting in siting the artillery's breaching pieces. For neither of these roles had officers been properly trained, suffering, in consequence, heavy casualties. More general daily tasks included building and maintaining roads, ditches, barriers, water supply, telegraph stations, magazines and smaller defensive forts and redoubts. A Lieutenant or Captain might find himself in charge of 1,000 or more Portuguese labourers with only two or three soldiers to help him.

For the officers themselves on field operations in the Peninsula, life was only a little less hard than the lives of their men. Officers and men alike were weakened by sickness caused by a variety of local maladies that had to be endured on the line of march. Letters sent home frequently contained requests for replacement items of uniform, some of necessity, some for a simple wish to look smart. Letters, newspapers and parcels from Britain usually took a month or two to arrive at a front-line regiment. On the march bivouacs or huts made from branches would be laid out under trees, if lodgings, barns or other cover was not available, and equipment hung on the branches. Officers messed by companies rather than battalions. In fine dry weather, life in the field might not be uncomfortable; in wet and cold weather, sleeping in wet clothes on wet mats, branches or the bare ground the reverse was true. Fleas, lice and mosquitoes were additional and severe summer and autumn discomforts. Ration beef and vegetables might be supplemented by game-birds or hares shot or trapped, all consumed in a mess trench lit by candles mounted in bayonet sockets. The local wine, although rough, was a welcome complement to the meals and dulled senses at difficult times. Cigars, when available, were very popular. Most brigade headquarters, and some regiments when in garrison, had proper Officers' Messes. Sometimes, as in Madrid and other Spanish cities, barracks provided shelter and a modicum of comfort. Officers, too, suffered as severely as their men if wounded. They were piled on carts and endured incredible discomfort, jolted on tracks or poor roads on their way to a field hospital, where treatment was often rough and ready and sometimes totally unskilled.

Off duty the practice of duelling had been greatly reduced but officers sometimes quarrelled violently; unofficial regimental courts of honour or wise peace-making by a Field Officer now usually settled such differences. Especially at times of reverse or misfortune, there was a good deal of grumbling in tents or other shelter. Overall, though, the long campaign and shared experience had created close feelings of brotherhood.

A number of officers' wives accompanied their husbands to Portugal and a busy social life grew up in Lisbon. Champagne was cheap and there were numbers of loose women for the unmarried. Card parties and gambling were also all available. Occasionally, passing through a town, a regiment's officers would be given a ball; language problems and different ideas of dancing created amusement for both British and Portuguese or Spaniards. A few wives followed their husbands on the march; one was described as holding an umbrella in one hand, her horse's reins in another. She was accompanied by a nanny goat for milk for her baby, a donkey on which travelled the baby and stores, an Irish nurse, her husband's servant, a dog and a cage of canaries.[10] Some wives had to nurse sick or wounded husbands, others to face up to the death of a husband. Husbands and wives with their children could sometimes become separated, neither knowing of the other's fate, in some cases with tragic consequences. A few officers married Portuguese or Spanish girls, on occasions eloping. Officers who misbehaved with a soldier's wife were severely disciplined.

Officers were also keen sightseers. Hunting, coursing and shooting all provided sport in periods of quiet. Cricket was played on several occasions. Pony, mule and donkey races together with dances and amateur theatricals were organised by officers to ease the monotonous life of soldiers. In a manner later to be copied by the Eighth Army in North Africa in the Second World War, an informality of officers' dress with individual personal embellishments appeared.

Some outstanding examples of regimental officer bravery merit mention as illustrating the spirit of the best of the officers. There was never a shortage of volunteers to lead a 'Forlorn hope' party and in most cases there was competition for the honour. Among the infantry epics was that of Lieutenant Macpherson of the 45th Foot, who although badly wounded took a French flag from one of the towers at Badajoz and replaced it with his red tunic.[11] In pitched battle officers stood in the centre of the square ready to strengthen the side or sides attacked; in the centre were also the regiment's Colours defended with the utmost tenacity by young Ensigns. At Waterloo the regimental Colour of the 69th Foot was defended by a sixteen-year-old Sandhurst cadet; despite twenty-two sabre wounds he killed three of his attackers.[12] The discipline and precision of the Guards battalions throughout the campaign, from Corunna to Waterloo led by their aristocratic or well-connected officers, represents one of the finest examples of infantry soldiering in the history of warfare.

Captain Dalrymple Ross's six-gun Horse Artillery battery, 'The Chestnut Troop', working with the Light Division, gained a reputation for making the guns fire from impossible platforms on high crags.[13] Another Horse Artilleryman, Captain Ramsay, finding his battery entirely surrounded by French cavalry at Fuentes de Onoro, limbered up his guns and at the gallop charged right through them.[14]

An event that vividly illustrates the teamwork of officers and men and caught the imagination of the whole army occurred at the siege of Burgos in 1812. Colonel Jones, the engineer in charge, exploded the mine to force the breach but was immediately hit by a bullet. A 'Forlorn hope' party of the 2nd Battalion of the 24th Foot, led by Lieutenant Fraser, rushed the breach against stiff French opposition to be followed by Captain Lepper seeking to enlarge it. Lieutenant Holmes at the same time led an assault over open ground against a heavily defended second gap; he was supported by Captain Coote with a second wave, Coote being wounded. Finally the remainder of the battalion, rallied by Captain Hedderwick, the senior surviving officer, cleared the way forward in a sweeping bayonet charge.[15]

A final proof of officers' commitment can be seen in casualties. Officers were killed or wounded in battle as much as, if not more than, their men. Twenty-five of the seventy-six officers of a brigade that fought at Barrosa in 1811 were killed or wounded. At Salamanca the 11th Foot lost three Subalterns killed, and the Lieutenant-Colonel, the Major, three Captains and eight Lieutenants were wounded, most seriously. At Quatre-Bras the 73rd at the end of the day had but one officer still on his feet; the Royal Scots lost thirty-one out of thirty-seven, four killed carrying the King's Colour. Out of 840 infantry officers at Quatre-Bras and Waterloo nearly half were killed or wounded, among them twenty-five out of the sixty-seven artillery officers.[16] At Waterloo out of sixty-three commanding officers eleven were killed and a further twenty-four wounded, some dying later. Thirteen out of twenty-four engineer officers were killed at Badajoz.

It must, however, be remembered that records and regimental histories record success and glory, only rarely failures. Shell-shock existed long before the 1914–18 war and one can assume there were victims of this also in this period. War needs led to some increase in the number of officers commissioned from the ranks, or serving in units for which commission purchase was not necessary. The majority, however, remained drawn from the aristocracy, minor

gentry or sons of clergy. Some junior officers were very young, bois-
terous, exuberant, late teenagers. The purchase system remained
the firm preference and policy of Wellington who believed that only
gentlemen could be relied upon not to act dishonourably and to
have an ideal and concern for something more than superficial military smartness.[17] His views also enjoyed increased support from the
London political establishment, seeing Bonapartism as a class as well
as a national threat.

Non-purchase promotion followed an officer's death, the next
senior taking over, an advancement that went all the way down the
officer ranks. In regiments that suffered heavy officer casualties the
survivors could do well. A number of officers not keen on active
service opted for half-pay; some even bought half-pay commissions
and of these some later entered full-pay service. In the units raised
for the war, commissions were granted without purchase, but these
commissions had no later market value. Officers wishing to make
a full military career sought commissions in older established
regiments, less likely to be disbanded for a peace dividend. The Royal
Artillery and Engineer officers remained commissioned without
purchase, with promotion by seniority. By 1814 there were over
700 artillery officers. The artillery usually fought in sub-units equivalent to a company or nowadays a battery, but called 'brigades' in
field or foot artillery, 'troops' in Horse Artillery, with as officers
a Captain and three Lieutenants or Ensigns. Sometimes brigades
or troops might be split into two detachments. The number of
engineer officers also increased dramatically to over 250 by 1814,
but there were never sufficient for all their tasks.

Personal self-respect, above all not to be found lacking in personal honour in the eyes of fellow officers, was the keynote of the
transformation of the louche young man about town or easy-going
country gentleman into a battlefield regimental officer.[18] Loss of
personal honour could lead to ostracism from an officer's peers. In
outward behaviour self-respect was marked by an easy superiority,

at times, particularly in the cavalry, arrogance. Although in an age of latitudinarism there was little open display of religion unless the Commanding Officer was a regular churchgoer, the Christian tradition was very strong, expressed in paternalism to soldiers, chivalry towards women and kindness towards the helpless.

Private income was all the more necessary in view of inflation, the on-going career needs of purchase in many regiments and, increasingly, the need for officers to help out with the day-to-day expenses within regiments where the wretchedly paid (or not paid at all, pay being months in arrears) soldiers were short of uniform or even food. The direct costs of a commission had increased: one for a Lieutenant in the infantry would cost £800, in the Grenadier Guards £1,700; for a Captain in the infantry the cost was £1,500, in the Guards £3,100; for a Major it was £2,600 in the infantry and £4,200 in the Guards. Besides the social prestige of the Guards, another reason for their higher price was that Guards officers continued to enjoy a rank higher than that within their regiment: a Guards Lieutenant, for example, ranked as a Captain, and a Captain as a Major or Lieutenant-Colonel. Officers' letters home often contained details of casualties, seniorities and advancement prospects and costs; others saw a few years' service in a smart regiment as a useful preliminary to a life in business or a country estate, foreshadowing the 'short-service commissions' of the 20th century. In practice for all commissions there were usually other additional charges and payments, and cavalry officers were expected to provide their own charger – of a high standard. Officers' private lifestyles depended very much on their own personal wealth, but in Britain women of various sorts and dubious relationships absorbed a large part of many a young officer's money, not a moral failure by the standards of the time.

Officers now carried swords, the spontoon being discarded, an indication that their duties were not in the front rank of foot soldiers. Officers of grenadier and light companies had the privilege of curved swords. Field officers wore epaulettes on both shoulders, Captains and Subalterns on the right shoulder only, with no rank distinction. Otherwise infantry officers' uniforms were little changed. A shorter coat was introduced in 1812 but officers continued to prefer the tricorne hat to a shako. Horse Artillery acquired the light cavalry blue uniforms with gold lacing still to be seen on the King's Troop on ceremonial occasions. Cavalry officers' tricorne hats were replaced by helmets. Some Scottish regiments, but not all, wore the kilt unless the weather was too cold as in the Peninsula in winter, or too hot as in India, when light trousers were issued.

Wellington took a bleak view about the competence of most of his officers, justifiable perhaps in the early years of his command but severe later. Those who sought the pleasures of Lisbon in excess were sharply reminded where their duties lay. Under his command officers learnt and were taught not only their professional skills, in particular attention to detail, but also concepts of responsibility and integrity. They were also increasingly responsible for the training and efficiency of their men. Officers in formations that Wellington considered to have performed badly were taken to task.[19] One regiment in which several officers had misbehaved badly was returned by Wellington to Britain and all its officers replaced. The winter months were used for training and reorganisation. In the winter of 1812–13, every battalion became capable of forming square from line, and into line from open column, in thirty seconds. Officers were also required to run cadre courses for NCOs.

No system of medal awards for bravery existed until Waterloo, for which a medal was issued to all ranks and a number of Field Officers were made Companions of the Order of the Bath (C.B.). Wellington as Commander-in-Chief might mention particular officers in dispatches; very occasionally an outstanding Lieutenant-Colonel or Major might receive a knighthood.

The rough nature of the rank and file was still seen in most regiments as ample justification for the severest punishments for disciplinary or criminal offences. Sentences of 800 or 1,000 lashes, or hanging in cases of the worst crimes, were not uncommon, both as a general deterrent and as a particular measure to protect the sound and meritorious soldiers. Wellington strongly approved. On a few occasions, appalled by the suffering, officers would reduce the number of lashes, or overlook an offence altogether to spare the soldier a whipping. Some commanding officers preferred other punishments such as solitary confinement. There was little or no rank and file resentment against severe punishment. While men stood in awe as whippings were carried out, there was no general anger against the officers who ordered them.

Mention of humour, and its value in linking together, was made earlier in this chapter. One example showing how officer–soldier relationships were changing is instructive. A Captain inspecting his company of the 95th noted that one soldier's biscuit ration tin was empty, the contents consumed contrary to orders. 'What have you done with your biscuit? Have you eaten it, Sir? Do you know it is against orders?' asked the Captain angrily. The rifleman replied, 'To be sure I do, but for God's sake, Sir, do you take me for a South American jackass that carries gold and eats straw?' Tension ended in laughter.[20] The personalities of individual officers, particularly those with charisma, either of stature or of character, could also play an important part in motivating soldiers.[21]

At home the military needs were leading to important developments in officer training and education. By 1806, following arrangements for reduced fees for the sons of officers, four companies of cadets, over 300 boys, were training at Great Marlow and two years later final approval was given for a purpose-built building at Sandhurst, on the Surrey–Berkshire border, the main structure to be in the Palladian country house style seen as suitable for gentlemen and following a design by James Wyatt, but to provide a military atmosphere and, to be surrounded by redoubts. The decision-making and building was very dilatory but cadets were moved in, in 1812, before the work was complete. Colours, then as now an enormously important symbol of loyalty and commitment, were presented to the College by the Queen, accompanied by the Prince Regent and the Duke of York, with great ceremony in 1813, the Colours then being consecrated in the newly completed chapel. A little later the Senior Division was moved to Farnham in Surrey where it was to remain for seven years. The two- to three-year Junior Division very quickly evolved into a single stream, combining Le Marchant's Junior Division and his proposed Second Division Commissioning Course. The curriculum included French, German, military geography and military history, together with drill, fencing, riding and swimming. A basic literary and elementary mathematics standard was required for admission, together with the approval of the College Governor. Examinations were held at the end of each year. The establishment provided for 200 cadets in four companies, 100 being sons of gentlemen, fifty destined for the regiments of the East India Company, and fifty at only nominal fees for the sons of officers who had been killed in action, were in reduced circumstances or had large families to support. Disciplinary problems, which had been serious with riots and violence at Great Marlow, were much reduced. The second part of the combined course covered the duties of junior regimental officers, geometry, trigonometry and military sketching. For this course there were two important examinations. Attendance on the course, though, was not obligatory, most officers still entering the service with no initial training. The 100 cadets of gentlemanly families and those destined for India paid an annual fee of 100 guineas (£105), while those who were orphans or the sons of officers in difficult circumstances paid only 31 guineas.

For the second part of the course, six months for future cavalry officers, less for the infantry, all had to pay mess charges to cover expenses, and prior to the start of the course had to have been approved by the commanding officer of a regiment or be a successor to a vacancy; if purchase was necessary the required sum would have had to have been paid. Those qualifying for a commission were styled 'Ensigns', and outstandingly able Ensigns could remain at the College without payment of fees and without purchase of commissions, a small but significant step forward.

The Royal Military Academy at Woolwich also developed in these years, alternating to meet the needs of the Army. A junior preliminary course for boys styled 'Ordnance Cadets' waiting for a vacancy opened at Marlow, but even when new purpose-designed buildings were completed at Woolwich – again to a Wyatt design – many juniors had to remain at Marlow or reside in the Royal Arsenal. By 1806 the establishment provided for 180 juniors and 128 High Establishment seniors. The accommodation problem was eased in 1810 by the decision of the East India Company to open their own college at Addiscombe, releasing some forty places at Woolwich.[22] Proper public examinations were reintroduced in 1811. The age of entry, ten in 1800, was progressively raised to fourteen and then fifteen. Of the twenty-nine seniors twenty-four were promoted, twelve each for the artillery and engineers. The best cadets could choose until each quota was exhausted, the first example of cadet choice of regiment procedures still an important part of a Sandhurst life, all cadets still having to appear before, and satisfy, regimental selection boards.

The fruits of these developments were, however, only to appear some way into the future. The Army in the Napoleonic War was essentially the Army of Wellington, an instrument forged by him during some of the stiffest campaigning undertaken up to that time. But the contrast between its dismal showing in the 1790s compared with its world-class performances in the war against the armies of Napoleon was also due to a number of other factors. The enemy was personalised, one everyone could understand, Napoleon, 'Old Boney'. Britain was behind its army and its officers; street celebrations followed the news of victories. Scores of men joined or were conscripted into the Militia or the newly formed local units of volunteers for home defence; these furnished recruits for the Regular regiments. Most infantry regiments themselves were now becoming identified with a particular region or county from which the rank and file and a few of the officers were drawn, so providing an internal cohesion and, in relation to other regiments, an increasing competitive spirit that served to develop efficiency.[23] The newly formed Scottish regiments joined the 1st and 42nd in making their special contribution to the British Army. The roughest of soldiers could walk tall in red and gold uniforms before campaign wear and tear. Food and rum supplies for the rank and file, both on the transport ships and in the Peninsula, were, except in times of reverse or withdrawal, greatly improved under Wellington's strict instructions.

Soldiers had confidence in the system. The very nature of French attacks, massed columns and the psychological warfare of deafening drumming, aroused an 'Old Trousers [the Rifles' name for the French] shall not get away with this' spirit, and regiments knew that steadiness in squares and well-controlled fire would prevail. Men were accordingly prepared willingly to obey their officers and drew inspiration from them when, as already noted they generally did, the officers led by example and with bravery. In turn, officers drew inspiration from the bravery of their men. As the long Iberian conflict wore on, officers gained much practical knowledge the hard way, becoming all the more competent. There were many occasions particularly in the years 1808–12 when, usually after a bloody encounter during a miserable winter retreat such as that to Corunna or after a prolonged siege such as those at Ciudad Rodrigo and Badajoz in 1812, discipline was broken by passion or sheer fatigue. Officers, even with gallows erected to hang the worst offenders, were unable to control orgies of violence, rape, paralytic drunkenness and looting. But by 1812 and in the 1813 advance into France the behaviour of the regiments improved and reached a standard high in comparison with those of other armies. Property was often targeted but people were respected, often soldiers giving of their rations to starving civilian women and children in Spain and, on entering into France, food and accommodation were paid for and severe disciplinary measures imposed on offenders who pillaged.

The British Army in the Napoleonic War, then, provides a very special further example of the now established paradox of the privileged easy-living gentleman displaying unexpected courage and skill in battle coupled with an appreciation that being an officer was again more than just a job. It was also a fortunate period, highlighting the triangular relationship of officer leadership, soldier followship and, in the final stages, public support from national society as a whole.

NOTES

1 Quoted in Barnett, *Britain and her Army*, 256–257.
2 These totals appear in Young and Lawford, *History of the British Army*, Chapter 11, by Antony Brett-James.
3 Shepperd, *Sandhurst*, ii.
4 For a full account of the military philosophy of the 1800 Rifle Corps see Arthur Bryant, *Jackets of Green* (London, Collins, 1972), i, and Sir William H. Cope, *The History of the Rifle Brigade* (London, Chatto and Windus, 1877), 5. The actual training document is *Regulations for the Rifle Corps formed at Blatchinton Barracks under the command of Colonel Manningham, August 15th 1800*, published in 1801.
5 The full version of Costello's memoirs, *Adventures of a Soldier*, was published in 1852. A valuable edited edition is that of Antony Brett-James, *Edward Costello: The Peninsula and Waterloo Campaigns* (London, Longmans, 1967).
6 Robinson, *Bloody Eleventh*, 260.
7 Lieutenant-Colonel R.J. Dickinson, *Officers Messes, Life and Customs in the Regiments* (Tunbridge Wells, Midas Books, 1977), 1.
8 The component units are set out in Butler, *Annals of the KRRC*, 45–46, 87–90.
9 'During the Peninsula War our men had divided the officers into two classes: the "come on" and the "go on".' Rifleman Costello's observation is recorded in Brett-James, *Costello*, 82.

10 Robinson, *Bloody Eleventh*, 341; W.F.K. Thompson (Editor), *An Ensign in the Peninsular War* (London, Michael Joseph, 1981), 213.

11 *A Short History of the Sherwood Foresters (Nottinghamshire and Derbyshire) Regiment* (Aldershot, Gale and Polden, 1940), 7.

12 John Keegan, *The Face of Battle* (Harmondsworth, Penguin, 1978), 187–188, describes this incident.

13 Sir Henry Newbolt, *The Story of the Oxfordshire and Buckinghamshire Light Infantry* (London, Country Life, 1915), 94.

14 Young and Lawford, *History of the British Army*, 108, 110–111.

15 Jack Adams, *The South Wales Borderers* (London, Hamish Hamilton, 1968), 64–65.

16 Young and Lawford, *History of the British Army*, 125.

17 Arthur Bryant, *The Age of Elegance* (London, Collins, 1950), 16, records Wellington's views.

18 Keegan, *Face of Battle*, 191–194, emphasises this personal aspect of officers' motivation.

19 Robinson, *Bloody Eleventh*, 445, quotes from one letter addressed to divisional and brigade commanders in which Wellington notes that from the moment the 1812 retreat from Burgos began officers lost control of their men.

20 Brett-James, *Costello*, 136.

21 An officer of the 95th Regiment noted that aristocratic officers possessed '. . . a degree of refinement, even in mischief, which commanded the respect of the soldiers . . .' Mark Urban, *Rifles* (London, Faber, 2003), 46.

22 Shepperd, *Sandhurst*, ii, iii; Hugh Thomas, *The Story of Sandhurst* (London, Hutchinson, 1961), i, ii; Brigadier Sir John Smyth, *Sandhurst* (London, Weidenfeld, 1961), i–iii.

23 *A List of the Officers of the Army* (London, War Office, 1783) notes county or in the case of Scotland regional titles, as for example: 'Third (or the East Kent) Regt. Of Foot, or the Buffs' and 'Eleventh (or the South Devons) Regt. Of Foot'. The War Office had circulated regimental agents on linkages in the previous year. Several regiments rejected the idea and others did not reply.

CHAPTER 6

THE OFFICER FROM WATERLOO
TO THE CRIMEA

The first fifty years of the 19th century furthered the paradox of
the anti-intellectual, hedonistic, sport-loving gentleman regimental
officer again generally displaying robustness, initiative and personal
bravery when needed. At first sight, the period appears to be one
of stagnation. It was, however, especially for the infantry, a period
of almost continuous colonial campaigning that taught flexibility
and improvisation and wrought, inconspicuous beneath the surface,
a small number of changes and formative developments to bear
fruit later.

The absence of any likely major Continental European enemy
led once more to demands for a peace dividend. Reductions of the
Army from its 1816 strength of 149,000 to 100,000 by 1821 followed.
Thirty-five infantry and eight cavalry regiments were disbanded. The
demands of Indian and colonial operations, however, led to small
increases in the 1830s, by 1837 to 109,000. Except for the excess
and untypical behaviour of a few officers, notably the Earl of
Cardigan in his command of two cavalry regiments, the general
public and press was little interested in the Army.[1] In addition, many
of the soldiers, including those in regiments linked to midland and
southern England, were Irish, adding to English indifference. The
popular support, so evident in the 1812–15 years, had evaporated
very quickly.

In military journals and elsewhere debate and discussion did take place. Some officers argued for a common training for all infantry regiments but with differing ideas as to what that training should be; others argued for more light infantry and rifle units. The infantry welcomed the percussion-cap musket, introduced from 1838 onwards, but opinion did not favour the issue of the Baker rifle to line regiments. The merits and tactical possibilities of the Minié rifle, which was authorised for all infantry in 1851, had not been fully appreciated by the outbreak of the Crimean War and one Division had not even been issued with it. For the cavalry, argument revolved around the question of the lance or sword, the chances of success for charges against squares, and the wider issue of how important cavalry actually was in any case. Artillery debate centred on the combat deployments and numbers of guns, horses and men, the sizes of guns and the merits or demerits of rockets, mortars and shrapnel, and whether a separate Royal Horse Artillery was necessary.[2] The impact of these debates on academic issues among regimental officers was virtually nil.[3] In practice, officers and NCOs trained their regiments for most of this period at single-unit level only, and in very old-fashioned and very complex drill evolutions modified only a little by Peninsula experience. Training centred on marching in columns on alignment at various distances, the officer keeping the distances accurately, deployment of close column into line, wheeling a close column, echelon marching of divisions into line and formation of a square from column. While district commands existed, no operational command division or brigade structures were created. Nor could the very varied internal security commitments in Britain or the even more varied types of overseas operations provide any general doctrine. In some regiments the colonial or Indian experience of officers, in particular application of tactics to terrain, was even denigrated. The reasons for this would seem to have been primarily social, such experience having been gained by officers obliged to live on their pay; tactlessness from officers with Indian experience may also have played a part. The few officers promoted from the ranks were not thought to have any particular experience or understanding of soldiers that might be valuable. In the event, the post-1815 infantry included an initial six, later eight, light infantry regiments and two rifle regiments each of two battalions. In ordinary line regiments one flank company was to be of light infantry, the other flank company being grenadier, though now with no particular role.

When the Minié rifle was introduced all regiments were finally organised on a common basis and given numbers or alphabet letters, 'No. 1 Company' or 'A Company'; light and grenadier companies retained only symbolic significance and, except in the matter of their green uniforms and social cachet, the rifle and light infantry regiments lost their distinctive structure. Regiments varied slightly in the number of companies, the average generally being six companies available for service and between four and one remaining as depot companies, the nucleus if necessary of a second battalion. Company strengths rose to between seventy-five and ninety men. A system of rotation, three years in the Mediterranean, three in the West Indies and three in North America before a home tour, was instituted in 1837 but service requirements occasioned many exceptions.

In the cavalry, four Light Dragoon regiments were converted into Lancers, a distinction being drawn between heavy sword cavalry (Dragoons and Hussars) and light cavalry (Lancers), and regiments were now reduced to a paper establishment of six squadrons each of two troops. Many regiments, however, were in practice composed only of two or three squadrons each of one or two troops, though each squadron now had a second cornet for troop command. The squadron now was often the operational sub-unit. The distinction between heavy and light cavalry was never very clear. Both were to train for the charge, but with light cavalry trained also for reconnaissance and outpost duties. The complex sequence of orders to be issued by officers was slightly reduced but still included twenty-one field evolutions covering space, keeping in line, advancing and retiring, heading and flanking military columns on the march, picquet guards for camps and patrolling. On operations or on the march, the squadron commander and the two troop leaders rode in front while the two or three very junior officers followed behind the rear file.

For a charge, officers would dress the regiment by squadrons, half-squadrons (troops), divisions (half-troops) and sub-divisions (quarter-troops) in one or two lines (the second being an immediate reserve) and order successively 'Trot', 'Gallop' and 'Charge' as the pace increased. After the charge, officers were to retire in columns of troops on each flank and reform behind the rear line. Officers on joining regiments were instructed in sword drill and the correct 'military seat' on horseback.[4] Heavy cavalry was not sent to India in the first half of the century; when a light cavalry regiment was sent its strength would be increased by as much as 25 per cent, an increase that led to problems of command with and for newly joined officers. Within the artillery, because of the inequality of overseas posting liabilities, and because in some colonies artillerymen might have to perform both roles, it was decided not to separate field and garrison artillery and, as a consequence of this division, the division of roles between gunners and drivers was ended. The artillery suffered particularly severely from the post-1815 reductions, its total strength being reduced to 6,000. Even the Woolwich field battery, supposedly a training team for others, was inadequately established. New units were raised only in 1846–47 but by 1853 there were still fewer than 100 guns ready for action. In some colonies local personnel, in some guise or other, were recruited as gunners. In Ireland, dismounted gunner companies were on occasions used as infantry for internal security duties. Fighting in India was almost continuous in these years, involving many British Regular regiments as well as those of the East India Company. In succession there were the Pindari War of 1812–17, the Gurkha War of 1814–16, the Third Mahratta War of 1817–19, the First Burma War of 1824–25, the disastrous First Afghan War of 1838–42, the Scinde and Gwalior campaigns of 1843–44, and the two hard-fought Sikh Wars of 1845–46 and 1848–49. On operations, the pattern generally followed throughout the whole British period in India was one British and two Indian, either sepoy or European, battalions in a brigade.

Campaigning was often arduous, officers and men being committed to battle after long and exhausting marches during which their columns were often harassed. The climate could vary from blazing heat to freezing cold. In the First Afghan War one whole regiment, the 44th Foot, was annihilated. At Ferozeshah, in the First Sikh War, two regiments lost over 300 men.

In general, traditional dispositions and tactics, carried out by well-disciplined troops led by capable regimental officers, proved effective against the less well-trained and armed Indian opponents. Well-controlled volley fire from infantry in lines with skirmishers on the wings on numerous occasions, a brilliant sabre cavalry charge at Ferozeshah and an equally brilliant lance cavalry charge breaking and trampling down Sikh squares at Aliwal, both in 1846, and the effective use of artillery, especially at Gujerat in 1849, all proved decisive. In several engagements, most notably at Aliwal and earlier at Ghuzni in 1839, there were particularly heavy officer casualties. The 31st Foot, for example in the battles of the First Sikh War, lost in total a Major, a Captain, four Lieutenants, three Ensigns and the Adjutant all killed or mortally wounded, together with a Lieutenant-Colonel, three Captains and six Lieutenants severely wounded and a further Captain, a Lieutenant and two Ensigns wounded.[5] Two examples from the history of the 16th Lancers at Aliwal illustrate the developing spirit of obligation among regimental officer leadership in these campaigns. One squadron commander later wrote 'I of course led the charge, at no point in the whole affair had I a man in front of me', and a Major very painfully wounded with a broken bayonet in his waist refused all medical treatment until his men had been attended to.[6]

Regiments on a normal march presented an unusual spectacle. 'War was habitually carried on with every provision for luxury and comfort.' A cavalry officer's personal retinue might include half a dozen camels and three bullock carts, often fine examples of woodwork for his personal baggage, two horses, a palanquin and bearers in which he was carried, and a score or more of servants and grooms. Behind might follow his wife on horseback, children on ponies and ill-assorted camp followers, including tent pitchers, stores, lascars, sutlers, food dealers and money changers.[7]

When not on operations in India officers had, as best they could, to cope with the problems of climate and boredom as these affected both their men and themselves. In hot weather soldiers would be paraded before dawn and then confined to their barrack blocks during the day, a wearisome round of daily life. In the men's barracks the only cooling would be damp wicker curtains over doors and windows, four men might be crowded on one bed, there were no facilities for cooling food or drink, and sanitation was often rudimentary. In the words of one regimental historian, 'A terrible listlessness descended on officers and men alike.'[8] Officers had to exercise careful supervision of their soldiers' food and ensure soldiers wore flannel belts and used woollen bedgowns. Officers might and generally did organise literacy classes, schools for the regiment's children, games, vegetable gardens, sports and dramatic productions, but the twin problems of sex and alcohol were in practice insoluble.[9]

Venereal disease rates for the rank and file varied between 20 per cent when units were on operations or in hill stations to 30 per cent or more when regiments were in or near urban areas. Monthly committees of officers inspected women living in cantonment areas; occasionally regiments would mount surprise patrols to round up all unmarried women for inspection, those being clean given a certificate and others drummed out. Consideration was given to the punishment of infected soldiers, but this was ruled as not permissible under military law. Alcohol was an equally difficult problem, soldiers believing heavy drinking could cure venereal disease. In some regiments, officers opened savings banks, but other officers were opposed to this, claiming that it was not desirable for soldiers to look to the future or their discharge. The same arguments arose over the desirability of temperance societies. Spirits were watered down and beer imported or brewed locally in their place, but the costs of beer were heavy, and many soldiers obtained the cheaper and more dangerous local brews by a variety of dubious means – even smuggling the beer into camps in boots.

One officer described his own life as being that of early morning and evening rides, learning an Indian language, Mess in the afternoon, reading, and writing letters: 'sadly sleepy and monotonous'. Some officers in this period acquired Indian mistresses or consorts, and in a few cases marriage followed. Officers usually lived in bungalows to which might be attached a small dwelling for consorts. Other nocturnal comfort was often gained by a servant called a punkah-wallah, whose task it was to keep the punkah, or fan, moving over the sleeping officer's body throughout the night.

Although India was the most important of the Imperial commitments, at various times, for periods long or short, cavalry regiments served in Portugal, Canada and South Africa, and the infantry in Gibraltar, Malta, the Ionian Islands, Portugal (in 1827), Australia, New Zealand, Iran, Ceylon, China, Burma, Mauritius, South Africa, Canada, St Helena, Jamaica and other West Indian islands. The duties and roles in combat of regimental officers were more varied than in India. In fortress colonies infantry officers and men might be called on to serve as gunners or simply be used as a labour force to build roads and fortifications. In Australia duties included policing penal settlements and the pursuit of 'bush rangers' (escaped convicts); detachments were also sent inland as the country was opened up and officers had to act as town commandants and magistrates or serve on juries. Officers and NCOs were used to help raise and train local volunteer units. In New Zealand assaults, sometimes by one or two companies, sometimes by one or two battalions, had to be made against fortified Maori posts, *pahs*, often defended with vigour, and military roads had to be constructed.[10] In hard fighting in China the Cameronians were attacked by Chinese armed with long spears in heavy rain when the old flintlock muskets were difficult to fire, their bayonets proving an inadequate answer. The British infantry themselves had to attack ports and cities defended by high stone walls. In Ceylon during the Kandian revolt an eighty-strong detachment of the 19th Foot had to fight off ten days of attack by 8,000 well-armed Kandians. In Burma attacks had to be mounted against high wooden stockades with flanking towers and ditches protected by artillery; attacks were often preceded by skirmishing operations in thick, hilly jungle and river creeks. In South Africa when needed for Kaffir War operations a company from an infantry regiment would be equipped with carbines, mounted and sent to protect colonists and their supply transport. Officers wore plain clothes, khaki not yet being instituted. Light infantry-style skirmishing was all important, and small rocket artillery sub-units proved useful both there and in Burma. In Canada 500 cavalry and over 10,000 infantry were committed in putting down the 1837–38 rising, but with regiments arriving ill-equipped for the Canadian winter. In the 11th Foot, freshly arrived from the Ionian Islands, officers had to lead men in overland moves on sleighs through the snow, passing long winter nights in log huts in the woods in which large open fires burned to keep men warm.[11] The transportation of units was a slow business; voyages to Australasia could last as long as six months. Some of the voyages were miserable – in one a ship designed to carry 850 was actually transporting 1,277, including 110 women and children.[12] Sometimes a ship carrying troops also carried convicts, some in chains.

Officers had to try to keep men fit with daily physical exercises and inspection of equipment, and combat boredom by organising entertainment and education, reading and writing for the illiterate.[13] On occasions, wives of officers or soldiers would add to the total number on board and add to the problems of order and morale. In the United Kingdom units from 1839 began to be moved by rail, saving time and money, under an officer train commander. Macadam roads also assisted the rapid movement of units, especially cavalry.

Such were the duties and roles of regimental officers, in most cases responsibilities of command and men's lives resting on quite junior captains and subalterns. Regimental histories abound with accounts of young officers gallantly leading assaults on forts or stockades, many losing their lives at the head of their men. In India cavalry Captains and Subalterns volunteered, when so permitted, to serve dismounted leading attacks.[14] There can be no doubt these examples of young officer leadership played decisive parts in the various campaigns' successes. The histories also note the terrible toll of disease, following life on a salt provisions diet, on officers and men alike, the chief killers being cholera, dysentery, yellow fever and malaria. Thirteen officers and over 400 men of the 2nd Foot, for example, died of disease in the West Indies in the years 1816–21.

Until 1829, there being no police force, troops (and the local Yeomanry regiments) had substantial and continuous internal security duties in Britain. Cavalry regiments were thought to be particularly suitable for this role, the horses adding a dimension of awe, and in general Regular regiments were preferred to the local Yeomanry. In controlling riots cavalry would often be deployed in troops or half-troops rather than squadrons, wherever possible in a line of horses, their riders with swords at the slope. Swords were used only when the troops were under serious attack, preferably using the flat rather than the blade. Generally, street patrolling proved effective with charges only a last resort. As early as 1816 the Royal Horse Guards had to be sent to control disorders in the Thames Valley, and in 1819 a cavalry regiment had to assist Yeomanry in containing a 60,000-strong riot in Manchester, at least eleven people being killed. The Grenadier Guards had to be deployed to contain riots in Smithfield, London. Political unrest in 1830 and 1831, following events in France and prior to the Reform Bill, was widespread. Peasantry in the south of England burned ricks and marched through the country demanding a living wage; in the north industrial labourers drilled, seemingly in preparation for civil war.

One of the worst events was the autumn 1831 riots in Bristol. Two cavalry, one infantry and one horse artillery unit had to be deployed and at least twelve civilians were killed. There were further disturbances in South Wales in 1841 over the cost of fuel; in the same year three squadrons of cavalry, a troop of horse artillery and infantry all had to be used to contain severe rioting in Manchester. From 1839 onwards repeated disorders and the need for military intervention occurred, now caused by the Chartist movement. Escorting of men arrested was often a dangerous duty. There were also invasion scares again, following events in France, involving the movement of troops to the south coast in 1846–47 and 1851–52. Regiments were also used on the coast to prevent revenue running and smuggling, and on a few occasions to restore order when boys rioted at major schools, including Eton and Harrow.

Ireland, where many infantry and cavalry regiments were stationed, presented continuous internal security challenges, day and night, from local pro-nationalist secret societies, Molly Maguires, Rockites, Whiteboys and Ribbonmen. The local Orangemen and Protestant yeomanry were also part of the problem. Officers were posted out with small detachments in the rural areas, and had to face the problems of morale and discipline, in particular drink, desertion and petty crime, that would arise when regiments were scattered in small out-posts. In the north, units had to try to prevent or intervene in sec-tarian disputes, particularly on anniversaries of the Battle of the Boyne. The elections in 1835 and the 1849–53 disturbances were the causes of special unrest and calls for the use of Army units as *gendarmerie*.

A major casualty of the post-1815 peace dividend was officer edu-cation. In 1817 the Sandhurst Junior Division instructing staff was reduced, the number of places reserved for orphans was cut to 80, so increasing the number of places for sons of serving officers who paid according to their rank; the fees for the remainder, some 120, were increased to £126 per year. By the end of the 1820s, orphan privileges were reduced to ten cadet scholars, and they were finally abolished in the 1830s. Other orphans and sons of junior officers were charged reduced fees of £40 and the overall cadet estab-lishment was reduced to 180. The instructing staff was also still further reduced.

The course was planned to cover four years, but any cadet over eighteen had to have special permission to remain. Sports – hockey, cricket, swimming, boating, riding and later fives – were encouraged. No alcohol, gambling or smoking was allowed on the campus. Senior cadets bullied juniors, there was much cadet braw-ling and the whole College atmosphere was spartan, with no anterooms, billiard rooms or canteen, and more Public School than military in its day-to-day life.[15] Cadets who failed the final examinations simply bought their commissions. Many commanding officers did not in any case like Sandhurst products. Wellington's introduction in 1849 of commissioning examinations for all infantry and cavalry officers purchasing commissions was only a relatively small step forward, as those who failed the examinations continued to buy their commissions. His second directive, that no Ensign could become a Lieutenant and no Lieutenant a Captain before satisfying a tribunal as to his knowledge and fitness, was not implemented prior to the outbreak of the Crimean War. The result of the neglect of professional initial training was that in practice officers learnt their battlefield tactical evolution and sword drills from their regimental NCOs in the early years of their service.

Woolwich, despite a recurrence of on-going and on occasions violent disciplinary problems, fared rather better. Although numbers were reduced progressively to sixty in the immediate post-1815 years, largely to prevent cadets remaining for many years at the Academy due to the blockages created by half-pay officers seeking regimental vacancies, in the 1820s they were increased slightly to an average of 125, with an annual intake of thirty-six. By the early 1830s an average of twenty-four received commissions each year. From 1831 fees were charged on a parental income base, ranging from £20 to £80 per year. Entrance was now by competitive examination (in practice too few candidates applied for any real competition) and the course was extended to include German, history and geography. First-year and final examinations became more rigorous. The age of entry was lowered to fourteen in 1848 and most cadets passed three and a half or four years at the Academy. Relatives were required to pay an initial 20 guineas (£21) for the cadet's uniform but otherwise no fees were charged and cadets were paid 28s 6d per day. As at Sandhurst, drink was forbidden (although smuggled in) and cadets bullied and brawled.[16]

The Senior Division fared worst of all. There being no major war menace and in consequence no division or brigade formations, little need was seen for any staff training in subjects such as organisation, movements, language or intelligence. Funding for the Senior Division was progressively reduced, ceasing entirely in 1832. The Senior Division was moved out of Farnham to reopen on the Sandhurst campus in 1821, student numbers fell to fifteen or less and there were very few applicants for entry. Few of those who received the course certificate served in staff appointments. Of 216 post-1836 graduates, only twenty served on staffs, in 1852 only seven.[17] Artillery and Engineers officers were ineligible for general staff appointments, a ban in practice ruling out the better educated and trained. Both Woolwich and the Sandhurst courses had to be self-supporting, a factor precluding course development.

Promotion and career development in the infantry and cavalry continued in the vast majority of cases to be by purchase. The limited number of cases of promotion by bravery or merit was achieved by brevet rank; this, however, did not apply to rank within the officer's regiment, so that for example a brevet Lieutenant-Colonel might still be only a Major in his regiment, an arrangement that could cause difficulties. If on the retirement of a Lieutenant-Colonel, the senior Major could not pay the costs of succeeding him, a Major from elsewhere who could pay would be found. In the Artillery and Engineers, promotion was by seniority only and exceedingly slow.

Regimental training in the years 1820–50 was badly under-funded, regiments often lacking a drill ground or a riding school; units were dispersed in small detachments and frequently moved. Elsewhere there were more encouraging developments in training including the opening of Arms Schools, for the Engineers at Chatham and for the Artillery at Shoeburyness, both in 1852, a musketry school for the infantry at Hythe in 1853, and training facilities for the cavalry at Maidstone. The need for training areas was also recognised, with the acquisition of land at Chobham where a two Division level exercise was held in 1853, and the purchase of land at Aldershot, also in 1853. By 1825 annual efficiency (fitness for role in modern terms) inspections had become more thorough – though much of course could still depend on the inspecting officer. Inspections now were to cover the qualifications of officers and NCOs, their expertise in their duties and unit administration, clothing, equipment, sickness rates, whether Captains could drill a regiment and Lieutenants a company, and whether the Officers' Mess was affordable for young officers. A competitive spirit between com-panies would attract favourable comment, though fewer questions appear to have been asked on actual training.[18] Annual confidential reports and a requirement for a medical certificate from an officer claiming to be unfit for duty were introduced, both measures seen as most ungentlemanly. The big reductions in the size of the Army after 1815 led to considerable turnover for several years in officer manning. Numbers of officers, providing they had three years of service, went on half-pay until a vacancy for which they could make an offer arose. The 'over-regulation' charges for commissions in regiments threatened with disbandment fell. Although a small number of officers spent long years in the service of a regiment or an artillery company, officers in many regiments were to come forward from half-pay lists. In the case of the 37th Foot, for example, of the twenty-one officers who joined in 1825 half came from half-pay and seven from other regiments; eleven left the regiment in under a year, with five more within two years. One officer had to wait twelve years before promotion to command a company.[19] The Artillery and Engineers suffered particularly severely, with the tedious process of seniority made worse by reductions in strengths.

The population of Great Britain increased fast in the 19th century, but the layering of society was extended into the new industrial and commercial classes, the Army both benefiting from and contributing to the on-going social stratification and gentrification. It continued to draw the overwhelming majority of its officers from these layered structures including, especially in the cavalry, 'a large sprinkling of the *nouveaux riches*, scions of the families of rich industrialists and East India merchants who took great pleasure in seeing their sons attired in the splendid uniforms of the period'.[20] Also, no doubt there was equal pleasure for both fathers and sons in seeing class status preserved and improved. From sources in both country and town more military families appeared.

After the 1828 repeal of the Test Act, Roman Catholics were able to serve as officers. In the Scottish regiments the proportion of English officers in this period varied, between a fifth and a quarter in kilted regiments, but much higher in most of the trews regiments.[21] Some resentment against English officers existed – but in turn many Scots officers became anglicised. Class self-confidence everywhere was complete, with no question over the propriety of the class system extending to the officering of the Army.

A measure of wealth was certainly needed, the very large majority of infantry and cavalry officers continuing to achieve their commissions by purchase. The number leaving Sandhurst for non-purchase commissions remained small but socially well-connected and, unless they had been royal pages, usually destined for less smart regiments. The number promoted from the ranks to be Cornets or Ensigns was even smaller. The costs of commission, however, continued to inflate – for a Cornet of cavalry £840, for an Ensign of infantry £450. In 1854 an infantry captaincy could cost a basic £1,800 but in practice a total of £2,400, and that for a cavalry lieutenant-colonelcy a basic £6,175 to which might have to be added as much as £7,000 or more in additional unofficial charges.[22] Infantry officers' prices were generally about a third less than those for the cavalry.

Lieutenant-Colonels could become full Colonels after three years and, if vacancies occurred, Major-Generals. Major-Generals, however, could not sell their commissions. In consequence many Lieutenant-Colonels either resigned or sold their commissions to an officer on half-pay, perhaps receiving a kickback if that officer later sold his commission.

Ambitious officers could and did advance their careers by judicious purchases and changing regiments. Others exchanged for reasons even less pleasant such as escaping from an unappealing regimental posting. In service officers had other expenses: a horse, a contribution to the band, mess life, etc. Misfortune could prove very expensive. A Hussar officer on royal escort duty was caught in a heavy rainstorm, ruining his uniform and giving his charger a fatal chill, a total expense of £700. If an officer died from natural causes while in service his financial investment was lost.

Uniforms, especially in the cavalry where regiments indulged themselves in brilliant, at times gaudy and frequently changing outfits with exotic headgear, were exceedingly expensive. The basic uniforms of a Light Dragoon officer in 1839 cost £134 13s 6d, a sum much greater than a year's pay; by the middle of the century, a Hussar's uniforms could cost over £300. Until 1822 officers were distinguishable by their head dress and the colour and splendour of their uniforms. In 1822 dress regulations prescribed rank badges: a crown and star for a Colonel, a crown for a Lieutenant-Colonel and a star for a Major, worn on epaulettes; by 1855 these were gold laced. Without lacing a crown and star signified a Captain, a crown a Lieutenant and a star an Ensign. The badges were worn on collar and cuffs in some regiments, on epaulettes in others.

Pay had risen but little, in real terms not at all. A cavalry Lieutenant-Colonel was paid a basic £365 per annum, a Lieutenant £118–130. Additional allowances were, however, paid for moving baggage and equipment, for living in barracks, for forage and for service in India (though the exchange rate for this allowance was set, deliberately, to be unfavourable). Some colonial administrations paid officers an additional allowance, but these were discretionary and could vary almost by year.[23] If not travelling with their regiments, officers until 1842 had to pay the costs of their passages overseas.

While cavalry officers generally had enough money to flaunt their wealth, infantry and artillery officers often had little to spare. These differences were reflected in the nature and style of regimental life, already in existence but to develop much further in these years. The cavalry, with its glittering uniforms designed, one can only surmise, to terrify the recipients of a cavalry charge, formed their own closed world. Musketry was held in disdain. Cavalry officers presented an air of languid boredom, yawning, pronouncing their r's as w's and interspersing conversation, when they made it, with haw haw noises.[24] The home service life of a cavalry officer provided for West End clubs, country house weekends, hunting and shooting. Officers entered national racing events and when overseas organised race meetings. In the Mess, heavy drinking was the form – but followed by hard riding the following morning.[25] Regimental messes were superbly furnished, regimental silver abounded, but the atmosphere does seem to have been more formal than friendly. Perhaps foreboding and the likelihood of death in a cavalry charge may have contributed to this exaggerated lifestyle.[26]

The style of mess life in most infantry regiments was more that of a close family within which younger members were cared for but in return expected to show respect to their seniors and not speak out of turn. Unofficial 'subalterns' courts' ensured conformity if a Cornet's or an Ensign's behaviour failed to conform.

Some officers remained clean-shaven, others grew moustaches or sported long side-curls. In the 1850s many officers grew beards, a practice to be banned after the Crimean War. On a few, now rare, occasions duelling occurred, but the practice had ended by the Crimean War. When a fierce quarrel between officers broke out a field officer, chosen by the officers involved, would hear both sides and arbitrate.[27] In all messes small cherished customs asserted the regiment's individuality – drinking the Royal Toast seated, passing Napoleon's chamber-pot filled with champagne around. And in most messes rough and tumble mess games would follow after dinner, as they do to the present day.

From 1812, officers who had been wounded received a pension according to rank, £300 for a Lieutenant-Colonel, £50 for an Ensign. Pensions for widows were regularised a little later. Loss of an eye or limb was not seen as a bar to further service provided the officer was fit enough to march and fight.

Slowly the progressive ideas of Sir John Moore and the Light Division trickled down into other infantry and cavalry regiments, emulation and encouragement replacing fear and repression.

The long years that infantry regiments served overseas, in which officers and men had to live and work together, served greatly to improve mutual understanding. In the cavalry a common love of horses often linked men and officers. More regiments awarded their own medals and badges: in the words of the historian Sir John Fortescue, 'Regimental officers worked busily to counter the mischief of the state.'[28] After the Peninsula officers increasingly saw their soldiers as human beings, no longer the scum of society. Many officers believed punishments had been and were still too brutal and sought other methods of punishment. In 1812 a maximum of 300 lashes was imposed, reduced to 200 in 1832. In 1836 a Royal Commission recommended prison sentences rather than flogging, but heavy lash sentences or other corporal punishments continued in some regiments through to 1846 when a maximum of fifty lashes was imposed. In 1830 regiments were ordered to keep a Defaulter's Book, a measure which served greatly to reduce the number of brutal punishments. When more enlightened ideas were rejected, the regiment fell into a 'frightful state of insubordination', as was the case in the early 1830s with the 13th Foot in India, with the murder of an officer and several NCOs. This regiment's response to any sign of insubordination remained a minimum of 300 lashes, but its historian commented that its soldiers still followed their officers and the regiment acquitted itself well a little later in the first Afghan War.[29]

Disciplinary punishments nevertheless continued to be severe, a death sentence being awarded for not only mutiny and desertion but insubordination, sodomy and other sexual offences. For irregularities of equipment, however, officers came to impose more moderate punishment – a period in stocks, bread and water diet, reporting every hour to the orderly sergeant, stopping a grog ration, or extra drills and guard duties. Officers convicted of offences were invited to retire rather than be dismissed and could thereby sell their commissions.

Until the end of the 1840s regiments stationed in Britain as well as overseas were expected to organise unit alcohol canteens. In barracks a block for the rich and another for recruits were often provided and inspected by the duty captain of the week. In 1847 coffee shops began to replace the alcohol canteens. As in India, some regiments provided reading rooms or libraries for their men and in most barracks provision was made for games, especially cricket and football, but physical training was not made compulsory. Officers in some regiments organised theatrical shows. The regiment's school, obligatory from 1812 though in practice instituted much earlier in a number of regiments, was another concern of regimental officers, classes being for the regiments' children or their illiterate fathers. Regiments, too, were continually required to produce returns – how many Bibles were available for soldiers, or how many nights per week did soldiers sleep in barracks.

Essentially the basis of the officer–soldier relationship in these years was summed up later in the century by Lord Wolseley: 'the very prejudices of the English gentleman only serve to make him the more popular with his soldiers ... the officer demanded from his men an implicit obedience not only because he was their officer but also as their social superior and, as he believed, their natural born leader ...'[30] It can be argued that this squirearchic relationship only began seriously to unravel on the beaches of Dunkirk in 1940.

NOTES

1 Cecil Woodham-Smith, *The Reason Why* (London, Constable, 1953), iii, iv, provides details of Cardigan's idiosyncratic despotism and press interest.

2 The various arguments are examined in detail in Hew Strachan, *From Waterloo to Balaclava: Tactics, Technology and the British Army 1815–1854* (Cambridge University Press, 1985).

3 Cowper, *King's Own*, II, 55, provides a clear example: 'After Waterloo the officers' interest in the art of war had rapidly declined.'

4 The Marquess of Anglesey, *A History of the British Cavalry 1816 to 1919* (London, Leo Cooper, 1973), I, 96–105.

5 Colonel Hugh W. Pearse, *The History of the East Surrey Regiment* (London, Spottiswoode, 1916), 177.

6 Colonel Henry Graham, *The Sixteenth, The Queen's Light Dragoons (Lancers) 1759–1912* (Devizes, privately published, 1912), 75.

7 Shepperd, *The Ninth Queen's Royal Lancers 1715–1936*, 103, 109.

8 S.H.F. Johnston, *The History of the Cameronians (Scottish Rifles)* (Aldershot, Gale and Polden, 1957), I, 231.

9 The issues are discussed by Douglas M. Peers in 'Imperial vice, sex, drink and the health of British troops in north Indian cantonments', a chapter in David Killingray and David Omissi (Editors), *Guardians of Empire* (Manchester University Press, 1999), ii. British medical officer policies are considered later in this work.

10 Lieutenant-Colonel Russell Gurney, *History of the Northamptonshire Regiment 1742–1934* (Aldershot, Gale and Polden, 1935), I, xviii, xix.

11 W. Aggett, *Bloody Eleventh*, II, 53.

12 Hugh Cook, *The North Staffordshire Regiment* (London, Leo Cooper, 1979), 38.

13 Graham, *Northampton Regiment*, 188, notes that a troopship transporting this regiment became a 'floating scholastic institution'.

14 A good example appears in Graham, *The Sixteenth, The Queen's Light Dragoons*, 75.

15 Shepperd, *Sandhurst*, 43.

16 Guggisberg, *The Shop*, iii.

17 Brian Bond, *The Victorian Army and the Staff College* (London, Eyre Methuen, 1972), 53, 59–60.

18 Atkinson, *Hampshire Regiment*, 174.

19 Atkinson, *Hampshire Regiment*, 171

20 Lieutenant-Colonel L.B. Oatts, *I Serve: A History of the Third Carabiniers* (privately published, 1966), 122.

21 Diana M. Henderson, *Highland Soldier* (Edinburgh, John Donald, 1989), 90–91.

22 Anglesey, *British Cavalry*, 161. Anglesey also notes the astonishing prices paid by Cardigan for the command of his two regiments, at least £35,000

for command of the 15th Hussars and, later, over £40,000 for the 11th Husssars. A table of all the official prices appears in T.A. Heathcote, *The Indian Army* (Newton Abbot, David and Charles, 1974), 118.

23 Aggett, *Bloody Eleventh*, II, notes daily allowances of between 15 shillings for a Lieutenant-Colonel and 5 shillings for an Ensign being paid in New South Wales.

24 Woodham-Smith, *Reason Why*, 139–140, records these affectations.

25 '. . . the effects of evening libations in brandy and port being regularly worked off in hard exercise by lunch time the following day'. Oatts, *Third Carabiniers*, 13.

26 To this author some cavalry marches – *Coburg*, *Moses in Egypt*, *John Peel* – seem to carry a note of foreboding. The motto of one regiment was, and still is, 'Death or Glory' – in that order.

27 A.D.L. Carey and Stouppe McCance, *Regimental Records of the Royal Welsh Fusiliers* (London, Forster Groom, 1923), 51, gives an account of one such arbitration.

28 Quoted in Anglesey, *British Cavalry*, 150–151. Campaign medals for all ranks who served in the Peninsula were at last authorised in 1847 despite objections that they were ostentatious.

29 Hamish Popham, *The Somerset Light Infantry (Prince Albert's)* (London, Hamish Hamilton, 1908), 51–52.

30 Quoted in Bond, *Victorian Army and the Staff College*, 20.

CHAPTER 7

THE CRIMEA AND THE
INDIAN MUTINY

The first sixty years of the 19th century ended with two major military commitments for which the Army was poorly prepared: the Crimean War (1854–56) and the insurrection in India known as the Indian Mutiny (1857–58). Both campaigns, in the case of the Crimea taken to an extreme degree, saw the worst and best of the Army, the worst being wretchedly inadequate preparation, staff work and command, the best being the courage and discipline of regiments, with as in the past numerous individual acts of leadership and bravery by regimental officers. For the Crimea a force of four infantry Divisions, one cavalry Division, sixty-six guns, and 27,000 men was despatched. Each infantry Division had two brigades of three battalions; the cavalry Division had a Heavy Brigade and a Light Brigade. Brigade staffs, with again a brigade major but now also 'A' and 'Q' staff captains for personnel and equipment respectively appeared.

Field operations remained essentially those of the Wellington era developed to a new perfection, in particular with the new Minié rifle. Infantry officers had to keep their advancing lines sufficiently well dressed for volley firing while under fire and over open and difficult terrain. Sometimes infantry lines would outflank Russian units and attack by echelon. On a few occasions officers had to lead companies through woods by the novelty of compass bearing.

Picquets played an important role – pairs of soldiers provided by one company posted around an area held by a regiment with an officer-led patrol moving constantly around the picquet outposts. Skirmishing was developed with the concept of sharpshooters, patrols of selected men, one patrol from each division, usually sixty-strong and led by a Captain, specifically tasked to harass Russian artillery but often used for other missions. The orders for the attack on the Redan defensive fieldwork, in the event unsuccessful, provided for a covering fire party of 100 commanded by a field Officer, a first storming party of 500 led by two field Officers, and a working party of 100 led by a field Officer, with the remainder of the brigade to follow.[1]

The army's artillery was strengthened with the support of larger pieces from warships and Royal Marine Artillery. Each Division had one or two Royal Artillery batteries with four 9 pdr. and two 24 pdr. guns; the Royal Horse Artillery troops still retained 6 pdr. guns and used them in pursuit operations as well as normal fire support. There were in addition siege artillery 18 pdr. howitzers, which over difficult ground provided officers with all the problems of man-handling. Engineer officers had particular duties before the walls of Sevastopol, constructing gun positions, trenches and saps.

The few cavalry charges began with the training manual walk–trot–gallop charge sequence, a directing squadron setting the pace, but in the resulting mêlées officer commands were 'Close in' and 'Rally'. Lines were meticulously dressed before an advance began; wheeling movements were ordered by sword signals from the leading officer.[2]

All officers had, of course, to lead in the general battlefield conditions of the time – the Allies' numerical inferiority, the noise of guns, cries of wounded men and injured horses, smoke and fog. After major engagements they had to come to terms with the wreckage, human and material, of the field – dead and wounded men, some still in agony, dead horses, abandoned rifles and other equipment scattered around. The pointlessness of some of the operations, most notably the charge of the Light Brigade, and the heavy casualties that resulted from these, were also challenges to morale.

In the early months of the campaign regimental officers had other burdens which they should not have had, all arising from years of financial stringency, collapsed logistic arrangements and poor command at formation level. Departure from Britain had been exciting, with champagne and flowers from crowds of well-wishers. But on the voyages horses, particularly those in sailing ships, fell ill and died – an emotional blow for a young officer devoted to his charger. On arrival in Bulgaria forage was inadequate and horses starved. Cholera, typhus and dysentery struck the regiments, with dozens of men dying and the only occupation being that of burial parties. Medicines were in short supply or simply not available. Food was limited to biscuit and salted pork. Morale slumped, even among officers, some of whom in their gloom neglected their turnout. Matters were not eased by a spate of orders and requests for returns, all of little relevance, from some formation commanders.

Worse was to follow when the force began to disembark on the Crimean peninsula on 14th September 1854. The available shipping being inadequate, essential stores, in particular tentage and medical supplies, were left behind. The small percentage of soldiers (drawn by lot) whose wives had accompanied them were concerned over the fate of many hundreds left behind in Bulgaria, a concern voiced to their officers. Soldiers had to land without knapsacks and with only a blanket roll. Officers had, nevertheless, to land in full dress uniform with swords. Neither the soldier's blanket nor his uniform were waterproof and soldiers had to sleep on the ground in all conditions until mid-October. Disease spread further and when the advance on the Alma began many soldiers collapsed from illness and fatigue. Officers were, however, able to draw on colonial field experience, and British Army field hygiene, latrines and sanitation were notably superior to those of the French contingents. But by November companies were reduced to some 60 per cent of their strengths. Officers had the task of somehow maintaining morale, alertness on picquet duty and a fighting spirit, all increasingly difficult as the weather worsened. Even when some tentage and equipment arrived many essential stores, food, medical supplies, fuel and wood for fires remained short. The tents were too thin to provide any real shelter from the cold. For many soldiers the winter of 1854–55 remained one of wet blankets in trenches, the first but by no means the last experience of the British Army in this type of static warfare, and one at the time viewed by many officers with disdain as lacking in fighting spirit. Heavy rain and, later, extreme cold resulted not only in further cholera and dysentery but also frostbite, gangrene, scurvy and tuberculosis. If the sick or wounded survived the 300-mile sea journey to the base hospital at Scutari, the appalling conditions further increased the death rate. Horses and mules also died by the score, obliging officers and soldiers to manhandle stores the eight or more miles from Balaklava to their positions. In 1855, and after a change of government in London, conditions improved, adequate stores arrived and engineers laid a light railway from Balaklava to the front.

Credit for the Army's heroic achievements in the Crimea is rightly given to the rank and file soldiers. But these men would not have achieved so much had it not been for the leadership of their regimental officers, leadership by bravery, by exhortation and by shared hardship. Crimea is a classic example of the importance in war of the regimental officer and the NCO. The exceptional poor performance of one unit, the 63rd Foot, appears to have been due to the fact that a number of its officers, including the commanding officer, were newly arrived in the Regiment, inconsistent in their discipline and not always attentive to detail in their duties. In addition, a number of the unit's NCOs had been killed.[3]

The Crimean campaign led to a decision to expand the Army, twenty-six additional infantry battalions being authorised in 1857–58. Hurried training of replacement drafts of officers and men in regimental depot companies arriving in the Crimea ill-prepared was seen as a weakness in the regimental system of the time. Transport by sea remained as unpleasant an experience as ever: one regiment's journey from Britain to Calcutta lasted 141 days during which soldiers took turns to sleep in such accommodation as was available; for the second half of the journey rations were reduced to half, with three pints of brackish water, half a pound of very hard dry biscuit and six ounces of salted pork per day.[4] Officers shared the experience, and had somehow to maintain morale. The war also saw, for the first time, communication between London and the field by wireless telegraphy.

The military operations following the outbreak of the Indian Mutiny were principally carried out by regiments of the East India Company's presidencies. However, some twenty British Regular Army infantry and eleven cavalry regiments were all involved. These had to face the conditions of heat or extreme cold and disease already described, but although serious uniform and supply problems existed, they were not on the same scale as the appalling shortfalls experienced in the Crimea. As before, the British battalions were generally one in a brigade including two other Company units.

The campaigns in different areas of northern India were hard fought, the mutineers and their supporters having artillery, military skills and experience. The reoccupation of Delhi, involving four brigades, each with a British battalion, and two British cavalry regiments, was a major operation. Elsewhere, regiments led by their officers might have to march twenty miles a day in extreme heat for several days to engage mutineers, relieve beleaguered towns and garrisons or escort Europeans. One regiment, the 52nd, actually covered forty-two miles in twenty hours in the extreme Punjabi hot season, following this with a twenty-five mile night march, and on again the following day, but were still capable of mounting a bayonet attack.[5] Columns on the march often came under harassing sniper fire. The campaigns included several pitched battles, skirmishing, cavalry charges into squares, entries into defended cities and forts, clearing cities of mutineers and small pursuit groups chasing defeated mutineers in flight, these latter giving special opportunities to junior officers.

The massacre of British women and children at Cawnpore affected the attitude of all troops, including the British Regular units in India, and led predictably to no quarter being given to mutineers, pillaging, punitive burning of villages harbouring mutineers and other revenge killings. Officers would not, often could not, limit these actions, generally seeing them as salutary retribution. Artillery officers even issued parade orders for the blowing of mutineers from the guns. The repression is the worst event in the history of the British officer, explicable, but not excusable, only by the fact that most of the British murdered and mutilated by the mutineers came from the same social classes as the officers.

The number of Army officers awarded the newly instituted Victoria Cross (V.C.) for bravery in the field in the Crimea and in the Indian Mutiny is a measure of the gallantry and leadership displayed in regiments. For conspicuous courage in the Crimea, the V.C. was awarded to one Colonel, one Lieutenant-Colonel, five Majors, nine Captains, eleven Lieutenants, one Ensign and one medical officer. In the Indian operations, the majority of the awards went to officers and men of the regiments of the East India Company, but from British Regular Army regiments recipients included two Majors, seven Captains, seventeen Lieutenants, one Cornet and four medical officers.[6]

Most of the V.C.s awarded were for acts of individual bravery and leadership of men, but some illustrate the ethos of the officers in the conflict in the Crimea. Lieutenant Clifford of the Rifle Brigade, a Roman Catholic, led an assault charge against the Russian lines during which he personally saved the life of one of his men. Lieutenant Elphinstone of the Royal Engineers, after leading a party to recover scaling ladders after an unsuccessful attack, led his men again to search for wounded lying close to the Redan; in this work he personally carried twenty men to safety. Lieutenant Graham, also an engineer, and Captain Davis, an artilleryman, were awarded their medals for similar life-saving work. In India, Lieutenant Wadeson of the Gordon Highlanders and Captain Fraser of the 7th Hussars won their awards for saving the lives of soldiers while under fire. Surgeon Jee of the Seaforth Highlanders rescued wounded men, tended them throughout a night in the open and under very heavy fire, and then got many of them to safety, again under fire, the following morning. Lieutenant Hackett of the 23rd Foot received his V.C. for rescuing a dangerously wounded corporal lying exposed under heavy fire. Captain Wilmot of the Rifle Brigade won his award for single-handedly using all the rifles of his four-man patrol, providing covering fire while three of his men evacuated the fourth who had been wounded.[7]

Officer casualties in the Crimea are also an indication of their involvement and were proportionately higher than those of soldiers. In total 158 officers, the flower of the Army, were killed in action, thirty-nine at Inkerman alone and fifty-one more dying later of wounds received. A further fifty-five died of disease.[8] A large number of non-purchase commissions suddenly became available, many of the vacancies being filled by the promotion of NCOs. The average age of cavalry and infantry Majors dropped to 32 or 33.[9] The events in both the Crimea and the Indian Mutiny increased pride in the regiments involved.

In one respect the suffering of the soldiers in the Crimea, especially the hardship created by the breakdown of the commissariat and the medical service, was not totally in vain. Thanks to a war correspondent, W.M. Russell of *The Times*, the first in this field, media attention in the form of press reporting for the first time drew the attention of the British public to the scandalous state of the military system, the attention marking a lasting sea-change in the relationship between the public and the Army. Events such as the charge of the Light Brigade, the Guards and the Highlanders at the battle of the Alma, the 93rd Foot's fighting at the battle of Inkerman and the tenacity of the 32nd during the siege of Lucknow caught the public imagination in an era of intense patriotism and Imperial adventure. In respect, therefore, of regimental officers for at least three decades the result was a more sympathetic public understanding. If things went wrong, blame was placed at higher levels. This was an important measure of reform, partly as a result of public opinion, and pressure was to follow.

NOTES

1 *Cadogan's Crimea* (London, Hamish Hamilton, 1979), 274–275. This work is an abridged edition of the letters sent from the Crimea by Lieutenant-Colonel Somerset J. Gough Calthorpe, a staff officer.

2 These can still be seen as the Household Cavalry passes the Sovereign at the annual Trooping of the Colour ceremony.

3 The event is analysed in Kirke, 'Social structures', 338–342.

4 Michael Mann, *The Regimental History of the 1st Queen's Dragoon Guards* (Norwich, M. Russell, 1993), 232.

5 Booth, *Oxfordshire and Buckinghamshire*, 78.

6 Philip A. Wilkins, *The History of the Victoria Cross* (London, Constable, 1904), 1–184.

7 The names of these individuals and their reasons for their awards have been set out because of their particular significance in the history of officers. Numerous officers were awarded the V.C. in later wars; some are noted but space cannot permit all of the names being recorded.

8 *Cadogan's Crimea*, 267.

9 The average age for Majors serving in British regiments in India appears to have been higher – 37 for cavalry and 42 for infantry. Heathcote, *Indian Army*, 133.

CHAPTER 8

THE VICTORIAN ARMY OFFICER

The second half of the 19th century was to follow the same pattern as the first, in that a number of useful reforms were effected but nevertheless still failed to produce Army officers properly prepared for the end of the century's major conflict, the Second South African War. Again, though on occasions there appeared to be a threat from France (the first threats leading to the formation in the 1850s of the Rifle Volunteers, the forebear of the Territorial Army), there was no continuous immediate liability for a European force.[1] If there was to be a major war it was believed that this would be in Asia, defending India against Russia. Other overseas colonial and imperial commitments, often serious and by the 1880s large-scale, were on-going and more pressing.

The first reforms, an immediate reaction to the scandals of the Crimea, were concerned with logistics and medical requirements; these are considered in a later chapter. Many of the reforms both to combat arms and support that were to follow in later decades were in part reflections of the changes in society, the growth of industry, scientific and technological developments, the rise of professionalism in civilian walks of life and Victorian Christian revivalism. The four major reforms to affect the front-line combat regiments were those initiated by Edward Cardwell in his years at the War Office from 1868 to 1872. At the top, in 1870, Cardwell reduced the number of divisions in authority that had so weakened the Army by centring power in the hands of two men, the Secretary of State for War and the Commander-in-Chief. To follow were the progressive abolition of flogging, being limited in 1867 to men on active service, further limited in 1870 and finally ended in 1889. In its place officers could award Field Punishment No. 1, lashing a man to a gun wheel for periods of time, or sentences of penal servitude. Next came the ending of the purchase of commissions in the cavalry and infantry in 1871, a measure not sought by the officers themselves and only secured amid sharp political controversy.[2] Finally, under Cardwell in 1871 and later under Childers in 1881, came the organisation of the infantry into regiments of two battalions, each regiment with a local, usually county, affiliation and a regimental depot often built in a castle style.[3] (Regiments numbered 1 to 25 already had two battalions.) The depot barracks included single soldier blocks, rows of small houses for married men and accommodation in or near the barracks for officers.

The two-battalion system was intended to provide for one of the battalions to serve overseas, the other to be at home, so equalising periods spent abroad. In practice this all too often proved unfeasible because of operational needs for drafts overseas, a shortage of recruits reducing the home battalion to a shadow strength, or financial cuts imposed upon the home battalion. The reform was not popular at the outset, many officers being reluctant to lose a prized and proud regimental number in place of a county with which in some cases they had had no previous connection. This was later to change. Sixty-six military districts each headed by a Lieutenant-Colonel with a small administrative brigade staff corresponding to a county or region were created to coordinate the Regular regiments, Militia, Yeomanry and Rifle Volunteers; it was hoped these latter would furnish recruits for the Regular units. Infantry weaponry changed, regiments firstly in 1857 receiving the .45 Enfield Rifle Musket and then a little later the first .577 breech-loading rifle, the

Snider, with from 1871 the 0.45 Martin Henry rifle. In 1889 the Lee Metford .303 breech-loading bolt-operated rifle with a magazine was introduced, in turn to be replaced by the Lee Enfield in 1899–1900. Officers began to give more serious attention to range training.[4] Machine-guns were initially seen as too expensive, but after Royal Artillery experiments with the less than satisfactory Gatling and Gardner guns two Maxim machine-guns began to be issued to each battalion from 1890, though the initial issue was often two per brigade only. Experiments were also made with hand-grenades but they were seen as more dangerous to the thrower than to the target. The structure of battalions was altered with in 1862 the reduction from ten companies to eight, the former elite grenadier and light companies being finally abolished. Each of the company's two Subalterns was responsible for a 'half company', a structure that was to prove unwieldy.

The cavalry were issued with carbine versions of the rifles. Until the 1899 Boer War tactics were to change but little, the infantry retaining square and line volley firing, though in the 1880s detachments were given mounted infantry training. Cavalry training remained centred on the charge, reconnaissance and column escort. In 1892 cavalry regiments finally adopted a three-service squadron structure. The artillery long resisted breech-loading guns. The field artillery's basic weapons were 13 and 17 pdr. guns and the Horse Artillery's 9 or 13 pdrs. Heavier siege weapons included 25 and 40 pdrs and 6-inch howitzers. Only in 1885 was the need for change finally accepted, breech-loaded quick-firing guns and smokeless powder providing new opportunities for artillery battery officers. More far-seeing was the 1856 amalgamation of the officers' Corps of Royal Engineers with the Royal Sappers and Miners to form the Royal Engineers, the corps in the Army the least concerned with gentlemanly amateurism. The late 19th century's technological advances provided officers of the Royal Engineers with the greatest need for change – in Britain itself with defensive structures around naval ports, advances in railway technology and bridging, searchlights, the invention of the contact mine and the development of balloons for aerial observation.

In 1881 as a consequence of the ending of purchase the rank structure in regiments was again fundamentally changed: command of companies, squadrons and batteries was made over to Majors. For this 137 Majors became Lieutenant-Colonels, and 613 Captains became Majors. They were, however, not permitted an issue horse and were not to receive the extra pay for three years in order to reduce the expense.

In 1861 some 24,000 men from the European regiments of the East India Company, whose rule had now been replaced, formed three new cavalry regiments and nine new infantry battalions, some as new regiments, some as second battalions of existing regiments. Lax discipline was tightened. Artillerymen of the three Company Presidencies' forces transferred to the Royal Artillery.[5] In addition one cavalry unit and one infantry unit were raised in Britain. The integration of the Company officers was not without friction, some of these officers being seen as social inferiors with family origins in commerce, 'trade'.

There remained no General Staff or permanent structure of operational Divisions or brigades. Overseas, brigades and 'Field Forces' were assembled for particular operations and destructured when the operation was over, a practice once again leaving many such forces ill prepared.

The ending of the system of purchasing commissions cost the taxpayer over £7,000,000 in compensation payments to officers who saw their financial investment programme ending. As first proposed, it was intended only to stop the initial purchase for a Cornet or an Ensign, but a Royal Commission reported that the compensation payable, that of the regulation tariff, would not cover the existing irregular additional payments, and Cardwell accordingly decided to end the whole practice and system and replace it with pensions.

The anomalies of the system, in particular its want of profession-alism at a time when other professions were working to organise and set standards, were all obvious arguments. At the time the reform made virtually no change in the nature of the officer corps. There were several reasons for this. First was the layering of society and the costs of being an officer over and above his pay, £200–£300 per year for an infantry officer, two or three times that amount in the Guards and the cavalry. Pay remained unaltered, but officers received compensation for the loss of the sale value of their com-missions and a system of pensions based on years of service was introduced. Also important was the preference for selection of future regimental officers from the growing number of fee-paying board-ing Public Schools, their discipline now restored. They were spar-tan, with senior boys responsible for the discipline and welfare of juniors, hierarchic and snobbish, with a curriculum classical rather than scientific, and had compulsory worship on Sundays. Sport and membership of the School's cadet corps could count more than aca-demic achievement.[6] Morality and self-discipline were viewed as equat-ing with courage. The foundations for future regimental life were here carefully laid and, most important of all, the attributes of an officer and a gentleman were inculcated.[7] Family traditions of service with particular regiments were appearing. The age was one of a strong military culture with pride in imperial expansion. Lastly, but by no means least, there continued to be the expectation in respect of what their officers should be among rank and file soldiers. These fac-tors all ensured that the overwhelming majority of officers still came from the minor gentry, the rapidly growing bourgeoisie and the aristocracy. There were of course exceptions, the most notable being Field-Marshal Sir William Robertson who had joined the cavalry as a trooper, and the unfortunate Major-General Sir Hector Macdonald who had joined the infantry as a private.

Cardwell's abolition of purchase was motivated not only for the obvious anomalies and injustices of the system but also by his hopes of fluidity of transfer of officers as well as men from the reserves and the Militia, impossible if the top of the pyramid of the regimental system was the purchased possession of the unit by its Colonel. In this he was to be disappointed. Depots and more seriously under-strength home service battalions became training institutions rather than a source of regiments ready for a crisis. The two major results of the reorganised regimental system, however, could not have been fully foreseen. Firstly, and the more important, the firm linking of regiments with counties or regions added a new and very strong linkage bonding officers, men, and officers and men together, in a system unequalled in combat loyalty and courage, and to be the envy of many other armies. It also affected public opinion: the officers of the local regiment were now part of the county establishment and, for more ordinary people, the soldiers were 'our boys', not some alien military presence forced upon them. Church parades and regimental occasions attracted public interest and support. Of lesser importance – but not entirely to be brushed aside – critics have noted the system to be costly (and it had to be trimmed after the Second World War) and one tending to limit officers to a nar-row conformity, their energies devoted to their regiment with its social and sporting life, rather than the development of their talents and imaginations to the full in the wider interests of the Army, so leaving them often ill-fitted for senior command or staff duties.[8]

The period saw Army officers, despite some colonial garrison reductions, still engaged in the widest variety of tasks and, par-ticularly for junior officers, adventures. Officers were to lead their men on operations in India, Afghanistan, Burma, Malaya, China, Jamaica, Barbados, British Honduras, Canada, New Zea-land, Southern Africa, West Africa, notably the Gold Coast, Sudan, Ethiopia and Egypt. Some of their work was colonial assertion or pacification against primary resistance, others punitive expeditions, all too often with very harsh retribution on local opposition, including blowing them from guns on ceremonial parade. In some operations, particularly in India and Egypt, regiments were committed in brigade or field force formations sometimes entirely British, sometimes with Indian regiments, and in Canada and New Zealand with locally recruited colonist units. On other occasions regiments and battalions operated on their own, frequently furnishing sub-unit size columns for particular tasks, and in the 1890s small detachments, usually the battalions' machine-gun teams under a Subaltern, would be sent out to operate with local units and police.

Terrain, climate and disease, cholera, dysentery and malaria, were in many campaigns a far more serious adversary than the enemy force. The risk of disease could affect operational planning. In both Napier's 1867–68 punitive expedition to Magdala in Ethiopia and Wolseley's 1873–74 Ashanti pacification campaign speed was essential – the campaigning had to be finished before the rains brought fevers. Burma in 1885–92 with its mixture of mountain, monsoon and malaria tested the health of officers and men to the limit.

Napier's march to Magdala across mountains and ravines with no roads or even tracks was of special difficulty; there was virtually no fresh water supply on the route, the altitude created a rarefied atmosphere and temperatures varied between 110°F at midday to freezing at night. The campaign owed all to the engineers who built a small port on the Red Sea. Engineers were also decisive in Canada: after long preliminary journeys by boat and rail, miles of road had to be built of felled tree trunks. Logistics played an ever-increasing vital role. In Afghanistan in 1880–81, when column sizes grew to over 10,000 men, as many as 10,000 animals, horses, ponies, mules, donkeys and camels were needed since wheeled transport, even for guns, was impracticable. Napier's Magdala march required 36,000 animals and over 12,000 porters and servants. Marches would begin early in the morning before dawn, with a stop of twenty minutes for a frugal breakfast at 0800 hrs and with ten-minute halts every hour thereafter. Some twenty miles, on occasions more, would be covered per day even in trying heat.

Tactics varied according to circumstances. Close-order line attacks could succeed, as they did in China, but could bring about disaster as happened in New Zealand in 1863. The traditional solid square and volley firing stood the Black Watch in good stead in the Ashanti campaign of 1873–74 and, despite failure at Isandhlwana when the seven-company square of the 24th Foot was overrun, officers and men alike being massacred, it saw success again when at Ulundi 20,000 Zulus were lured into attacking a square.[9] Final hollow square successes were secured against mass charges by dervishes in the Sudan in 1896–99, the square being strengthened by redoubts and zariba wire or thornbush-protected perimeters. One square had been broken at Tamai in 1884 but was quickly reformed. The last and very spectacular success of square and volley was at Omdurman in 1898, with over 10,000 dervishes being killed in fruitless attacks for fewer than fifty British and Egyptian dead. Officers varied the exact format of the square, loose across open terrain but closing when attack threatened. Wolseley set officers of two divisions the novel task of leading a night approach march and a dawn attack at Tel el Kabir in Egypt in 1882. Operations in Burma in the 1885–92 campaign were later called 'The Subalterns' War', young officers leading pursuit groups to round up insurgents in precipitous hills and jungle, with heavy rain and carnivorous animals to add to their concerns. Prior to the Zulu War, operations in South Africa were also based on small column groups.

In the Sudan infantry officers could find themselves and their men mounted on camels for rapid movement. At Magdala officers led the final assaults on Emperor Theodore's strongholds in very traditional manner with scaling ladder parties. Reverses happened. The worst, already noted, was that of Isandhlwana, but the well-known defeat at Majuba at the hands of the Boers in 1881 and the failure of the Gordon Relief Expedition in 1884–85 were both severe setbacks. Less well known, the 66th Foot suffered severely at

Maiwand in the Second Afghan War in 1880, when overrun by vastly superior numbers. The battalion lost ten officers and 265 soldiers killed, with thirty-two more wounded. The regiment's officers rallied their surviving men for the last stand. Desertion, in both Canada and South Africa, remained a problem for officers.

Large-scale cavalry charges were infrequent, but lance charges were made with success against the Zulus; in South Africa squadrons of British cavalry would work with locally raised horse and mounted infantry, often firing carbines from the saddle. In the various operations in India, officers led squadron- or troop-sized charges, sometimes with Indian units and not always with success. In Egypt cavalry was used for encirclement, protection for the guns of the Horse Artillery, reconnaissance and pursuit of fugitives, and often simply as mobile mounted infantry. The most famous charges in this period were those of the Household Cavalry by moonlight in Egypt in 1881 and of the 21st Lancers at Omdurman in the Sudan in 1897; among the Lancers' officers was the young Winston Churchill. Artillery played an increasingly important role in these late 19th century operations. New pieces, including 16 pdr. guns, were used to great effect at Tel el Kabir, and 2½-inch guns were carried by camel in the Sudan in 1884. In India 9 pdr. guns were pulled by horse or bullock, or mounted on mules or elephants. In these operations, officers and guns were still at the front. In the 1897 North-West Frontier operations rocket artillery was used to good effect. Perhaps the greatest engineering achievement was Major Girouard's 200-mile-long railway in the Sudan. The Royal Engineers deployed their first signals telegraph company in the Ashanti campaign of 1873. Signals communications, in India especially, were made very much more efficient by the use of heliograph.

Operations against opponents that were organised into something like a European field army, possessing artillery and effective small-arms fire, were the most risky. In Egypt Wolseley, with 20,000 men, was opposed by 30,000 men with sixty guns. While Wolseley was successful, Colley suffered his defeat and death at Majuba as the Boers were well equipped with excellent rifles and skilled in fire and movement.

Finally, law and order operations, in Ireland against Fenian partisans and on a few occasions of industrial unrest in Britain, notably miners' riots in 1893, remained necessary.[10]

In recognition of the resources and bravery shown in these operations Queen Victoria authorised a new award, the Distinguished Service Order (D.S.O.) for officers in 1896. A number of V.C.s were awarded to officers for service in these campaigns, some again reflecting the sense of concern and obligation for soldiers. In New Zealand, for example, in 1865 Captain Shaw of the 18th Foot led a party of four soldiers to rescue a badly wounded soldier under heavy fire at thirty yards' range. Lieutenant Marling of the 60th Rifles was awarded for rescuing a wounded soldier under heavy fire in the Sudan in 1884. Two medical officers, Surgeons Crimmin and Le Quesne, won their awards for tending wounded under fire in Burma in 1889, Le Quesne himself being wounded. Perhaps the most famous of the many awards were those for the gallant defence of Rorke's Drift Post in the 1879 Zulu War. Lieutenant Chard of the Royal Engineers, Lieutenant Bromhead of the 24th Foot and Surgeon-Major Reynolds, three of the V.C. winners, became national heroes.[11]

In operations in India the luxury lifestyle of the early 19th century finished. Officers now shared most of the discomforts of their soldiers on campaigns, though sometimes (but increasingly rarely) on horseback on the march rather than on foot. In normal times, officers' social lives in India improved. In the cantonments – either a little distance from city centres or in hill stations – pleasant mess buildings with verandahs, gardens and tennis courts were laid out. Officers would have at least three or four personal servants, with several more if they possessed a number of horses and ponies. The number of churches, in particular garrison churches, increased. In smaller stations these churches often took one regiment at a time for the Sunday parades, early morning or evening. Officers became members of the local Europeans-only club; both clubs and regiments organised a variety of theatrical and sporting activities – some only for club members but many for all ranks. Officers who could afford the ponies played polo, others enjoyed pigsticking, big-game shooting, racing, cricket and tennis. In the cooler weather unmarried girls came out from Britain to visit relatives – and with good fortune find a handsome officer husband enjoying a gener-ous local leave in a hill station. Other officers married British nurses or teachers. More officers' wives came out to India to join their husbands, public health conditions having improved and quinine being available. With their arrival came the ending of asso-ciations with Indian women, hitherto regarded as necessary. Also, after much campaigning by medical officers, moralists and church authorities in the 1890s, all forms of military brothels were abol-ished. However, many commanding officers made covert arrange-ments for their men. Those that did not were liable to find a higher venereal disease rate in the unit.

Several officers in India and elsewhere made notable contribu-tions to the study of ornithology, entomology and archaeology as well as surveying and map-making.[12] Mount Everest is named after a Colonel of Engineers. Among others of particular note were Lieutenant-Colonel Champion's researches in botany, the ethnology and weapons collections of Lieutenant-Colonel Lane-Fox (later Pitt-Rivers), and Captain Warren's archaeological work in Jerusalem. Royal Engineers officers' activities included railway construction, the architectural design of prestige buildings (not only overseas – at home the Royal Albert Hall in London was the design of Captain Fowke), large-scale irrigation schemes in India and the delineation of frontiers.

In Britain too officers' lives were enlivened, and their mess bills enlarged, by more extensive social activities, in particular devotion to sport, especially cricket, hunting and shooting, balls and other mess functions. Officers could still take long periods of leave, often several months. The 'hard-riding' officer won general admiration. Officers' Messes became more wealthy, with silver tableware being bought or presented by officers together with expensive china dinner plates and cups, many of excellent design, always incorporating the regimental badge. All officers even in Britain had at least one, usually two, soldier servants, one for himself and one for his horse or horses. Wealthier officers continued to join expensive London clubs, sometimes politically linked to the Conservative Party, a fact not unnoticed by others. Etiquette, snobbish and rigid, governed day-to-day social life, with rituals of visiting cards, dancing partner lists and seating at dinner tables. Houses and marriage allowance became payable, but only to officers over thirty. Officers were expected, for reasons of military efficiency and general social convention, to follow the unwritten rule 'Captains may, Majors should, Colonels must', a code to last until the post-1945 years and in effect prohibiting marriage, except for the wealthy, for Lieutenants and junior Captains. This code, further, often left young officers, products of boys-only public schools, ill prepared for acquaintance with women. In many cases, officers suffered from inhibitions and communication difficulties with women of their own class (the women themselves often younger and equally ill prepared to meet men) and in consequence to compensate without inhibitions with women from other backgrounds.[13]

Officers wishing to marry had, and in theory still have, to seek their Commanding Officer's permission. If approved, and if the officer and his bride so wished, the custom of church-door guards of honour, brother officers or NCOs with swords, evolved. The few officers promoted from the ranks were rarely promoted beyond the rank of Captain; although accepted as brother officers, they were not expected to participate fully in the social life.

To last until the 1960s, and in some measure still surviving, was the Victorian age belief that officers, wives and families were expected to be Christian role models. Wives, headed by the Commanding Officer's wife, were expected to help as unpaid welfare assistants and counsellors with soldiers' domestic or family problems – an extension of the squirearchic pattern of officering. While some wives, unfortunately, on occasions went further, interfering in other regimental or garrison matters not their concern, their work and often very genuine interest played an important part in regimental life and was useful, welcomed by the rank and file and their wives, and not resented as condescending. In several regiments, officers opened regimental charities to assist widows and orphaned children. Officers' families were expected to accompany their husbands to Sunday church parades. Extramarital affairs were few. Divorce was unacceptable and virtually unheard of. Misbehaviour with another man's wife led to forced resignation from the Army. A curious exception to these conventions of behaviour was the cavalry officer Lieutenant French, the future Field-Marshal, who married very discreetly, divorced even more discreetly but went on to conduct several generally known extramarital affairs. No evidence of homosexuality among Victorian officers exists with one exception, Sir Hector Macdonald, who committed suicide when his private life became public.

Towards the end of the century, some middle-class opinion became critical of officers, seeing them as out of step with the rest of the nation, arrogant, apparently over-privileged and leading an out-of-date lifestyle, but paradoxically there was virtually no criticism of the traditional belief that the essential quality of an officer was that he must be a gentleman; the issues were simply of lifestyle and professional competence. For some, indeed, the very fact that officers were gentlemen ensured their interest in preserving the class structure. For others, in the middle class, a commission was the path for upward social mobility, gentrification or, if they were newly wealthy, in landed-estate social acceptability. In reverse, many landowners felt some obligation to serve, at least for a period of time.[14] Generally, though, in this age of proud imperialism there was much public support for the Army, its colonial operations being well written up in the press and in books, including fiction.

In the 1880s and 1890s, the Army overseas reluctantly parted from the brightly coloured dress of the past and uniforms, other than on ceremonial occasions, became khaki, adopted much earlier in India, at first informally through necessity but later regularised. The drabness of the colour led officers and NCOs to pay particular attention to the shine on those items of uniform – boots, buttons and badges – that were not khaki. Khaki was finally adopted for regiments in Britain rather later, in 1902. With khaki came the Sam Browne leather belt, named after an Indian Army cavalry officer who lost his left arm in battle and needed a belt and shoulder strap to secure his sword and scabbard to his left side. The rank badge system was revised, a Colonel's insignia becoming a crown and two stars, a Lieutenant-Colonel's a crown and one star, a Major's a crown, a Captain's two stars and a Lieutenant's one star. Cornets and Ensigns had no insignia until much later, in 1913, when Captains were given three stars, Lieutenants two and Second-Lieutenants one. Until the First World War these badges were worn on the lower sleeve of khaki service dress. In the new regimental depots and barracks officers daily ensured that soldiers' bedding and kit were laid out with meticulous precision. After the Crimea, officers were forbidden to grow beards; in 1896 shaving the upper lip was forbidden.

Another area of military life, sea transport, also saw slow improvement, with first the hiring of commercial steamships for long sea voyages and then the placing of troop transport contracts with specific shipping companies including the Peninsular and Oriental and the Union Line, now operating much larger steamships. Officers and their wives and children, when entitled, travelled first class, Warrant Officers second class, but even the third class provided for NCOs and soldiers was a far more comfortable experience than earlier travel. Even in the cramped conditions of the hired ships, officers were expected to dress for dinner every night.

Promotion remained a thorny issue. Promotion on merit was suspect and there was no agreement on what constituted merit; Sir George Colley, who passed out first at both Sandhurst and the Staff College, fell in disaster at Majuba. There could be, and were, anomalies in reporting, and a belief that more senior officers should be men of property remained strong. In consequence, promotion remained unstructured and some officers were awarded a more senior rank as a result of influence and connections. Sometimes, advancement went to junior officers who had specifically caught the eye of a leading General, the 'Ashanti ring' of officers who had served with distinction under Wolseley in the Gold Coast being the most important example.

Pay remained low, for a Lieutenant-Colonel still only £365 per annum, a Captain now £211, a Cornet £95; Guards, Cavalry, Artillery and Engineer officers received a slightly higher rate. All faced increasing out-of-pocket expenses and the rates were far below those earned in the civilian professions or government service. Again, paradoxically, this was seen as desirable in that the taxpayer saved money, the only people likely to want to be officers would be men of substance, and that in any case service as an officer was a matter of honour. Private income was therefore essential, at least £1,000 per annum in the Guards, £750 or more for the cavalry and £200 for the infantry. Some regiments required a prior assurance that aspirant officers would have sufficient private income, and there were cases of officers not able to meet the regimental lifestyle being bullied and harassed until they left. Even the most junior officers had a personal servant – in the infantry the platoon commander's runner – while Commanding Officers had two or three.

The changes and developments in officers' education and training appeared impressive but were in reality rather less so. Officers' anti-academic culture and a belief that character counted for more than training persisted. The variety of overseas tasks, the absence of any major land power adversary and the consequent uncertainty over exactly what was the Army's role continued throughout the rest of the century to mitigate against any formation of doctrine or solid education programme for officers.

There was, nevertheless, reaction to the obvious and monumental failures of staff and command in the Crimea. After study by several committees, and much debate in Parliament, in a Council for Military Education created in 1857 and elsewhere, a decision was reached to create a Staff College, distinct from the Royal Military College but within the same grounds in Camberley and until 1911 still in theory under command of the RMC.[15] Building the College premises began in 1859 and was finished in 1862. The initial arrangements provided for a two-year course with an instructing staff of nine, of whom four were to be serving officers styled 'professors'.

Admission was to be by competitive examination, good reports from regiments, at least three years' service and, if a Subaltern, proof of having passed a promotion examination. Thirty students – twenty-five from the Guards, infantry and cavalry and five from the Artillery – were to be admitted. Engineer officers were only admitted later, it being thought their initial training was sufficient. Provision was made for officers either to qualify by sitting the final examination without attending the College at all, or to be given exemption from the first year. The course included military history, drawing, military administration, military law, fortifications and reconnaissance, with as options a foreign language, science or mathematics. Study of military administration (one hour per week) was apparently thought sufficient instruction in matters of supply and movement. Teaching generally lacked inspiration and was often boringly pedantic. The final examination was marked in three grades and an order of merit, after which officers would be posted for six months, very soon progressively reduced to one month, to a regiment in a branch of the service other than their own. An average of some thirty officers entered the College each year in the 1860s. While it attracted a few of keen intellect (and also, it would seem, officers wishing to get married or avoid a posting overseas), the College for long made only limited appeal to men in a culture in which career ambition was that of regimental command. Service abroad, preventing preparation for the entrance examination, together with a regulation that, however able a second candidate might be, only one officer from any battalion could be accepted, and the dislike of the College held by many senior Generals who preferred officers who had not been at the College for staff appointments, all detracted from its reputation. Until the end of the purchase system, two years at the College – with no certainty of later career development – could also mean missed opportunities for regimental advancement and regimental life.

The course syllabus was slightly expanded following criticism in 1870, with road-making and military telegraphy now being included. In military administration more but still insufficient attention was given to transport of men, animals, stores and casualties, and field encampment. In the decade that followed the number of student officers at first increased but only to fall at the end of the 1870s. The College, however, became more practical with outdoor teaching and battlefield tours incorporated in the course and, notably in operations directed by Wolseley, more graduates of the College being selected for staff duties. The order of merit was abolished, but the curious anomaly by which an officer could sit the final examination and become 'p.s.c.' (Passed Staff College) without attending the course lasted until 1880.

Further improvements in the 1880s followed with a slight increase in numbers, thirty-two in 1886, now including officers from the Indian Army. Battalions could now offer more than one candidate and the Commander-in-Chief could nominate four candidates he thought promising. A Russian language option was added to the course and the final grading into three abolished, a simple distinction being awarded to a few. The quality of instruction improved greatly. In the 1890s the final examination was abolished and operational training centred increasingly on theoretical tactical problem solving, rather than fact cramming, with staff rides to place problems in a field context. The problems chosen for exercise study, however, were generally those of strategy and tactics rather than logistic procedures.

What did all this mean for the regimental officers, many of whom were young Lieutenants in their twenties? In peace it could serve an officer well. If he was ambitious he could apply for – and if able probably gain – staff training and career development, though in some cases at some disadvantage to his regimental career prospects. The College became more generally accepted except by the most traditional regimental officers. The British decision not to have a Staff Corps but to alternate regimental and staff postings gave many the best of both worlds, and spared the Army the arrogance of a *corps d'elite*. The course provided many with the companionship of officers of other branches of the Army and a much-needed insight into their duties. It certainly did provide them with much-enjoyed sport – cricket and hunting in particular. For war, however, as was to be seen at the end of the century, there remained major shortcomings. The absence of a General Staff to formulate a national strategy and doctrine lay at the root of these. As a consequence, low priority was attached to thorough preparation or training for the issue of orders or large-scale field logistics for a force of several divisions fighting a well-equipped and resourceful field army.[16] The regimental officer – and his men – were to pay a heavy price for these weaknesses.

The same half-measure reforms took place at Woolwich and at Sandhurst.[17] At the former, entrance by competitive examination replaced 'jobbing' nomination, and the minimum entry age was finally set at sixteen after a brief period at seventeen. Many boys had previously attended an Ordnance School at Carshalton from the age of eleven; some also entered, at various ages, from Addiscombe and Sandhurst. Although improvements in the buildings, food and facilities were made, discipline in the 1860s was still rowdy, with serious disorders in 1861 and 1864; thereafter high spirits were better contained. In the first years of the 1890s sports and games came to provide a healthier outlet, the annual cricket and athletics fixtures against Sandhurst being especially important in Woolwich cadets' lives. In the first years of the 1890s a process of 'bifurcation' began, with separate-stream two-year courses for future Engineers and future Artillerymen, the former being more rigorous and taxing. This was, however, ended in 1896.

At Sandhurst, the former entry by interview only was replaced by interview and a written examination, including mathematics, history, geography, drawing and Latin. Although not actually very testing and because for both Sandhurst and Woolwich the examinations were very competitive for the limited number of entrants, less confident candidates were often packed off to 'crammers', tutorial establishments that came to specialise in the entry tests.[18] The fees for the sons of officers were reduced and twenty nominated 'Queen's Cadets', sons of officers killed or deceased from disease, were accepted without fees. The majority of future line infantry and many cavalry officers now passed through Sandhurst, receiving priority over those nominated for a Direct Commission with or without purchase. The practice of Direct Commissioning continued, however, for some time – despite its formal abolition in 1859. Many commanding officers, particularly in the Guards, preferred the Direct Commission, one reason perhaps being that until its abolition the system of purchase removed motivation from the Sandhurst cadet with his commission already paid for. It was also possible for a Militia or a Yeomanry officer to transfer to the Regular Army after a not very testing examination and be exempt from attending Sandhurst. The Sandhurst course with its older cadets was now more professional, less like that of a public school. However, although food and other conditions of life were improved, discipline remained poor with a mutiny in 1862 and serious disorders again in 1864.

As a forerunner of changes to follow in the next decade, in 1862 the College's establishment was increased from 180 to 336 to provide for cadets destined for the Indian Army following the closure of Addiscombe, and the course was reduced from two years to one. The 1870s, following the abolition of purchase, were years of turbulence. A disastrous experiment of making the College course one for Second Lieutenants was introduced but they, and the Direct Commission cadets sent to Sandhurst, did virtually nothing, having no incentive. Other cadets had to wait for commissions until a Russian war scare in 1878 led to a need to bring regiments up to strength. Stability only returned in the late 1870s after a major policy decision that all future officers (except those for the Engineers and Artillery and a few entrants through the Militia) should attend Sandhurst as cadets. The establishment rose slowly from 200 to 360 and then on to 480. The course was lengthened to eighteen months with 120, later 160, admitted twice a year. The curriculum now covered military engineering, topography, administration and law, French and German, drill, equitation and physical training. Much of the classroom teaching was, however, poor and outdated; many cadets, doubtful of the value of any serious professional studies in the development of their careers and bored by emphasis on spit and polish, limited their intellectual and physical efforts to the sports fields.

The quality of combat training that young officers received in regiments after Woolwich or Sandhurst appears to have varied very considerably, and to have been affected by the duties of the unit at the time. For a young officer in England, there might be one, two or three regimental parades each week and one or two field days per month in the summer, with even less training in the autumn and winter hunting season. Above all other sports, hunting was seen as the best form of training for an officer. The traditional anti-academic culture continued, leaving the majority of officers with a casual approach, limited to their own arm of the service, to any professional study of war. For the small minority of officers that did make a serious theoretical study, military journal articles could be stimulating, especially those of the Royal Artillery and Royal Engineers. Some useful books on various aspects of warfare also appeared. More infantry officers attended shooting courses at Hythe. The specialist training of Engineers and Artillery officers advanced with developments in technology. For all, more professionalism entered into annual confidential reports and promotion tests. Perceived as most important, however, remained character training in all its aspects.

Here, improvement was visible. Relations between officers and men were well tempered by constant colonial campaigning in which they continued to learn, know and respect each other. The units' senior officers took care to instruct newly arrived Ensigns. 'The first and most important duty is the care and welfare of the men under his command', said the Second in Command of a Rifle Brigade battalion to a newly joined officer in 1899, going on to add that the young officer must get to know each individual man under his command so that the man would turn to him in any difficulty.[19] In other regiments new officers would be given a booklet setting out their duties and what was expected of them as leaders, together with advice on regimental customs and etiquette.[20] More practically, a young officer would be given a platoon with an experienced sergeant who would teach him quietly more than any booklet or manual. In cavalry regiments, morning and evening 'stables' provided officers and troopers opportunities to talk and know each other as human beings. While all this was constructive, there still remained a minority of poor officers – place seekers, social climbers, the gun-shy and the excessive drinkers – and there were cases in the colonial campaigns where officers put their own interests and safety before those of their men.

On the march, a few larger officers would carry the weapon of a soldier who appeared to be in difficulties, and at a campsite all officers were expected to see to their men's welfare before going to their own tents. In more normal times, sports, theatricals and company parties all developed comradeship that crossed class distinctions. The major danger to discipline was not any specific discontent but alcohol. An example of this occurred when men of a cavalry regiment extended excessive hospitality to soldiers of the Devonshire Regiment at Muttra, near Delhi, in 1884. Almost all the soldiers became very drunk, 600 men lost their good conduct badges and companies had to parade every day for a year.[21] One small-scale refusal-to-work protest by sixty men of the 19th Hussars in Dublin in 1877 seems to have been the result of the regiment's Colonel overworking his men. It was the only event of its kind in the century and hardly merited the charge of mutiny that faced its leaders.[22]

From 1893, Commanding Officers could award penal sentences with or without hard labour for fourteen days instead of the previous seven. Commanding Officers could also deprive a man of pay for damage or absence without leave. In these cases, soldiers were given the option of a court-martial. Minor punishments, extra duties or confinement to barracks, for up to twenty-eight days by a CO or seven by a squadron or company commander, were without appeal.[23] Defaulter soldiers were, and still are, marched in without belt or headdress, before a unit or sub-unit commander smartly dressed, usually in an office furnished and decorated with regimental insignia and properties. Junior officers due for reprimand received extra duty officer punishments, the number of days depending on the gravity of the offence.

A few large-scale exercises were held in the early 1870s but were then discontinued and not resumed until the mid-1890s.[24] By this time, areas around Aldershot, Frensham and (after 1890) Salisbury Plain had become available for training, and exercises with two or more Divisions were possible. In 1898 an exercise involving two Army Corps was held, revealing several minor operational procedure weaknesses, notably the absence of clear definitions of staff officers' duties. The major ones, the effect of the firepower of modern artillery and machine-guns on infantry and horsed cavalry, remained unnoticed in Britain – but not in Continental Europe or in South Africa.

NOTES

1 The 1st Rifle Volunteers paraded in the forecourt of Exeter Castle on 12th January 1852. The present-day Territorial Army infantry unit in Exeter carries on the name.

2 The legislation was thrown out by the House of Lords and only achieved by the administrative device of a Royal Warrant.

3 A good example, although now made over into maisonettes, survives at Stoughton, in Guildford, the depot of the former Queen's Royal Regiment; the castle-like keep dominates its area of the city.

4 Aggett, *Bloody Eleventh*, II, 105.

5 Until the 1930s the imperial Indian Army was not permitted artillery units. All artillery units in India were on British Army strengths and officered by British Army Regular officers on a tour of duty in the sub-continent, even though the gunners and limber personnel were Indian.

6 The university and school officers' training corps are described in Appendix 4.

7 As late as 1942 this author's Public School housemaster addressed new boys: 'Here the masters are the officers, the prefects are the sergeants and you are the soldiers.' Many Public Schools had a Sixth Form Army Class programme. Heathcote, *Indian Army*, 142, provides a table of the class origins of Sandhurst products in the years 1890–95; 49·6 per cent were sons of service officers, and of these 42·8 per cent were British Army, the remainder Navy or Indian Army. Other significant contributors were private gentlemen 13·7 per cent, sons of clergymen

6·9 per cent, Indian Civil Service 5·8 per cent and the legal profession 5·5 per cent. All other professions and occupations were each below 1 per cent; these included brewers, manufacturers, ship-owners, farmers and tradesmen.

8 'No officer had ever volunteered for the Staff College . . . They lived and fought as a regiment, without personal considerations . . .' Ian B. Hamilton, *The Happy Warrior: A Life of General Sir Ian Hamilton* (London, Cassell, 1966), 19, so describes the culture in the Gordon Highlanders when Hamilton applied for the Staff College in 1874.

9 The Ulundi square comprised five infantry battalions and four 9 pdr. guns around the perimeter enclosing a cavalry regiment and local levies, in all 5,000 men.

10 The major examples when troops were alerted were the London dock strike of 1889, the postal strike of 1890 and unrest in Wales in 1893. Aggett, *Bloody Eleventh*, II, 177, notes a rural case arising from disturbances among Cornish miners.

11 Wilkins, *Victoria Cross*, 192–193, 237–245, 276–277.

12 These and other examples appear in Ian Beckett, *The Victorians at War* (London and New York, Hambledon, 2003), vi.

13 An example, fictional but instructive, appears in C.S. Forester's perceptive novel *The General*, (London, Michael Joseph, 1936). The author is, however, a little unfair in his presentation of the military competence of officers. A useful and very frank overall picture of a young officer's professional, sporting and private life appears in General Sir Hubert Gough, *Soldiering On* (London, Arthur Barker, 1954), 34–35.

14 The issue is discussed at length but with interesting examples in Gwyn Harries-Jenkins, *The Army in Victorian Society* (London, Routledge, 1977), ii. Harries-Jenkins notes how many members of the landed nobility and gentry, after their service in the Army, served the public in other ways.

15 Bond, *Victorian Army and the Staff College*, ii–v, sets out in detail the foundations and development of the College.

16 In June 1891, the Secretary of State for War, Stanhope, issued a memorandum that was the nearest approach to a defence policy statement in the late Victorian era. Priorities were support for the civil power in Britain; the garrisons needed for India and strategically important colonies; with the Militia the ability to mobilise two Army Corps for the defence of Britain; and if finance permitted the ability to despatch an expeditionary force of two Army Corps and a Cavalry Division overseas. The likelihood of the latter was seen as 'improbable'.

17 Brigadier Sir John Smyth, *Sandhurst* (London, Weidenfeld, 1961), Part II; Shepperd, *Sandhurst*, v–vii.

18 Of the examination, William Robertson, at the time a sergeant-major, wrote later, 'The examination was very simple and was passed almost as a matter of course for it would have been an unforgiveable breach of etiquette for officers of one regiment to plough a candidate sent up by another.' Field-Marshal Sir William Robertson, *From Private to Field Marshal* (London, Constable, 1921), 32–33.

19 Bryant, *Jackets of Green*, 167.

20 A work widely read by junior officers was Captain S.T. Bannius, *Regimental Duties Made Easy* (Aldershot, Gale and Polden, 1901).

21 Aggett, *Bloody Eleventh*, II, 209–210.

22 Anglesey, *British Cavalry*, III, 76–79.

23 Anglesey, *British Cavalry*, III, 75; 17; Major S.T. Bannius, *Military Law Made Easy* (Aldershot, Gale and Polden, 1904), v, provides examples. The 1881 Army Act codified Statute Military Law.

24 Aggett, *Bloody Eleventh*, II, 172, for example, notes an exercise on Dartmoor involving 12,000 men taking place in 1872.

CHAPTER 9

THE EDWARDIAN ARMY OFFICER

The Victorian Army entered the Second South African War with regiments well disciplined but still holding the belief that thorough training in the traditional tactics of square, echelon, line and volley infantry, with a line-up of guns in the open at the front to provide overwhelming fire power, in turn followed by a dashing cavalry charge, would all once again bring victory. The campaign was seen as small-scale, likely to be short and causing few casualties. But the Army was to meet an opponent expert in fieldcraft, including mines and barbed wire and in particular use of cover to advance and mount a surprise attack; expert marksmen in rifle shooting and highly mobile on ponies capable of living on the rough terrain; and expert in the bold use of artillery in single or a pair of guns, sited concealed and using shrapnel and smokeless powder. The nature of the terrain, bare open veldt in some areas studded with rocky hillocks known as *kopjes*, of climate which could vary from extremes of heat to extremes of rain, hail and cold, and of water supply on occasions disastrously polluted, all added to the purely military difficulties. The original force of four divisions with cavalry and artillery had grown by 1901 to over 400,000 of which almost half were Yeomanry, Rifle Volunteers, Militia, Australians, New Zealanders, Canadians and South Africans. The series of early disasters under incompetent Generals in the last months of 1899 – Stormberg, Magersfontein, Colenso and the besieging of Mafeking, Kimberley and Ladysmith – were the result.

Thereafter, and under the better generalship of Roberts and Kitchener, regimental officers were able to draw on the discipline within regiments as they entered a learning curve, leading first to a clear conventional warfare victory, but calling for further learning in the final phase of the war when the Boers turned to commando guerrilla warfare. Far greater weaknesses were evident at command and staff levels as so few officers posted to staff appointments had had any previous staff training.

At the outset, infantry officers with swords and buttons brightly shining led their men in line attacks, with some success at Elandslaagte and Belmont, but presenting an excellent target and suffering heavy casualties. These attacks were, however, to fail, on occasions disastrously; at Magersfontein and at Spion Kop officers were reduced to trying to restore order after a rout. Morale slumped following these reverses, adding to regimental officers' problems increasingly compounded by lack of maps, reliable intelligence, inadequate reconnaissance and confused orders from formation commanders. The arrival of stores and supplies, too, was irregular and for a while some regiments had neither greatcoats nor blankets for nights, often rainy, in the open. Night marches could end in confusion as did attacks or big sweeps mounted without the necessary information about the ground, still less the enemy. Supply columns were ambushed. The nature of the ground more than tactical thinking then began to force change; division and brigade formations were broken up into columns. Attacks were launched by groups of 20–30 men in, to use a later term, 'blobs', forming half-company size rushes, by bounds and supported by artillery fire.[1] Unit fronts, no longer dominated by the square, widened as both sides sought to outflank each other; the widening gave company officers greater responsibilities, particularly as in big attacks men from different units became mixed up and required sorting out. But in these new styles, infantry officers led men in a number of spirited attacks with, generally, increasing success. Much of the campaign for the infantry, however, was spent in marching, often in great heat. Some regiments, or companies grouped from different regiments, became mounted infantry seated on Burmese Pegu ponies, a novel experience for young officers.

Food supplies varied: in some areas the wagon trains arrived safely and units were well fed; elsewhere, officers and men marched for days on bully beef and biscuits. Later in the war the Army's first emergency ration pack appeared, comprising two four-ounce tins, one of concentrated beef, the other of cocoa paste. These could be consumed neat, or boiled for an hour to produce thick soup and cocoa. When conditions permitted, officers set up field messes; a delicacy that produced mixed reactions was one of an extract of horse and local wild spinach, all flavoured by violet powder. The worst problem, however, facing regimental officers, and not properly understood by them, was disease, especially enteric fever, from dirty water. The war cost 6,000 men killed and 16,000 died of disease. The Boer War memorial of the Queen's Royal Regiment offers a regiment-level example; the Regiment's one battalion (reinforced by a small number of Rifle Volunteers) lost 43 killed or died of wounds, and 99 who died of disease.[2] It was an army victorious but weary that marched into Pretoria, regiments 'dressed in rags and broken boots'.[3]

In the last guerrilla phase of the war, railway lines and supply trains and columns were attacked by roving Boer commandos several hundred strong. One spectacular commando success was the destruction of a British force 1,300 strong, compelling 600 officers and men to surrender. Detachments from battalions led by Subalterns and Captains were sent out to guard blockhouses and outposts in fortified corridors and, when possible, to form columns, including artillery, to track and hunt down the commandos, a task made very difficult by the fact that their supply wagons moved much slower than the Boers. Officers were also obliged to take part, many finding the tasks distasteful, in the punitive burning of Boer farmsteads and the herding of women and children into concentration camps.

It was also not a great war for the cavalry officer, pre-war close-order drill evolutions being of little value. Much of their work was limited to leading patrols, and providing screening and cover for columns of troops and supply wagons, sometimes as much as fifteen miles long, on the march. In the final guerrilla phase of the war, cavalry squadrons led by junior officers were useful as pursuit groups, using rifles rather than swords or lances. There were, however, a few useful cavalry charges, when the shock value of cavalry could be used to advantage, notably a spectacularly successful one at Klip Drift when the Boers were put to flight. Cavalry also did much valuable work dismounted jointly with infantry. They suffered from the same problem as the artillery, shortage of quality fodder for the horses; at the outset the artillery also faced ammunition shortages. Artillery officers fired a variety of weapons, the majority being 15 pdr. field guns and the largest being 5-inch guns and 6-inch howitzers; they absorbed valuable lessons in the concealed siting of guns, indirect fire and firing in support of the infantry. In the final phase of the war, in addition to supplying one or two guns to a pursuit column, some batteries were temporarily converted to a mounted infantry role, which was novel and exciting for young Artillery officers.

Royal Engineer officers were responsible firstly for signal communications, heliograph, flags, searchlights and lamps, but also for railway construction, armoured trains, steam traction engines and, as always, bridge construction, a notable feat being the construction in February 1900 of a bridge over the Tugela river while under heavy fire. Also, for the first time, Engineer officers were involved in aerial reconnaissance from twenty-four tethered balloons communicating with the ground by signals telephone and a combat intelligence unit, the Field Intelligence Department, was created which, by the end of the war included 132 officers.

In general, officers very unjustly saw the Boers as an 'other', comparable with the non-white adversaries elsewhere in the Empire, a perception fuelled by allegations of breaches of local white-flag surrender agreements. They respected, and feared, Boer fire power but noted that the Boers (whose rifles had no bayonets) were in turn afraid of cold steel – bayonets, swords or lances. In fact, the Boers were often generous in victory and in matters such as temporary truces to collect wounded or bury dead. These factors, contributing to a curious Darwinian belief that the British race might be in decay (occasioned also by the poor physical state of many recruits), led to a view that offensive spirit must be restored.

Numerous awards of the Victoria Cross and Distinguished Service Order were made to officers who fought in the Boer War. Several once more showed obligation as well as great personal courage, notably Lieutenant Norwood of the 5th Dragoons Guards, Lieutenant Parsons of the Essex Regiment, Major Brown of the 14th Hussars, Lieutenant Dugdale of the 5th Lancers and Lieutenant Milbank of the 10th Hussars, who all received their awards for rescuing soldiers while under fire.

The Army's regiments had few other commitments in the first fourteen years of the 20th century. The North-West Frontier of India was relatively quiet, requiring no major field force operations. A battalion was posted to China as part of an international force guarding the Tientsin/Beijing railway and other units continued to serve in colonies. Individual officers opted to serve in small-scale but nevertheless fierce campaigns in Somaliland, the Gold Coast and Nigeria. Industrial unrest in Britain such as the 1910 strike of miners in Monmouthshire, railway unrest in Derby in 1911 and a dock strike in 1912 all required troops to support the police. Some individual Regular officers were posted to units of the new Territorial Force (T.F.), as instructors and administrators, not a very onerous task at the time as funds for the training of T.F. units were very limited.[4]

The Army's evident shortcomings in South Africa, together with the ever clearer realisation that the military power and ambitions of imperial Germany must mean the end of 'splendid isolation' from Continental affairs, led to a decade of far-reaching reform, supported by public opinion. A number of committees, of which the War Office (Reconstitution) Committee was the most important, considered different issues and a reforming Minister, Richard Haldane, at the War Office from 1906 set in place the necessary changes.

Most important, though affecting the daily lives of regimental officers only indirectly, was the long overdue creation in 1908 of a General Staff headed by an Army Council. The post of Commander-in-Chief was abolished; instead there were to be the military members of the Army Council, the Chief of the General Staff (from 1909 the 'Imperial General Staff'), responsible for operations, intelligence and overall policy, the Adjutant-General responsible for personnel welfare and recruitment, the Quartermaster-General responsible for equipment and its supply, and the Master-General of the Ordnance responsible for artillery and engineering works. There was to be also one civilian member, the Financial Secretary. Below these senior generals were general staff directorates for the variety of duties, the most important being the Director of Military Operations, the Director of Military Training and the Director of Staff Duties; others concerned recruiting, medicine, the T.F., etc. Across the country military districts were created for administration, freeing units and their Commanding Officers for training.

The field Army was reconstituted by Haldane on a permanent basis of formations, six infantry and one cavalry Divisions. By August 1914 each infantry Division, 18,000 men, comprised three infantry brigades of four battalions, with a squadron of cavalry and four field artillery brigades (each of which comprised three batteries of field guns and one to three batteries of howitzers), all supported by a garrison artillery heavy battery, two engineer field companies and medical units. The cavalry Division was formed initially of three, later of five brigades each including three regiments, together with five Horse Artillery batteries.[5] This force, organised into two Army Corps, was to be available for action fifteen days after general mobilisation. It was to be supported, for home defence, by fourteen T.F. Divisions, fourteen mounted brigades and field artillery, its units commanded by Territorials while formation commanders and most staff officers were Regular officers.

At regimental level, infantry training absorbed the main lessons of South Africa, 'advancing in small squads by rushes', using ground tactically in fire and movement, camouflage, digging in and shooting accurately at medium and long ranges. The traditional emphasis on ability to march long distances with greatcoat, blanket, rations and rifle was also maintained.[6] By 1907 the short magazine Lee Enfield rifle was in general use. By 1913–14, battalions had been restructured into four companies each with a company commander, a second-in-command Captain and four platoons, the platoon now providing the youngest officers with a responsibility of their own as platoon commanders. Battalions also received an increase of six officers for depot and T.F. training, and to cover for the absence of officers at Staff College or in staff appointments. Training itself became much more professional and rigorous, following principles set out in several manuals, of which the most important was the two-part *field Service Regulations of 1909*, covering operations and organisation and administration. Within cavalry regiments, each of the three sabre squadrons now comprised four troops; squadrons were commanded by Majors or Captains, troops by Subalterns. Against critics, cavalry officers maintained their own special *élan* and the speed of the horse charge with its shock value could still make a vital contribution to any battle. All regiments were now issued with two Maxim machine-guns – an issue not welcomed by many of the more traditional officers – and sword cavalry regiments received a new pointed sword. Other regiments, after some controversy, retained lances. The machine-guns reflected the new cavalry training requirement, the ability to fight dismounted with rifle or carbine. Officers were also instructed to place more emphasis on the reconnaissance role of cavalry, and a few interested themselves in aircraft and radio communication.

In the artillery, the distinction (as much social as of role) between the Royal Horse Artillery, Royal Field Artillery and Royal Garrison Artillery remained. In the RHA and RFA three or four batteries each commanded by a Major, self-accounting and proud of its individual name and traditions, formed a brigade commanded by a Lieutenant-Colonel, with a brigade Major and an Adjutant. The battery commander was assisted by a Captain and two or three Subalterns. Two RHA batteries were independent. Subalterns commanded sections of two guns. The RGA remained organised in companies, heavy and mountain batteries. The RFA received the new and very efficient 18 pdr. field gun and 4.5-inch howitzer. The RHA received 13 pdrs. The RGA were equipped with 60 pdr. pieces and a few very heavy guns. Training, however, remained very amateurish, not properly related to maps, and the Boer lessons of indirect fire were soon forgotten; much communication was by megaphone. Royal Engineer officers became responsible for flying and aerial navigation, and it was from the Royal Engineers that the Royal Flying Corps was formed in 1912. Large-scale exercises practising the new formations and their staffs were held in the autumn of the last pre-1914 years, land on Salisbury Plain and elsewhere being acquired for the training.

Staff officers were now trained in common standardised operational procedures and responsibilities. Apart from a small number of places at the College filled by nomination, entrance was by a now very real competitive examination. The Staff College course was progressively brought up to date, notably in the period when the future Field-Marshal Lord Rawlinson was Commandant. The course inculcated an ethos of duty and service, the subjects taught being more practical, broader and less mechanistic in presentation.

Rawlinson's successor, Sir Henry Wilson, added Service and Medical Corps officers to the directing staff, and increased the number of student officers. The lessons of the Boer War and the Russo-Japanese war were studied, including issues of administration and logistics. Wilson furthered theoretical studies of a war in defence of Belgium and France. Staff rides set exercises involving not only the issue of orders but complex logistics and medical problems. Robertson, Wilson's successor, with notable prescience introduced the study of retreat. Although staff and student officer relations were friendly and often informal – particularly when hunting or on the sports field – pressure and stress were applied for the first time. Almost all Commanding Officers agreed the College's work was vital and most came, still sometimes grudgingly, to respect its products.

In career development initially eight years of service and 'p.s.c.' gained an officer a general staff appointment, which he would hold for four years before returning to regimental duty. A few officers who had held a staff appointment but had not been to the College were exempted from the first year of the two-year course and its first-year examination. A little later the eight years' service requirement was dropped. Accelerated promotion – by brevet rank – could be gained for p.s.c. officers and by a few others.[7] The terms General Staff Officer, GSO 1, 2 and 3, came into use and Staff College graduates, even if only Captains, wore red hatbands when in staff appointments, a practice sometimes arousing resentment. Financial restrictions precluded the posting of more than two Staff College-trained officers to any one divisional headquarters.

The two cadet colleges also came under critical scrutiny, especially Sandhurst where the inadequacies of the changes of the late 19th century were now highlighted, in particular the culture of gentlemanly disdain for any serious professionalism. The outbreak of the war in South Africa led to early commissioning of cadets and the shortening of courses – one of only three months added to the unsatisfactory state of affairs. A committee on the education and training of officers found little fault with Woolwich, where the shortening of courses had been better managed and the standard course soon returned to two years, with emphasis not only on the capabilities of new quick-firing guns but also of signalling and field telephones. Sandhurst was initially directed to provide a two-year course, later shortened to one year and then extended to eighteen months. Much greater emphasis was placed on outdoor training – rifle and revolver shooting, machine-guns, minor tactics and signalling, including morse and semaphore. Cadet numbers ranged between 600 and 700, a range of new buildings was opened, and the course now ended with a stiff two-day outdoor examination period, only two three-hour papers being taken indoors.[8]

Despite the looming menace of German military power, one major crisis momentarily threatened to tear the Army apart. In 1912 the Liberal government introduced legislation, the Home Rule Bill, to provide for a measure of devolution to Ireland under a Dublin-based administration. In the next eighteen months excitement, especially in Ulster, reached the point of hysteria. Protestant 'Volunteers' in the four northern counties began drilling and parading *en masse*, determined to resist any control by Dublin. Regiments were deployed, initially to maintain order at rowdy meetings. As the crisis deepened, it appeared that some ministers in the Government were planning to use Army regiments and the Royal Navy by show of force to coerce, and perhaps even by the use of force, to disarm the Volunteers and impose Home Rule. A number of officers, including Sir John French (Chief of the Imperial General Staff), Gough (the commander of a cavalry brigade at the Curragh thirty miles from Dublin) and many regimental officers, were Ulstermen. At a meeting General Fergusson, the local division commander, and Gough were given an option, apparently in excess of War Office proposals, that officers domiciled in Ulster could take leave or accept a posting elsewhere; others would be required to obey orders or be dismissed with loss of pension. Gough put the option to a meeting of officers. A large number, including fifty of the fifty-five officers of the Curragh brigade and six of the thirteen officers of the attached RHA brigade, opted for dismissal in the event of their being ordered to initiate active military operations against Ulster.[9] Other officers in infantry and artillery units, both in Ireland and in Britain, expressed support or voiced their reservations and resentment. An appeal was made by General Paget, the Commander-in-Chief of forces in Ireland, to the cavalry brigade officers in which he took it upon himself to draw officers' attention to their loyalty to the King, an appeal made without reference to the King himself, a fact which later came to be known. Paget recaptured a few waverers but only added to the painful division of loyalties among others and many more elsewhere as they learnt of the crisis.[10] Journalists swarmed around the little camp. Ordered to return to London, Gough and the cavalry Colonels, after some stormy meetings in the War Office, gained a promise endorsed by French that the Army would not be used for coercion. They returned to the Curragh as heroes to their officers and men. But the events became public and press knowledge; the Government was accused of a surrender to cavalry Colonels – 'the people versus the Army'. The Prime Minister, Asquith, was forced to say that any action by any group of men in the service of the Crown to assert what they would or would not do was unacceptable. As a result, French and the Adjutant-General, Ewart, resigned and were replaced.

A new Army Order was issued in which superior officers were forbidden to ask their subordinates what attitude they would take in any further contingencies; officers and soldiers were forbidden to ask for assurances about any order they might receive, and all were reminded of their duties to support the civil power in the protection of life and property – but noticeably there was no mention of any forcible imposition of government policy.

As summer followed the spring, the cause of Protestant Ulster gained support in Britain, and in Ulster the Volunteers obtained quantities of firearms. It was clear that civil war in Ireland would now be the result of Home Rule unless Ulster was in large measure excluded. Talk and the drafting of revised legislation – never in the event enacted – continued through June and July until the outbreak of war shelved the whole issue for the time being.

The importance of the event, known in history (somewhat exaggerated) as the 'Curragh Mutiny', is that it represents the one occasion in the British Army when a large number of the Army's officers, not only those posted to Ireland, planned, and were known to be planning, resignation rather than obey orders they suspected of being likely to lead to civil bloodshed. If their suspicions were correct that plans involving battleships and mass transportation of troops from England forcibly to suppress the Ulster Volunteers were in hand, and evidence suggests a strong probability in the political hysteria of the time, criticism should lie with the political direction and not with officers faced with orders of dubious moral legality. The unpopularity incurred by the Army was soon to be forgotten, but the dislike and distrust of politicians among Army officers was to last very much longer.

Socially the years 1902–14 were *la belle époque* for the Army's officers in every branch of the Service in Britain or overseas. Training was not totally time-consuming, often finishing by lunchtime and so providing officers with ample opportunities for sport, hunting, shooting and social activities. A few officers bought a car. There were, however, very different styles of officers' mess life. Osbert Sitwell, projected suddenly from a comfortable existence as a Yeomanry officer into firstly a Hussar regiment in Aldershot and then later the Grenadier Guards in London, describes both with, perhaps, some literary embroidering.[11]

In the Aldershot cavalry barracks, 'an enormous barracks, an exotic edifice of iron pillars and verandahs facing north', the daily routine for officers (with 'port-nipped faces') as well as soldiers was proclaimed by bugle, beginning with Riding School at 0600 hrs. Field exercises after breakfast were followed by morning 'Stables'; two hours of drill after lunch were followed by evening 'Stables', a lecture and finally, for officers, dinner in the Mess. In the Mess itself by day, 'no one spoke except to mumble grumpily to himself'. The regimental band filled the gap at dinners even when 'guests from other cavalry regiments were fortunate enough to be invited to sample our particular brand of speechlessness'. Newspapers were limited to the (Conservative) *Morning Post* and a racing paper. Newly joined officers were expected to remain silent, though after two years they might converse, on suitable subjects such as horses or dogs, to their exact equals.

It was with relief that Sitwell was transferred to the Grenadier Guards whose officers, although from the same monied back-ground as the Hussars, lived and behaved totally differently. When not on ceremonial duties training centred on marching, twenty to thirty miles each day. Social life was restricted only by gentlemanly conventions, though some guidance might be given to young officers if – for example – they wished to travel outside London any distance north of the Thames without good reason.

The British Regular Army that stood at the outbreak of the First World War was the largest peacetime force in its history to date, with an establishment of 260,000, within which there were thirty-two regiments of cavalry, 154 battalions of infantry, thirteen brigades of Horse and forty-nine brigades of Field Artillery, nine mountain batteries, eighty-seven companies and twelve heavy bat-teries of Garrison Artillery, fifty-two plus ten depot companies of Royal Engineers, together with fifteen signal sub-units and two bridging trains, fifty horse, twenty mechanised and five supply companies of the Army Service Corps, thirty-five companies of the Royal Army Medical Corps and thirteen Veterinary Corps Sections. Thirty-two officers from various regiments were under instruction in the newly formed Royal Flying Corps.[12] At long last, in January 1914, rates of pay were increased from their early 19th century rates.

The Army's distribution provided officers, and many of their men as well, with worldwide opportunities for travel and sport. In India were eight cavalry regiments, forty-four infantry battalions and twenty Horse or Field artillery Brigades (seventy batteries, not counting eleven garrison coast defence companies), together with Engineers and Service corps units and sub-units. Elsewhere cavalry and infantry were still serving in South Africa, and infantry and artillery officers were serving in Egypt, Aden, Sudan, Malta, Gibraltar, Malaya, Ceylon, Burma, Mauritius, Hong Kong and Bermuda. It was not surprising, then, that Aurelle, André Maurois's fictional First World War French interpreter attached to a British battalion, noted that he now understood that 'this world is a great park laid out by a gardener god for the gentlemen of the United Kingdom'.[13]

Although this world began to unravel on 4th August 1914, the British Army had, nevertheless, by that date completed a remarkable twelve-year transition from a colonial bush warfare force to a very efficient, albeit small, field force, with well-trained Regular soldiers and competent regimental and staff officers, well trusted and respected by their followers.

NOTES

1 An interesting description of this change actually taking place in one engagement appears in Herbert Fairlie Wood, *The King's Royal Rifle Corps* (London, Leo Cooper, 1967), 77.

2 The Memorial is in Holy Trinity Church, Guildford.

3 Geoffrey Powell, *The Green Howards* (London, Leo Cooper, 1968), 74.

4 One Regular adjutant even discharged his duties in the autumn when there was no hunting or fishing, and no training, by telegram from the south of France. Lieutenant-General Sir Adrian Carton de Wiart, *Happy Odyssey* (London, Jonathan Cape, 1950), 44.

5   The units comprising the force, the original British Expeditionary Force, are set out in David Lomas, *Mons 1914* (London, Osprey, 1998), 16–18.

6   Aggett, *Bloody Eleventh*, II, 417.

7   Bond, *Victorian Army and the Staff College*, vii–x, describes in detail the changes and developments at the College.

8   Shepperd, *Sandhurst*, vii–ix.

9   A.P. Ryan, *Mutiny at the Curragh* (London, Macmillan, 1956), 132. It should be noted that the officers indicated that they would be prepared to preserve law and order, and property.

10 David Scott Daniell, *4th Hussars* (Aldershot, Gale and Polden, 1959), 239, records of the officers present at Paget's appeal, 'They were shocked and bewildered . . . as they were expected to sacrifice their training and their careers or fight men whose Protestant principles and loyalty they shared'.

11 Osbert Sitwell, *Great Morning* (London, Macmillan, 1948), iv. According to Sitwell the lectures, with one exception, covered topics such as the care of horses and the importance of cavalry in the coming war. The exception was one given by the future Lord Plumer.

12 *The Army List, 1913*. These totals cover all Regular Army units but do not include certain Special Service battalions. It should be remembered that most of the battalions based in Britain were under strength, some very badly so.

13 André Maurois, trans. Thurfrida Wake, *Colonel Bramble* (London, Jonathan Cape, 1932), 40.

CHAPTER 10

THE REGULAR OFFICER, 1914–18

The British Army in the First World War should be judged, with now the wisdom of history, as one of the most remarkable institutions to appear in the long history of the British Isles. Its component parts, the 1914 Regular Army, the Territorial Force and Kitchener's New Army, for four long years showed a sustained fighting spirit in France and Flanders unmatched by any of the other contestants and equalled only by those of the Army that fought at Gallipoli, in Macedonia, in Italy or in the Middle East. For the first time in her history, Britain fielded a mass mobilisation Army, the seven Divisions that crossed the Channel in mid-August 1914 having grown to over fifty by 1918. But the resilience shown by officers and men of these new battalions and formations was the result of training and modelling on the style and pattern set by regimental officers and NCOs of the Regular Army, in particular the 'Old Contemptibles', as the original British Expeditionary Force (BEF) came to be known.

This work is primarily concerned with the duties and lives of unit-level Regular officers; only limited space can be given to the special features of the Territorial or New Army personnel. Also outside the scope of this work must lie the controversies over the competence or otherwise of senior commanders, detailed narratives of the successive major operations, the rival merits of different divisions, or the comparisons that have been made between British and Dominion formations.

But it can be noted at the outset that violence of the Western Front, and the deaths, suffering and hardships endured by front-line soldiers, were all shared equally by personnel of each of the three components of the BEF. No one had foreseen the new dimensions of battlefield horrors – the thunder of mass artillery barrages sometimes lasting for several days, the effect on human bodies of machine-gun fire, artillery shrapnel or flame-throwers, the cries from 'no-man's-land' of wounded men and maimed horses, the sights and smells of decomposing corpses and carcasses, the awesome patterns of light from starshells, flares, tracer, Verey lights and explosions, the fear of an unseen opponent tunnelling beneath. These were the conditions under which regimental officers had to command and lead men into operations with every likelihood of being killed. All, with the exception of Lord Kitchener, had believed that the war would be short. Prolonged defensive warfare had not been foreseen; soldiers had not been trained or equipped to live for days or weeks unwashed and in filthy uniforms, in mud at times waist deep, in waterlogged, insanitary trenches or ditches with rats, lice and, in summer, mosquitoes for company. Above all, no one was – or ever could be – psychologically prepared for the heavy casualties of battle, the loss of comrades and friends.

Where did all the officers needed for the immense expansion come from? A brief initial summary is necessary. At the outset, many came from Public School and University Cadet Corps, especially those holding Certificate A or B, already imbued with concepts of duty, honour and self-sacrifice. Others came from men who by their class status seemed suitable even if they had no previous military training. New Army battalions were on formation officered – usually in numbers far short of establishment – only by elderly retired Regular officers of varying physical and mental fitness. Indian Army officers on leave in Britain were ordered to join the new units.

Plate 18 An Army Chaplain at a burial in the trenches, 1915. Imperial War Museum.

Plate 19 A Queen Alexandra's Nurse at work in a hospital train in the First World War. Courtesy of Queen Alexandra's Royal Army Nursing Corps.

Plate 20 Mechanisation 1937. A Cavalry officer with the old and the new. Courtesy of the Regimental Museum of the The Queen's Dragoon Guards.

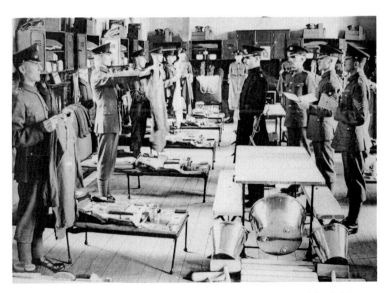

Plate 21 Kit Inspection, Irish Guards, *c.*1930s. Courtesy of the Irish Guards.

Plate 22 Coldstream Guards Officers at Sidi Barrani, Western Desert, 1940. Photo by kind permission of the Regimental Lieutenant-Colonel Coldstream Guards.

Plate 23 A Troop Leader's car before setting out on patrol. Courtesy of the Regimental Museum of the The Queen's Dragoon Guards.

Plate 24 Stress: Officers of the Devonshire Regiment after prolonged jungle operations, Burma campaign. Imperial War Museum.

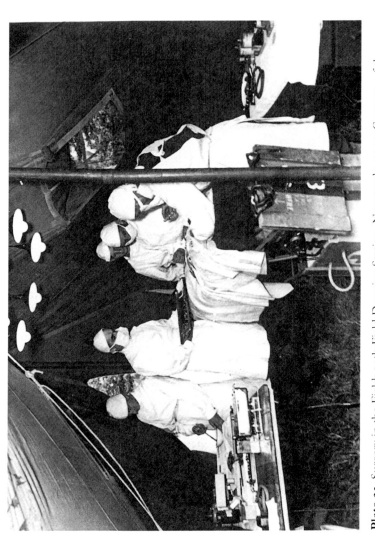

Plate 25 Surgery in the Field: 13th Field Dressing Station, Normandy, 1944. Courtesy of the Trustees of the Army Medical Services Museum.

Plate 26 The British Officers of the 40th Pathans (late the 5th Bn, the 14th Punjab Regiment) in various orders of dress, Edwardian era.

Plate 27 Indian Army Cavalry Polo Champions, 1913. British Officers of the 18th King George's Own Lancers.

OFFICERS MESS: THE MESS ROOM

Plate 28 An Indian Army British Officers' Mess; 39th Royal Garwhal Rifles. A vanished world.

Plate 29 King's Commission British and Viceroy's Commission Indian Officers of the 1st Bn Guides Infantry, 1917.

Plate 30 Patrol returning from an operation in Malaya. The patrol commander, a lieutenant, is second from the left. Courtesy of the Cameronian Association and Sir John Baynes.

Plate 31 Major A. Hartley and Captain B. Dace, Royal Engineers, working on an unexploded German bomb in 1959. For his work Major Hartley was awarded the George Medal. Courtesy of the Institution of Royal Engineers.

Plate 32 A lieutenant and his platoon of Royal Welch Fusiliers about to set out on patrol, Belfast, 1981. Courtesy of The Royal Welch Fusiliers.

Plate 33 A major of the Scots Guards directing operations in Belfast, 1992. Courtesy of The Scots Guards.

Plate 34 Captain Caroline Lovell, Royal Engineers, of 73 Armoured Engineer Squadron, training at a NATO fuel depot in Germany for work she was later to do in Basra. Courtesy of the Institution of Royal Engineers.

Plate 35 21st Century soldiering. Peace support in Basra. © Crown
Copyright/MOD

Some of the New Army 'Pals' battalions chose their own officers. A number of Midland and Northern units were given officers from the South. Some were given a crash training course, others simply posted to battalions to be trained along with their soldiers. From February 1916 officer cadet battalions were raised, to train over 100,000 officers in country houses or on university campuses by the end of the war.

The two cadet colleges were placed under considerable strain. At the outbreak of war, they lost most of their best instructors and the numbers replacing them were reduced.[1] As the war progressed, both colleges had a constant turnover of instructors, these being officers who were recovering from wounds and not yet fit to return to the front.

At Woolwich, senior cadets were commissioned at once in August 1914, and shortened courses provided the juniors. Six-month courses for Artillery and Engineer officers were then introduced but these had to be lengthened to twelve months in 1917, largely due to the fall in educational standards of school-leaver applicants. A total of 1,629 cadets were commissioned from the Academy during the war.

At Sandhurst, too, cadets were immediately given their Commissions. For Regular Army cadets an emergency three-month short course was introduced, but this was found to be unsatisfactory and the course was lengthened progressively to six, eight and finally twelve months. From 1914 to 1916, a special cavalry cadet company existed. Lodged at first and temporarily in the Staff College building, fifteen one-month courses for New Army officers were provided by the College. Among the cadets were a large number of NCOs selected for commissions. Sandhurst's total of cadets commissioned in the war years amounted to 5,131. In all, 3,274 Sandhurst commissioned officers lost their lives and thirty-five were awarded the V.C.

In both colleges fees were abolished for the duration of the war and the entry age limits changed to sixteen-and-a-half to twenty-five.

Instruction at the Staff College was closed down at the outbreak of war, and only resumed in 1917 with four-month courses for experienced GSO2 grade officers selected for possible GSO1 appointments. The consequences of this gap in training are considered later in this chapter.

What were the experiences of the regimental officer in this first truly National British conflict? This work will focus on the experiences of officers on the Western Front, in Belgium and in France, where the vast majority of the Army was committed.[2] Experiences in Italy and Macedonia were comparable, in Gallipoli and Iraq (Mesopotamia) worse, but in 1917–18 in Egypt and Palestine exhilarating. At the outset, it needs to be emphasised that while this work sets out the role of officers in all units in all theatres, they worked in partnership with their NCOs, in particular Warrant Officers and Sergeants, dependent on their loyalty and support, and very frequently drawing inspiration and personal courage from their example. Leadership more than ever became a two-way relationship.

The infantry, as always, formed the highest percentage of the soldiers on the Western Front.[3] For the infantry officer the most testing moments, requiring all that he could summon up to contribute in command, leadership and courage, were, of course, those when he led his unit or sub-unit 'over the top' against enemy wire and fire, or he steadied his men at a time of an enemy onslaught on his own trench lines, either likely to lead to confusion. These were, however, the moments of high drama, and much of the front-line officer's life was less dangerous or relatively safe.

In attack, platoon commanders, armed only with a revolver, would lead at the head of their platoons, closely supported by bombers to throw grenades into enemy trenches and bayonet men to complete the 'clearing up'. In big attacks second and third waves would follow, all on extended fronts. Company and battalion commanders generally also led from the front. In 1916 infantry officers had to learn how to work with lifting artillery barrages. When the Lewis light machine-gun was issued in increasing numbers, movement and machine-gun covering fire tactics could be developed.[4] In 1918, as an improvement on flares, an improvised system by which a ground indicator device could guide aircraft towards targets was devised and used by infantry officers. After attacks, Commanding Officers would, with their subordinates, analyse and draw lessons, particularly if success had not be achieved. Lessons learnt would be passed up to formations, resulting in a general improvement in tactics.

How did officers feel when leading their soldiers in these attacks, with men whom they had trained and whom they trusted falling beside and behind them? For some a single motivation, for others a mixture of extremes amounting to a personal struggle.[5] From memoirs one can identify several themes: a patriotic view that if King and Empire required one to do this duty then it must be done; for others a more grimly rational 'ours not to reason why'; for many the honour of the regiment and a need – despite nagging, naked personal fear – not to show that fear before soldiers or other officers; for a few a Christian duty in a war against evil; for a number an adventure or a sporting opportunity with only the risks of any blood sport. For many, particularly at first, there was a sense of exhilaration: 'this is it' after weeks of training and preparation. While killing Germans was the duty only a few relished the killing, and these generally did so in an atypical sense of vengeance following the deaths of comrades. Colonels would sometimes lead an attack wearing gloves and armed only with a walking stick. By 1917 exhilaration had largely gone and weariness was replacing enthusiasm, but the return of movement gave all a morale boost that maintained fighting spirit.

Before a major attack, officers would be carefully prepared for their roles, instruction would be given on terrain models, and sometimes replica ground areas prepared from maps and air observation. Precise orders would be prepared, issued and perhaps rehearsed, including detailed instructions for diversionary attacks, the assembly of the attacking force, the start of the assault, the clearing of enemy trenches and the consolidation of the few yards of ground gained. Officers were responsible for security and camouflage, and for ensuring their men were rested and fed prior to the attack.

It was generally far from all quiet on the Western Front. Even if no major operations were in progress, infantry officers would be ordered to lead trench raids, to reconnoitre terrain, to capture a prisoner so as to identify the units of the enemy opposite, or to take out an enemy machine-gun post causing trouble. Such parties might be one of an officer and a dozen men, and would be supported with covering fire from flanking platoons or companies. Senior officers considered such local attacks to be valuable training for young officers and desirable for maintaining fighting spirit.

If an officer was wounded and fallen to the ground, much would depend on luck. If he was fortunate, he would be picked up by stretcher-bearers quickly, but many had to be left in no-man's-land where they died, including some whose lives could have been saved. A battalion had sixteen stretcher-bearers; sometimes more men would be drafted in for the work from the band or pioneers. The casualty would then be taken by stretcher, handcart or wagons on tram lines laid in some trenches to a Regimental Aid Post, and from there by ambulance to Dressing Stations or Casualty Clearing Stations, and thence by ambulance train to base hospitals or back to Britain. Such travel was generally very uncomfortable, the ambulances having no springs and the trains being improvised.

There does not appear to have been any privileged treatment for officer casualties in the front-line arrangements. In Britain, however, comfortable London town and country houses were converted into hospitals and convalescent homes for officers who were treated very hospitably and attended by leading physicians and surgeons.[6] Widows of officers received pensions, and disability payments were also awarded.

When a brigade was in the front line, the usual pattern was that of two battalions up, one in support and one resting; later after the reductions, it was two up and one in reserve. Duties changed every eight days. Within the battalions at the front, one or two companies would be in the first-line trenches, the others only a little distance further back, duties being rotated. All companies had continually to improve or, after rain, drain and repair their defences using timber stakes, sandbags or material from nearby wrecked buildings. The work was dirty; nights were often either sleepless, interrupted by enemy harassing fire or broken by the morning and evening 'stand to'.

In the first line officers, if they slept at all, could doze in scrapes or niches in the trenches; further back, sleep meant 'funk holes', small dugouts, sometimes made more comfortable and drier with planking, but these could not always be covered, officers and men remaining wet. In some advantaged areas, there were company head-quarters dugouts and a Mess for the company officers, at least one of whom, of course, was always forward in the first line. Another might have special observation duties, crawling a few yards at a time into no-man's-land, or visiting men in listening posts ahead of the first line. Another might be the company orderly officer respons-ible for the feeding of men and rum issues. Those not on specific duties played cards, read, ate, dozed (if really lucky, in pyjamas), and for sport caught rats. Food varied but was generally good if monotonous, in times of activity perhaps only tinned bully beef and tea. Many officers received food parcels from home. All would have routine administrative duties to discharge; pay, returns, defaulters, letter censorship and condolence letters to relatives of men killed. Sometimes a venereal disease rate had to be reported. Finally, all officers were involved in the arrival, distribution and local training of fresh drafts of men unaccustomed to their new life of danger, filth, cold and rain in evil-smelling trenches. When not in the front line, officers' duties might include rifle, foot and kit inspections, practising gun drills, supervising working parties, digging support and rear defences, filling sandbags, moving stores on lines of communication, commanding parties for laying telephone line and burial parties for the dead and dead horses. Some units were tasked with guarding road bridges or junctions, or formation headquarters. Parades might have to be arranged for visiting senior officers or divine service. Buildings chosen for rest areas were often cold and draughty and, if possible, had to be improved. Also, whenever possible, officers organised sports, usually football, in rest periods.

One officer, interestingly, analysed his life in the year 1916.[7] He spent sixty-five days of the year in front-line trenches, with a further thirty-six in nearby close supporting positions, a total of 101 under fire. A further 120 were spent in reserve positions from which he might be called, either because of fighting, or because he was needed for a working party. Of the remaining seventy-two days, twenty-one were spent on courses in schools, ten sick in hospital, seventeen on leave in England, nine days at a base camp and fourteen travelling. The 101 days at the front were spent in the form of twelve 'tours' in the trenches varying from one to thirteen days (the Somme). In these, he participated in one direct attack, two bombing actions, one action in which his unit held the front line while other units attacked, and one trench raid.

Battalions were often very short of officers, even in quiet periods perhaps sixteen or less, and fewer after engagements in which a number of officers were killed. Companies were often commanded by Lieutenants. In 1915 and early 1916, many Regular officers were committed to the training of New Army units; a number of training courses for infantry officers were set up but these frequently suffered from the reluctance of unit commanders to release their best officers to act as instructors. The courses covered signals, mortars and machine-guns, grenades and bombing, gas warfare, tactics and unit administration.

The heavy machine-guns issued before the outbreak of war were mostly withdrawn and with their officers grouped into Machine-Gun Companies, later Battalions, vehicle-mounted so as to provide concentrated machine-gun fire when required. Trench mortars were also not issued to units but special mortar battalions were provided to brigades to meet particular needs, particularly gas bombardment.

The nature of the infantry officer's duties exposing them to the greatest danger meant that they suffered proportionately the highest casualty rates in the Army. In 1916–17 it was estimated that the average life expectancy of a newly joined Subaltern in the front line was, at best, one month.

With trenches, wire and machine-guns all ending the war of movement, artillery soon became the most important, if not the most numerous, part of the Army, although in the first eighteen months fire-power was handicapped by acute ammunition shortage. Battery equipments and strengths varied according to the availability of weapons; in 1914, for example, Territorial Force batteries might have only four guns, usually updated 15 pdrs. As the war progressed, guns began to wear out after firing 3,000 rounds and, again, batteries might not have all their weapons.

Throughout the war Regular, Territorial and New Army battery officers all continually learnt new tactical uses of artillery, and met problems for which even the Regulars had never been trained.[8] Guns often had to be moved over mud, and sited for firing, on lunar landscapes pockmarked by shell holes. In 1914, the lessons learned, or relearned, were the dangers of overexposure in the front line, the importance of indirect fire, the value of night firing and the need for high-explosive ammunition ('regarded as unsporting because it gave off yellow fumes which were rumoured to be poisonous') as well as shrapnel. In 1915, developments included the planned concentration of fire, the lifting barrage, the use of messages about targets sent down by telephone from balloons or reports from observer aircraft, the value of aerial photography, and recognition of the need for the development of gas shells and of anti-aircraft artillery. In 1916, officers were directing fire in barrages several days long with, as the infantry assaulted, creeping barrages twenty to fifty yards in front of advancing infantry, the barrage moving forward in bounds between three to eight minutes. In 1917 barrages, on occasions of four to five thousand guns and again lasting several days, were expected to produce total destruction of the enemy's defences. The year saw the greatest artillery duels in history, each side regarding his opponent's batteries as the prime target and the Germans frequently using gas. Batteries were expected to fire with precise accuracy and officers to be skilled in the techniques of artillery intelligence for counter-battery work – the observation of enemy gun flashes and the time that elapsed between flash and detonation. Barrages would also be fired on areas not selected for attack as a bluff or distraction. Smoke shells provided batteries with new opportunities for helping the infantry.

In 1918, with some return of movement, guns were required to move quickly so as to provide cover for ground newly acquired by the infantry. Batteries worked with tanks with only limited success, but with much greater success with aircraft, now capable of machine-gunning and bombing German trenches or troops on the move. In the last years of the war, the RGA's heavy guns, 6, 8 and 9.2 inch, all used for firing deep into enemy territory, were pulled by tractors, but for Field and Horse Artillery throughout the war, horses or mules pulled the guns, forage often being a concern for battery officers.

Unlike the infantry, artillery batteries generally could not be rotated for rest periods, so adding to the exhaustion of officers and men. In day-to-day living, officers would be responsible for their gun positions, guns usually being sunk one or two feet into the ground with perhaps a perimeter protection of tree trunks and camouflage netting. One officer would have the dangerous observation role forward with the infantry, moving with a signaller in and out by night to and from an observation post, a tree, a building or a shell hole slightly enlarged with sandbags. In quiet areas, men's lines and horse lines had to be inspected. At the front, if lucky, a battery might be sited near a group of farm buildings, providing shelter at night; by day, or elsewhere, officers and men would live in dugouts. Until late 1917 and 1918, batteries would only be moved at night, though with the 1917 advances battery officers used abandoned German posts, sometimes still containing dead Germans. Ammunition was brought up by night, often on the backs of batteries' horses.

Young officers attended short courses giving them a rudimentary knowledge of ballistics, registration, range tables and correction. In training and in quiet periods, officers supervised gun drill. Officers were also sent on specialist courses of several types, and general courses such as gas, tactics and unit administration.

For Regular Army cavalry officers, the trench warfare of the Western Front was a frustrating but not entirely negative experience, leaving them nevertheless envious of the successes of mounted units (Regular, Territorial Force Yeomanry or Imperial) in the Middle East.[9] In the August–September 1914 retreat, regiments displayed skill and secured success in reconnaissance, skirmishing and harassing advancing German columns and screening British columns, but regiments, in particular officers, took heavy casualties. By the First Battle of Ypres, cavalry troopers and their officers were manning trench lines. Thereafter, there being no breakthrough to exploit until the last months of the war, cavalry officers could only lead their men in duties lacking in glamour, regiments being used as mobile infantry when needed to plug a gap, or small-scale junior officer-led work including scouting, escort of prisoners of war, the protection of headquarters and staff, or simply use their troopers as military labour. The cavalry divisions, formed into one, later two, Corps, were broken up in 1916; a dismounted cavalry division existed in 1916–17 and again briefly in 1917; and one Corps was reconstituted in 1918. With the return of movement in 1917–18,

detachments from both sword and lance regiments, led by Field
Officers or Subalterns, made a number of charges, at first small-
scale sub-unit level attacks.[10] In August 1918 three divisions of the
Cavalry Corps made brigade-sized assaults on the German Amiens
defence line with much success. Smaller unit-level charges continued until September, in some cases supported by Household
Cavalry machine-guns and infantry. Major problems throughout were
the costs of horsed regiments, the supply of forage and the difficulties, on clogged roads, of deploying the regiments at rare moments
of opportunity.

Many Regular officers went on promotion to serve in New
Army or Yeomanry regiments or formations; others secured staff
appointments or were attracted to flying or armoured or lorried
machine-gun units, one being the Household Cavalry. Officers
who remained with regiments generally led a less dangerous and
uncomfortable existence than their infantry counterparts, living in
tented camps. Some specific courses for cavalry regimental officers
were held, in particular on the crossing of trench lines; officers also
attended other general courses including machine-gunnery.

Engineer officers were involved in a very wide variety of duties.
The most spectacular was mining, the June 1917 Third Battle of
Ypres opening with the explosion of nineteen large mines that had
taken two years to prepare. They were also required to prepare,
or supervise others preparing, defensive strong points or other
fortifications, building bridges, light railways and roads near the front,
and ports, inland waterways and coastal shipping elsewhere.

In addition, at this time Royal Engineers officers were initially
responsible for communications. They remained responsible for
major lines, while units trained their own signallers. Six-foot-deep
trenches had to be dug for cables; labour parties, soldiers from
other arms, or Chinese labourers had to be supervised for this work.
Other Engineer officers were responsible for despatch riders, signal
lamps, heliographs and carrier pigeons. Officers had to learn voice

discipline for field telephone systems and principles of signals security.

Many Engineer officers were involved in the evolution of the tank, a number leading tanks in the early tank engagements. When poison gas was released from containers in 1915, Engineer officers were responsible for its launch. Other officers, mostly recruited for the war, were responsible for camouflage design. An 'Intelligence Corps' was formed during the war; its personnel did not have a common cap-badge but wore green arm and cap bands. Some officers came from Regular Army regiments but the majority came from civilian life, including a number of German-speakers who were concerned with prisoner questioning and captured documents. Others worked in air photography, in signals intelligence, in the intelligence staffs of formation headquarters or in field security.[11] The officers of the newly formed Tank Corps came from several sources, as well as the Engineers, infantry, artillery and the Royal Naval Air Service. At first, tanks were organised into companies of twenty-five, later changed to battalions of seventy. The mechanical unreliability of the machines and the limited experience of the officers were major handicaps for the new weapon system, and were compounded by the fumes that arose when the engines overheated. By August 1918, over 400 tanks were in service in France. Their successes were real but limited, more of significance for the future than at the time. Despite much ingenuity and battlefield courage, tanks were never decisive.

Royal Flying Corps officers came from the Regular, Territorial and New Armies. They lived a life generally very much more comfortable and secure on the ground, but of the greatest risk and danger in the air. Most transferred to the Royal Air Force when it was formed on 1st April 1918.

For all branches of the Army, training manuals of steadily improving quality were produced throughout the war for the instruction of officers. An Inspector of Training was appointed to raise the standards and also to standardise operational procedures across the five field Army commands.

In general, Western Front divisions retained their identities of origin – Regular, New Army or Territorial Force – but within them, either for 'stiffening' with Regular units or as a result of casualties, a measure of mixture did occur. At the opening of the Somme battle in July 1916, one of the four Regular divisions still contained only Regular battalions, two now had a New Army brigade as well as two Regular ones, and one had one New Army battalion and one Dominion. Three of the New Army divisions had one Regular battalion in each brigade, but the other four New Army divisions had no Regulars.[12] By the summer of 1918 little had changed; the 5th Division's three infantry brigades, each still of four battalions, included one New Army battalion in two of the brigades and two New Army battalions in the third, each brigade with a trench mortar battalion.[13] The mixing continued down to battalion levels. Regular battalions would sometimes have New Army officers (one suspects carefully selected) posted to them and New Army battalions would have a few Regular officers. For a young Regular officer there were, if they wanted it, prospects of rapid promotion; a pre-war Captain could easily find himself commanding a New Army battalion. But in general, Regular officers preferred to stay and serve with Regular battalions, with other officers of the same upbringing, values and view of society and the world rather than in the company of New Army officers who might be suspiciously clever or from the commercial or even lower classes. The need to replace casualties could govern the distribution of units; for individual officers there was a general understanding that an officer should not have to change his regimental cap badge and identity unless he volunteered to do so. As the war progressed, raising ever-worsening manpower problems, divisions were reduced in size by cutting in most divisions the number of infantry battalions per brigade from four to three, and within infantry companies, by a reduction from four platoons to three.

Staff work in 1914, in particular the movement of the BEF across the Channel and its subsequent orderly retreat, well illustrated the wisdom and success of the pre-war reforms at the Staff College. In the years 1915–17 six-week-long staff courses followed by attachments at an *ad hoc* college in France and from 1916 also in Britain were arranged; in 1917 the Camberley Staff College reopened but again only provided short courses. Staff officers with their red cap bands and clean uniforms worked in division head-quarters usually located in buildings that were dry and often warm. They were often resented by line regimental officers who felt the staff were escaping from the realities of the war, despite the fact that numbers of Staff College graduates had been killed in 1914 with more to die later, and that the officers selected for the short wartime courses were mostly Regulars from combat regiments. Some graduates from the Indian Army Staff College at Quetta also served in staff appointments, mostly in the Middle East.

Within the constraints of the trench warfare situation, much staff work was good. When in the late summer of 1918 real movement returned, the staff work needed to maintain the momentum of advance and coordinate infantry, artillery, cavalry, engineers, tanks and aircraft was of a high standard.[14] A major weakness at the assessment level, though not in its collection, was operational intelligence.

Although numerous awards of the Victoria Cross and the Distinguished Service Order were made, the war saw an increased need for the recognition of bravery or other especially meritorious service of both officers and men. The Military Cross (M.C.), a bravery award, was created for officers, with an equivalent Military Medal (M.M.), for all other ranks in 1915. The Order of the British Empire, an award for outstanding service, was also created in 1917 with a Military Division within which, in practice, Captains and Majors might become Members (M.B.E.) and more usually Lieutenant-Colonels and Colonels Officers (O.B.E.). Some officers were also awarded Allied medals; some were well earned while others 'came with the rations'. Uniforms were unaltered on the Western Front except that officers and men alike wore steel helmets. Personnel in the Middle East wore shirt and shorts in hot weather. Religious belief was important for many officers and some soldiers in the war, and officers headed their units or sub-units at church parades and services. There were, however, shortages of Chaplains, sometimes only two or three for a division.

Unless major operations were imminent or in progress, officers of the BEF were entitled to one or two periods, usually two weeks, of home leave in Britain per year. In Belgium or France, during quiet periods, officers might slip away to a local inn or small restaurant for an evening 'away from it all'. A lucky few secured a few days in Paris. Leave appears to have been one of the few advantages officers had over their men, whose leave entitlement was less.

Although not commissioned, the 1914–18 war saw the first appearance of formed women's units (other than nurses) in the British Army in the Women's Army Auxiliary Corps, WAAC.[15] WAAC personnel served in a variety of roles, mainly administration, catering and driving, but also intelligence. The WAAC's formation was opposed by many officers, a major reason being that if the Corps were to have commissioned officers, men would have to salute them. In consequence, the Corps had its own rank structure; Controllers, Administrators, Deputy and Assistant Administrators, with Forewomen and Deputy Forewomen as NCOs. Badges of rank for the officers were roses and *fleurs-de-lis*. The work of the Corps was recognised in 1918 when it was restyled Queen Mary's Army Auxiliary Corps.

The British public supported the front-line regiments, though not always their senior formation commanders, fully during the war – to such an extent that fit-looking young men in plain clothes, very likely to be service personnel on leave, were liable to be given white feathers by vigilantes or suffer some other form of abuse. The war was represented to a receptive British public as a Manichaean struggle between the good and civilised against the barbarian 'Hun' who murdered Belgian civilians, torpedoed merchant ships and sent Zeppelins to bomb civilian cities. An important factor in this support was the careful control of press reporting which played down checks and reverses, magnified successes and concealed from home readers the full horrors of trench warfare when at its worst. This control was at first exercised by Kitchener's arbitrary outlawing of journalist war correspondents, issuing orders for their arrest, but from 1915 selected reporters were co-opted and integrated into the military system to produce controlled, censored and sanitised accounts. Had the public been fully informed of the actual conditions of the Western Front, press pressure might have led to a radical change. In the event, the outcry came only after the war was over.[16]

While on many occasions soldiers were critical of individual regimental officers, there was never any serious unrest, protest or refusal to follow by rank and file against officers as a body. There were several reasons for this, perhaps the most important for most being pride in the regiment. British society was still cohesive overall, despite class differences; class conflict was only to emerge in the post-1918 years. Soldiers, even those in the New Army, were still prepared to accept social superiors, in a number of cases their superiors in their peacetime lives, as officers. Officers shared the hardships of trench life with their men, and generally suffered and were seen to suffer proportionally much heavier casualties. Soldiers accepted the situation, knowing that their officers could do little to improve conditions and were not responsible for them. New Army officers, many middle class, followed and often extended the benevolent sense of obligation towards soldiers that marked the pre-1914 Regular Army; in return for this measure of respect for them as individuals, their soldiers accepted authority. General goodwill, with a slightly less formal discipline, characterised both the Territorial and New Army regiments. Many soldiers found this sense of obligation and care a surprising and marked improvement on their pre-war civil employer–employee relationships.

The cumulative effect of the enormous numbers of New Army and Territorial officers and men on the career Regular officers is not entirely clear. It seems generally, and predictably, true that Regular officers found working with Territorials easier than with those of the New Army. On occasions, when New Army officers failed to measure up to the standards of Regular officers with whom they were working, there was friction (on one occasion a newly joined Subaltern arriving at a smart Regular infantry battalion in the line was immediately sent back to London to acquire proper uniform). Equally, New Army officers, arriving with either original ideas or equipment such as gas, distrusted by Regular officers, were not always welcome. But overall, the relationship was a working one. In the longer term, two consequences can be argued. Firstly, from these wider contacts, the stress of the war and the censoring of soldiers' letters home, it seems that Regular officers who went on to serve after the war had a better understanding of their soldiers and the social conditions from which they were recruited, and an extended sympathy for soldiers' personal problems and difficulties. Secondly, the experience of the trenches was so traumatic (many officers either refused or were very reluctant to talk about the war except to the few people whom they knew would understand) that on their return to peacetime, soldiering officers simply wanted a return to the *belle époque* of the pre-1914 years. They hoped never again to have to repeat 1914–18, a hope not without a sclerotic influence, conscious and subconscious, on senior officers' thinking in the years to follow.

NOTES

1 Sheppard, *Sandhurst*, 116–121, 123–128.
2 Of special value in recounting the actual fighting methods used on the Western Front are the different chapters in Paddy Griffith (Editor), *British Fighting Methods in the Great War* (London, Frank Cass,

1996). Many memoirs and biographies describe the actual day-to-day lives of officers, from which it is possible to put together the composite account that follows.

3 Griffith, 'The extent of tactical mobility in the British Army', in Griffith, *British Fighting Methods*, i, 1–22, provides an excellent general introduction while focusing on the infantry.

4 In 1916 Lewis guns were issued generally on a scale of two per company; in 1917 the issue had increased to four and by 1918 to eight.

5 Charles Edmonds, *A Subaltern's War* (London, Peter Davis, 1929), 35, commenting on the personal tensions between ardour and fear, summarised this 'strange sense of dual personality' in which 'Always the struggle within, fought behind the dark curtains which screen the hidden springs of conduct, was more real than the physical struggle without and the practical details of life passed by like an illusion.'

6 One such, 17 Park Lane, London, is described in Carton de Wiart, *Happy Odyssey*, 54, 64, 77, 86–87. It should be noted, however, that good arrangements were made, often in seaside hotels, for soldiers' convalescence. After the war, a number of schemes, generally Utopian and unsuccessful, were set up for disabled ex-officers. One of the most unfortunate was in Kenya.

7 Edmonds, *Subaltern's War*, 120–121. This work is an excellent account of a young officer's war in 1916–17.

8 Jonathan Bailey, 'British artillery in the Great War', in Griffith, *British Fighting Methods*, ii, 23–49, summarises the wartime developments. Also 'Gunners' in Nigel Steel and Peter Hart, *Paschendaele: The Sacrificial Ground* (London, Cassell, 2000), vii, is of special value, and includes a number of personal memoirs. Also useful is a work by an RGA officer, Arthur Behread, *As From Kemmel Hill* (London, Eyre and Spottiswoode, 1963).

9 Stephen Badsey, 'Cavalry and the Breakthrough Doctrine', in Griffith, *British Fighting Methods*, vii, 138–174, usefully corrects the generally held view that cavalry achieved little or nothing on the Western Front.

10 Examples appear in Atkinson, *Royal Dragoons*, 453–454, and Michael Brander, *The 10th Royal Hussars* (London, Leo Cooper, 1969), 98–99.

11 For a more detailed account see Anthony Clayton, *Forearmed: The History of the Intelligence Corps* (London, Brasseys, 1994), i–iv.

12 Keegan, *Face of Battle*, 219.

13 Brigadier-General A.H. Hussey and Major D.S. Inman, *The Fifth Division in the Great War* (London, Nisbet, 1921), Appendix 1.

14 The specific logistic problems are set out later in Chapter 13.

15 Shelford Bidwell, *The Women's Royal Army Corps* (London, Leo Cooper, 1977), i, ii. The idea of women serving was not new; various semi-official groups had existed before the war.

16 This subject is examined in Martin J. Farrar, *News from the Front: War Correspondents on the Western Front* (Stroud, Sutton, 1998).

CHAPTER 11

THE REGULAR OFFICER BETWEEN
THE TWO WORLD WARS

Historians have not treated the British Army in the inter-war years very kindly, dismissing it as merely an Imperial *gendarmerie*, writers concentrating their attention on the Army's serious shortcomings in the spring of 1940 and offering less serious but equally sharp criticism of its officers exemplified in Low's famous cartoon figure, Colonel Blimp. This criticism is based on a perception that the inter-war years were a single whole period, which in military terms they were not. The last four years, 1935–39, saw revolutionary developments in technology, notably the monoplane fighter and bomber, the big aircraft-carrier, and improved radio command and control of armoured fighting vehicles, now capable of moving at speed. These developments abruptly rendered the national strategies of several countries, France and Japan as well as Britain, strategies that had been realistic in the first fifteen years of peace, to be dangerously obsolete.

In these first fifteen years the British Army had been a very professional force for what had been its primary role, and what it was in the event to do well: an army for Asia or North Africa, for the defence of India's North-West Frontier against invasion, and in Egypt against an attack by Mussolini, mounted from Libya. Even if it had had the will, the Army had neither the lead time nor the funding to change in the last four years to a force capable of arresting a

181

German *blitzkrieg*. For this the blame lies with the political direction and its belated recognition of the need to rearm, the senior military officers whose gaze was too often limited either to the past or to the day-to-day demands of Imperial security, and the general anti-military mood of the British public; it does not lie with the Army's regimental officers.

Certainly the wide range of commitments faced by the Army in both the 1920s and 1930s gave a priority to the contemporary problems.[1] In the 1920s the Army at the outset faced major operational commitments in Ireland, Egypt, Iraq and India, and smaller-scale operations in Turkey, Sudan, Palestine and China (Shanghai). In the years 1919–21 and again in 1926 industrial unrest in Britain required substantial military involvement. A British Army of the Rhine had to form part of the Allied occupation force in Germany, and battalions had to be deployed in 1919–20 to maintain order while plebiscites were held in Silesia, East Prussia, Burgenland, Danzig (Gdansk) and Fiume. Battalions were also involved in the short-lived anti-Bolshevik operations in northern Russia and the Caucasus. The 1930s saw, again, major commitments in India and from 1936 in Palestine, with smaller-scale operations in Egypt, Cyprus, Burma, China (Tientsin) and Jamaica. In both the 1920s and 1930s one or two battalions were needed as garrisons for Gibraltar, Malta, Aden, Sudan, Hong Kong and the West Indies and from the later 1930s Malaya. In the Asian duties Indian Army units also participated, in the sub-continent itself playing the lead roles; in many operations, including those in Britain, the Royal Navy and Royal Air Force played important roles.

In 1928, after the disbandment of eight Irish battalions and some cavalry and other reductions, the Army totalled 137 infantry battalions, twenty-three cavalry regiments, forty-three artillery brigades (thirty-two field, five light, three medium, one heavy, two anti-aircraft), thirty-four coast defence emplacements, six British-officered Indian mountain batteries, four tank battalions and eleven armoured-car companies.

Until 1932 military strategy was governed by a rule that held that Britain would not be engaged in any major war for ten years. The Army was expected to be able to mount an expeditionary force (not necessarily for Europe) of four or five infantry divisions and one mobile one. For the two major Imperial duties in 1928, a year typical of the core inter-war year period, in India there were forty-five British Army infantry battalions, eleven cavalry regiments, sixty-five artillery batteries and eight armoured-car companies, while in Egypt there were one cavalry and two infantry brigades, six artillery batteries and a small number of tanks and armoured cars. Although championed by a few far-seeing officers, mechanisation was slow and viewed with distaste within the Army. An experimental Mechanised Force of medium and light tanks, armoured-cars, artillery, either towed or mounted on half-tracks, and machine-gun infantry was established in 1927; it was to be disbanded the next year. A second such force in 1931 which actually practised deep penetration was unfortunately even more short-lived. Late 1930s' planning was intended to have two armoured divisions ready by 1939, one in Britain and one in Egypt, but neither was properly organised, trained or equipped. Neither the infantry nor the artillery had effective anti-tank equipment. Transport, however, had been entirely motorised by September 1939. Most training manuals reflected the lessons learnt from the final months of the First World War, though one for mechanised forces was issued in 1931. There were, however, three manuals of the greatest importance produced as a result of experience in India, in particular the disastrous massacre at Amritsar in India in 1919. There some 380 men, women and juveniles attending a nationalist demonstration were shot by soldiers of a Gurkha regiment on the orders of an Indian Army brigadier, Dyer. Demonstration had been vociferous but not militant. Dyer, an excitable, harsh and intolerant officer who had been born in India seven years after the Mutiny and brought up in its aftermath, however, saw the demonstration as the start of a new nationalist uprising, to be suppressed, if necessary brutally. The consequences were tragic.

The manuals that followed were the first edition of *Duties in Aid of the Civil Power*, which appeared in 1923, *Notes on Imperial Policing* in 1934 and a revised edition of *Duties in Aid* in 1937, all forming the first doctrine instructions for regimental officers, accepting the political dimension of maintaining or restoring law and order. These two manuals laid the foundation of British counter-insurgency doctrine and, supplemented by experience in Bengal and Palestine in the years 1934–39, were to form the basis of the post-1945 decolonisation campaign tactics. Within the limits of funding and availability of equipment, the standard of training for the operations expected at the time was high. Everywhere in the Army officers ensured a return to pre-1914 standards of parade drill and dress, discipline and care of arms and equipment. The pace of life in Britain was, however, less strenuous, many afternoons being free for administration, ranging from cadre courses to audit boards and foot inspections, and sport.

Operations overseas could be very testing, perhaps the most exacting throughout the period being the North-West Frontier of India, 'the Grim' to British soldiers. Both in the immediate post-war months and throughout the 1930s conflict amounted to conventional war, 1919 seeing an attempted invasion of Afghanistan, followed by British and Indian Army regiments setting forth from massive fortress encampments protected by wire and machine-gun posts to penetrate into Baluchistan and Waziristan. In the 1930s infantry officers at the head of their units or sub-units in extended columns, their routes reconnoitred by cavalry and screened by picquets commanded by Subalterns on mountainsides, with mountain artillery guns on mules available for support, all formed an exciting adventure for a young officer. Valleys would be cleared by men led by their officers in extended line, and villages burnt as a punitive measure. In the 1930s *lashkars*, bands sometimes of several thousand men, would attack British and Indian-held outposts or forces; their repulse often developed into an all-arms battle involving two or three brigades, light tanks, aircraft and medium, field and mountain artillery. For the infantry it was said that the bitter cold mountains of the North-West Frontier were the world's finest school of infantry; certainly if officers were not well trained or had not trained their soldiers well in observation, use of ground, camouflage and accurate shooting, their lives were in serious danger.

Also in India, over the whole period regimental officers learnt to control anti-British or Hindu versus Muslim communal disorders, the learning later forming the manuals' doctrine. The basic principles here were the use of minimum numbers and 'good temper'. The display of power in the form of flag marches was often sufficient to cool passions both in India and elsewhere. In more serious situations where power had to be converted to force, standard procedures were evolved. Officers were to carry only revolvers; platoons were to march either on one side only of a street, or in box formation, soldiers facing outwards at the rear and the head of the box and alternately inwards and outwards on the roadsides, with the officer and bugler in the middle of the box. Officers were to order buglers to herald the reading of a Riot Act, in the form of a banner in the appropriate language. If necessary charges would be made in two waves, fire was only to be opened after a warning and the aim should be the arrest of disturbance leaders. Drives by armoured cars, cavalry or lorry-borne infantry escorted by armoured cars were to operate by bounds supported by reserves. Officers were to ensure secrecy and surprise in cordon and search operations. Platoons were instructed on street clearing and house searching, with certificates of no damage obtained from the owner, and on the protection of women. Officers commanding armoured vehicles were to use them as infrequently as possible to avoid familiarity, never to stop and if opening fire to use only single rounds.

Regrettably these principles and practices had not been properly learnt in Ireland. Though the worst excesses of the security forces in the 1919–21 period were not committed by Regular Army units, fracas and beatings-up did occur following incidents and abuse. The Army was war-weary and not yet trained for this type of conflict. The mere display of power, battalions on the march, often made matters worse. Passions ran particularly high after the murder of twelve British Army officers, some in front of their wives, in November 1920. For the regimental officer, work in the brief and unsuccessful campaign was the leading of small parties and patrols usually in rubber-soled shoes in pursuit of individuals 'on the run', raiding illegal printing presses or bomb factories or leading men in large cross-country 'sweeps', curfew patrols, protecting loyalists, guarding prisons and keeping roads open. Sometimes in large cordon and search operations infantrymen would be supported by armoured vehicles or searchlights. In late 1920 patrols and infantry ambushes would be sent out for three or four days, but units on the move were often ambushed or mined on roads by the insurgents and officers and soldiers had to live behind barbed wire protection. Officers had also to serve on drumhead summary military courts, a task made difficult by defendants refusing to plead.[2] In 1920 forty battalions and eight cavalry regiments were serving in Ireland in the campaign.

In Britain industrial unrest made heavy demands on the military. In 1919 steel-helmeted officers and men were on the streets of Liverpool and Glasgow securing public buildings, providing transport for commuters in London and securing railway lines in Yorkshire. In 1920 infantry and armoured-car regiments were sent for similar duties to several cities. In 1921 eleven infantry and three cavalry regiments were moved to the London area, the Guards camping in Kensington Gardens; troops were also out on the streets of Glasgow. Regimental depots were tasked to supply arms to civilian volunteers. Thirty-six infantry battalions had to be deployed in the

1926 General Strike, displaying power in marches, securing Hyde Park and manning barricades in Whitehall. Other units, including armoured cars, escorted food distribution.

In the brief intervention in northern Russia infantry officers found difficulty in maintaining any enthusiasm in the icy cold and dark winter of 1918–19; on one occasion two battalions refused orders, though soon afterwards relenting. In Egypt officers led flying columns of infantry and armoured cars in pursuit of insurgents and organised river transport rescue of Europeans cut off. For the rest of the 1920s troops had on occasions to appear in the streets of Egyptian cities. The Iraq rising, in stifling heat, was on a larger scale, with columns of battalions forming four corners of a diamond formation supported by pack artillery, machine-guns and aircraft all engaging in pitched battle and then imposing collective communal punishments. Company- or platoon-sized detachments held hurriedly built blockhouses on key lines of communication. The ground operations ended in the Kurdistan mountains and swampy valleys in 1923 with columns mounted on mules and camels, picquets screening them from hillsides and aircraft bombing insurgents. In Sudan in 1924 a two-battalion attack in the streets of Khartoum was necessary to put down mutinous Sudanese soldiers. In 1927 instability and local violence arising from warlord feuding led to the despatch of battalions to Shanghai and Tientsin in China as part of an international force. The decade ended in 1929 with the need to deploy two battalions in Jerusalem and Tel-Aviv to support locally recruited forces, protect Jewish settlers and search out Arab attackers.

In the 1930s the large scale of Frontier operations has already been noted. Forts now had wireless and some a searchlight; officers' and soldiers' accommodation would be half below ground to avoid snipers, soldiers sleeping with their rifles chained to them or in a pit beneath them. Infantry manned the perimeters of forts and camps, within which were the all-important 3.7-inch mountain howitzers and their big Missouri mules. All marching was by fire and movement bounds, no two with ever the same pattern, with officers mounted on ponies. The Indian situation was also worsened by violence by large 'Red Shirt' crowds in the towns of the North-West Frontier Province, worsening nationalist and inter-communal violence in many other cities, an arson campaign in Assam, and most difficult of all a terrorist campaign of targeted killings and assassinations in the difficult terrain of Bengal, where flag marches often had to be in single file. Troops frequently had to open fire on leaders of rioting demonstrations, with severe punitive measures taken by the police.

A rising in Burma in 1930 required operations very similar to those of the 19th century. In mountainous and jungle areas and with heavy rain, platoon officers led snatch parties in pursuit of insurgent leaders. Infantry company officers had the unusual task of running an armoured train; platoon patrols would have their supplies and ammunition carried by mules or an elephant, one elephant being able to carry all a platoon needed for three days.

Other smaller-scale uses of British Regular troops to restore order in the 1930s were in Cyprus in 1930–31 and in Jamaica – normally a very popular posting as subalterns met American girls from cruise liners – in 1938. On occasions also, troops appeared on the streets of Egyptian cities.

The most serious of the internal security commitments in a colony was, however, that of Palestine, the on-going arrival of Jews, many fleeing real or anticipated persecution in Europe, leading to an Arab uprising opening in 1936 and mounting in scale and ferocious violence until the outbreak of war. The early stages differed little from India with assertions of control of streets, escorts, snatch parties and protection of Jewish settlers. The Arabs, well-funded and able to resume an apparently normal life as shepherds or farmers after a night of violence, turned to sabotage, ambushes and larger attacks. These required armoured-car and mounted cavalry sweeps with two or more battalions and aircraft to contain them. In 1938 in protest against British attempts to limit immigration, Jewish groups turned from retaliation against the Arabs to attacks on the British. The style of operations now moved to more work at night, motorised flying columns of half, one or two company sizes with radio, and machine-guns and mortars firing if necessary while on the move. Some columns included field artillery. For pursuit in the hills, horses, mules and donkeys were used to move units into assembly areas for cordons and searches. The precursor of the later Special Air Service Regiment, the Special Night Squads, commando-style snatch squads, were tasked to kill insurgents sabotaging oil pipelines or engaged in arms smuggling. Some fifteen of these squads, the brainchild of Major Orde Wingate, were formed and were very successful. Finally, Regular Army battalions once again found themselves on the streets of Belfast controlling sectarian violence from 1932 to 1935.

A common feature of all these operations, from the North-West Frontier to Palestine and Belfast, was the responsibilities that fell upon the regimental officers, even the most junior. Within the infantry, battalions retained the structure of four companies each of three platoons; progressively further specialist platoons or sections were added, including pioneers, signals, mortars and machine-guns, with in the 1930s anti-tank and anti-aircraft platoons (the latter with no weapon other than a machine-gun). Most battalions appear to have lost their machine-guns in the 1930s, but in return motor transport and tracked Bren light machine-gun carrier platoons were issued.

Officers commanding and serving in regimental depots had to train soldier recruits; in some northern regiments recruits were so unfit from under-nourishment that their strength first had to be built up. Other duties included helping school and university training corps, recruiting marches and local ceremonial. Training – for units of all arms – continued to run on an annual cycle of individual training beginning in the autumn, with collective training from April to

September and finishing with large-scale exercises. Most home-based units were, however, very much under strength, with infantry companies less than twenty strong and flags representing men and weapons on exercise. Congenial and generally not very exacting postings for Captains included the duties of Adjutant of a Territorial Army unit, for Majors and Lieutenant-Colonels staff duties or deputy or full military attaché at an embassy abroad.

The year 1919 saw the last horsed cavalry full regimental charge in the Army's history. In operations against resurgent Turkish nationalists the 20th Hussars attacked resisters. The charge, led by the officers, was traditional. Trumpets sounded, two squadrons abreast in column of troops, a third in depth, all with sabres in hand, made the charge, regrouped and charged back.[3] But the following years were overshadowed by the rumours, plans and reality of conversion from horses to armoured-cars and light tanks. This was a painful process for many (but not all, some young soldiers seeing a bright second career at work in garages) which began in 1928 and was largely complete by 1939. The culture of the horse remained, however, officers possessing their own or using the few 'Government Chargers' supplied to regiments and so continuing to enter equestrian sporting events. Cavalry on horses were used on flag marches in India in the 1920s, and with armoured-cars in cordon and search operations in Palestine in the late 1930s.

Artillery officers faced major changes. In 1924 the separate branches – Horse, Field and Garrison – were amalgamated, though RHA regiments continued to wear their own cap badge and tunic buttons. A posting to the RHA became now the aim of many, particularly the ambitious. New weapons and fire control systems were introduced, among them medium, anti-aircraft and anti-tank guns, the most important being the very successful 25 pdr. field gun. The basic field unit structure remained, until 1938, a battery of three sections, each of two field guns, the battery commanded by a Major assisted by a Captain and three Subalterns, of which the senior was the gun position officer. Three or four batteries, the fourth being howitzers, formed a brigade, the Lieutenant-Colonel's command, and three brigades were allotted to divisions. Slightly different structures existed in home-based batteries and with medium and mountain units. The late 1930s saw three fundamental changes: brigades became regiments, batteries ceased to be self-accounting and much real power passed from the battery commander to the regiment commander, and the 25 pdr. began to replace both the 18 pdr. and the howitzer in field regiments, these latter now being composed of two twelve-gun batteries each of three four-gun troops. Horses, so much a part of Royal Artillery life in action, routine life and ceremonial, were replaced in mechanisation.[4]

During the war the Engineers had found the greatly increased signals work that fell on officers too difficult to combine with field engineering. In consequence in 1920 the Royal Corps of Signals was formed in which officers and men could concentrate on communications. Thinking about tanks was confused by two particular issues: cavalry regiments wishing to retain a reconnaissance role after mechanisation preferred light tanks, and the fact that medium tanks were of no use in India. Their value as a breakthrough or anti-tank instrument was only recognised by lone voices.

The social life of officers was as full and varied as in the years before 1914 but in most regiments on a lower scale, money being tighter, and regiments wishing to attract and keep the sons of former officers.[5] Regimental custom remained stiff with much social formality in some regiments, Colonels and Majors calling junior Lieutenants only by their surnames even in the Mess; in others, notably Guards and cavalry, the style was more relaxed, with Christian names for all except the Commanding Officer. In Messes 'shop' (i.e. work) and politics were forbidden subjects, women were allowed in the Mess only on specific social occasions and, generally, though not everywhere, standing of drinks between members was not allowed. Evenings would be spent playing card games or billiards.

In India, Indian servants stood behind officers' chairs at mealtimes, available for errands.[6] Single officers were expected to dine in Mess in the mess kit uniform every weekday, married officers at least twice a week; regimental balls and other functions were frequently arranged. Larger institutions and regiments or groups of wealthier regiments maintained a sailing club with yachts; the School of Artillery at Larkhill, the Staff College at Camberley and other large garrison centres maintained a drag hunt or beagles or both. Sport remained all-important, though unit teams had to be captained by an officer. Most officers of the rank of Captain or above ran a private motor car, while Commanding Officers had an official vehicle. Some young officers bought motorcycles, not always meeting the approval of Commanding Officers in 'smart' regiments. In India and Egypt, clubs where officers mixed with the local white community continued to provide the focus of a rich social and sports life. Routine life changed little from what it had been in the 19th century. In the hot weather soldiers were confined to barracks in the heat of the day, drink and venereal disease among soldiers remaining a problem for regimental officers.

Although pay was little changed and remained low, housing for officers and their families improved with new building in the 1930s. Officers' housing was separate from that for the rank and file, the size of house depending on seniority and size of family, with a few larger houses tied to particular posts. The need to rent houses for married officers on waiting lists was reduced; in India comfortable bungalows were built for married officers in the hill stations, while the unmarried had rooms in barracks, forts or bungalows that were often distinctly primitive with plumbing the responsibility of Indian servants. More thought was given to the career development of officers, with better prospects for at least eventual promotion to Major. The same constraints on marriage and marriage allowance, however, remained as did views on divorce, where resignation was still expected if an officer was the 'guilty party'. Officers everywhere had servants and Commanding Officers had drivers. Regimental medical officers looked after all ranks and their wives and families. Many officers kept pet dogs, which if well behaved were permitted in the Mess.

Inevitably, in an organisation as inward-looking – and as alienated from the rest of society – as the Army, there were little social distinctions: officers of the Guards looked down on everyone else, within the cavalry Dragoons looked down on Lancers, in the infantry the Rifle and Light Infantry regiments claimed a social cachet, and within a county or region one of several regiments would have a particular social status. In the Royal Artillery acceptance into an RHA regiment was as much a social as a professional status. The distinctions would sometimes extend to sport, the Guards and Cavalry officers playing polo and less wealthier officers pig-sticking in India or point-to-point in England if they possessed horses; otherwise ball games, hunting, fishing, shooting or golf filled free afternoons. Young officers destined for Indian Army regiments serving an initial attachment to a British battalion were, in some regiments, treated as second-class citizens.

Officers no longer had to grow moustaches. Uniforms were altered after the war, finally replacing the showy cuff rank badges with less conspicuous stars and crowns on epaulettes; only officers of the rank of Colonel and above, even if staff trained and in a staff appointment, were now entitled to red cap-bands. With mechanisation – and because in the public mind it was associated with excessive militarism – the custom of wearing peaked cap, tunic, riding breeches and boots began to change, though it was to last for many years and still exists for Adjutants in some regiments. The introduction of battledress and berets or side-caps in 1939 dealt this custom a further blow. With battledress, rank badges, in most regiments woven cloth but in some metal, were worn on epaulettes and all officers wore their tunic neck button open to display khaki collar and tie as a distinctive feature. Although battledress was the issue uniform, officers were still expected to purchase service dress uniforms, mess kit, peaked caps and perhaps side-caps from approved Bond Street regimental tailors. 'British Warm' light overcoats were also very popular and permitted for wear when not on parade with troops. Officers continued to carry canes; in most regiments instructions directed that the cane could not be swaggered but only swung strictly parallel to the ground.

One or two regiments became known for their willingness occasionally to accept a Jewish officer who otherwise met the regiment's professional and social requirement; similarly the occasional European aristocrat exile would be accepted in a fashionable regiment. Predictably, being associated with the replacement of the horse, the Royal Tank Corps remained the least socially prestigious of the front-line combat regiments. A minority of Royal Engineers officers gave the Corps, generally more free from social snobberies than elsewhere, a lasting reputation for mild eccentricity or a puritanical form of Christianity.[7] In the remaining Irish regiments were some officers from the former Protestant ascendancy in the south. Northern Ireland continued to produce a number of outstanding officers, among them the future Field-Marshals Alexander, Montgomery and Templer. In the Scottish regiments the number of English officers declined sharply, though their Scots successors were little different from their English opposite numbers who became Scots by adoption.[8]

The class-based social background of officers in the inter-war years remained; in the Royal Artillery, for example, at least ninety per cent of the officers had been educated at the better-known Public Schools and brought up to accept responsibility in the service of an Empire whose permanence and worth were taken for granted.[9] A few, one or two in each artillery brigade, were wartime promotions from the ranks with only limited promotion prospects. In general these conditions applied also to the infantry. Each unit, cavalry, artillery or infantry, had a promoted Sergeant or Warrant

Officer as a Quartermaster on a special Quartermaster's commission. Despite the level of pay there was no shortage of young artillery officers, among them now a few university graduates. A Lieutenant's pay per day was 13s in 1923, later reduced to 12s 4d – about £18 a month from which in most units £10 would be spent in mess bills, with also extra duty pay for servants and a groom. Accommodation, basic food up to the value of five shillings per week and, if the unit retained horses, forage were free. Marriage allowance, one shilling per day, remained payable only to officers over thirty. The young regimental officer was cheerful, carefree and inclined to arrogance; his superiors, particularly if they had had war experience, were more reserved and cautious. Promotion in the 1920s and most of the 1930s was slow, taking perhaps twelve or more years before a Subaltern could become a Captain, but was alleviated by the fact that a number of Subalterns and Captains left after a few years in the Army to pursue more lucrative careers elsewhere. In any gap between postings an officer was placed on half-pay, a serious matter for a Major or Lieutenant-Colonel with a family.

Transport by sea for all regiments now became very much more enjoyable, most voyages being in handsome four-masted liners owned by the Bibby Line and named after English counties. Officers travelled in comfortable cabins. Wives and families could accompany officers to most overseas postings. Children, however, were often left behind at boarding school, with relatives or in the care of kindly spinsters who provided substitute homes with both comfort and affection.[10]

The initial training of officers in the cadet colleges was uneven, that in Woolwich being a great deal more professional than at Sandhurst.[11] Common to both was an entry requirement of School Certificate, passing a Civil Service test, an entry age of eighteen and a very high (90–95%) proportion of Public School boys who set the tone of life.[12] Both colleges required fees to be paid, and Sandhurst faced falling numbers throughout the period. At

Woolwich the eighteen-month course included basic military training together with military science, drill, tactics, trench and bridge construction, military history, a measure of British politics, Imperial and international affairs and options including further science and language subjects. The operation of the internal combustion engine was taught, but cadets were not taught to drive and were forbidden from driving or riding motorcycles in vacations. Equitation and sport were seen as of prime importance, prowess on the games or hunting field being the mark of a good cadet. Royal Signals cadets joined the RMA in 1924. After Woolwich artillerymen went on to the Larkhill School of Artillery, engineers to the School of Military Engineering and, for the most promising, for two years to Cambridge University, and signals officers to the new School of Signals. In 1939 with war imminent, courses were shortened.

Sandhurst began the period with a two-year course, shortened later in 1924 to eighteen months, to save money. Its entrants included a number of the titled or heirs to titles, many from traditional military families and some from Indian Army or Colonial Service families, but numbers were always short. Fees on paper were £200 rising over time to £400, but King's scholarships and other grants existed for the sons of serving or deceased officers. From 1922 a limited number of promoted NCOs under the age of twenty-four were accepted. These were called 'Army Cadets' rather than 'Gentlemen Cadets' and generally went to support service corps on commissioning. Sport was viewed even more emphatically than at Woolwich, success in some sports, notably boxing, fencing and riding, being recorded in inter-company competitions. Riding was obligatory for all: cadets who went hunting or entered events were excused the day's training, and horses were hired locally by cadets who could afford to do so. Riding and other accident victims were expected to bear any suffering without complaint, as befitted a gentleman.

Cadet life remained rumbustuous, often wild, with bullying and ragging. Cadets who were thought not to conform or who committed petty pilfering of another's property were brutally handled by their peers. Drink was in theory controlled, in practice exceeded. Cadets were not allowed cars, though some kept one in nearby Bagshot. Bicycles were issued to all – and bicycle drill practised. London was not far away for those who could afford it. One or two local professional ladies were available. The 'finishing school' lifestyle included instruction in writing cheques, answering invitations and the importance of engraved rather than printed visiting cards.[13]

The military training was extended to include trench digging of all types, use of all infantry weapons, drill (including ceremonial) and church parades every Saturday and Sunday. Civilian academics taught military history and Imperial geography, with science or language subjects as options. For cadets, being gentlemen, no formal leadership training was thought necessary, and there was no training for living in the field or field exercises, this all being left to regiments. Later in a junior officer's career, specialist courses – for machine-guns, mortars and gas warfare for infantry officers, signals courses for Royal Signals Officers and supply courses for Service Corps officers – were provided usually at Captain level. In sum, however, an officer's training was adequate for the squirearchical style of officering and the duties of the Army in Asia, but was to prove woefully inadequate for the European war to come.[14] Preparation for the Staff College examination and the College course itself provided little stimulus. The mindset of officers changed little from the day they left Sandhurst; any questioning of received wisdom and practice was seen at best as uncalled for, if not dangerously radical.[15]

In 1939, after much debate, a second attempt at introducing a women's corps in the Army was made with the creation of the Auxiliary Territorial Service (ATS) as part of the Territorial Army. Its duties were similar to those of the QMAAC of 1918. Again the question of commission and rank arose. ATS officers were now styled Commander (equivalent to a Subaltern), Senior Commandant (Major) and Controller (Colonel). No pre-war provision for their training was made, leading to friction when inexperience was evident. Acceptance and welcome in Officers' Messes varied and was at its best in anti-aircraft artillery.[16]

In the immediate post-Armistice months discipline broke down in several barracks and regiments, including Guards battalions, in protest at delays in demobilisation. There was also in 1920 a mutiny in an Irish battalion, the 1st Connaught Rangers, in India, largely a by-product of the Irish situation. Both events were the product of exceptional contemporary circumstances. Otherwise the general relationship between officers and soldiers changed little in the Regular Army in the inter-war years despite the anti-militarism and developing class animosity in society as a whole, the 'officer class' being a popular target. Soldiers came, if not immediately, to view the Army and their officers with appreciation. Many had joined as a consequence of unemployment, often pure hunger, others as a result of a petty misdemeanour, frequently a consequence of poverty, where a magistrate had offered the choice of the Army or a custodial sentence. The Army provided food, sport, regimental companionships, travel, education if a soldier was illiterate and help in finding a job after service was over. Officers were aware that their soldiers were now better educated, and also aware of their soldiers' personal and welfare problems, with which they felt more personally concerned.

Right up to the outbreak of war the bulk of the Army was distributed around the Empire, in Egypt, India, Malaya and the colonies. Sustained political opposition to the acceptance of any substantial European commitment continued until 1939. The growing German menace belatedly led to expansion, the doubling of the Territorial Army and the introduction of conscription, all intended to create an Army of six Regular and twenty-six Territorial divisions.

While the doubling led to a sudden increase in promotion prospects for Regular regimental officers in the provision of cadres and staffs, it left the Army ill-prepared for the outbreak of war so soon afterwards.

In September 1939 all that could be despatched immediately to France was four infantry divisions. Almost all the infantry battalions had the excellent new Bren light machine-gun section weapon and two-inch mortars, a platoon of the more effective three-inch mortars and a reconnaissance platoon of ten tracked Bren gun carriers, but for anti-tank protection there was only the almost useless anti-tank rifle. No battalions had any specific anti-aircraft weapons, soldiers being told to use their Bren or Lewis guns. The divisional artillery, three regiments, had either the new 25 pdr. gun or an improved 18 pdr. gun capable of firing 25 pdr. ammunition; the anti-tank batteries had only the inadequate 2 pdr. gun. Each division also had a regiment of light tanks, some Regular, others Territorial Army, additional Bren gun carriers and a machine-gun infantry battalion. The divisions were grouped into two Corps, each of which possessed additional field, medium and anti-aircraft guns.

The whole, even when increased in the months before May 1940, highlighted the failures of pre-1939 preparation with its absence of armoured formations and efficient anti-tank weaponry. The very real virtues of the inter-war Army – steadiness, discipline and good shooting – were unable to prevent its defeat, though they could prevent that defeat from turning into rout and catastrophe.

NOTES

1 A full account of all the military commitments and operations can be found in Anthony Clayton, *The British Empire as a Superpower 1919–39* (London, Macmillan, and Atlanta, University of Georgia, 1986).

2 A useful brief summary account appears in Gordon Blight, *The History of the Royal Berkshire Regiment, 1920–1927* (London, Staples, 1953), ii. The early chapters form a very interesting account of the life of an infantry regiment in the 1919–39 years.

3 Lieutenant-Colonel L.B. Oatts, *Emperor's Chambermaids: The Story of the 14th/20th King's Hussars* (London, Ward Lock, 1973), 415–416. This book's curious title derives from the capture of Napoleon's chamber pot by the 14th Light Dragoons after the battle of Vittoria.

4 A perceptive account of Royal Artillery officers and regimental life in the 1930s at the time of mechanisation, the abdication crisis, German and Italian rearmament and the artillery structure changes appears in a novel by Gilbert Frankau, *The Royal Regiment* (London, Hutchinson, 1938). The main plot is thin, but the background and officers' views and attitudes are instructive.

5 Thomas, *Story of Sandhurst*, 189, quotes from a memoir written by Lord Belhaven, a Sandhurst cadet in 1924: 'The regiment which I hoped to join, the Royal Scots Fusiliers, was then an expensive one but it had shortly to cut expenses to the bone to allow the sons of its former officers to join it. It was the same everywhere, even to a certain extent in the Brigade of Guards and the Cavalry.'

6 Lieutenant-Colonel R.E.R. Robinson kindly gave me this insight into mess life of the period.

7 The tradition began in the 19th century in the days of General Gordon, and was referred to elsewhere in the Army as 'mad, married and Methodist'. The most famous example in the 20th century was, perhaps, General Sir William Dobbie whose Christian faith and simple lifestyle were to prove inspirational when Dobbie was Governor of Malta in the worst days of the Second World War.

8 For example, Earl Wavell, the most famous Black Watch officer of the 20th century, came from a Hampshire family.

9 *The History of the Royal Artillery 1919–1939* (privately published by the Royal Artillery Institution, 1978), 15.

10 The author recalls one such home in Exmouth run by Miss Sweet. Among her charges was the future sculptress Dame Elizabeth Frink who recalled this home with affection.

11 Sheppard, *Sandhurst*, x, provides an account of life in both Colleges; of the Sandhurst course Lord Carrington later wrote 'The curriculum was peculiar, and seemed to have little coherence and not much relevance to our future duties except in the most basic physical sense.

Drill dominated life.': Carrington, *Reflect on Things Past* (London, Collins, 1988), 21. John Masters, *Bugles and a Tiger* (London, Michael Joseph, 1956), ii, describes day-to-day life and the cadets' code of honour, often enforced very brutally.

12 At Sandhurst, for example, the College's magazine, *The R.M.C. Journal*, carried photographs of members of the various major games teams. Under team members' names were carefully recorded their former Public Schools. Any competitors from other schools were simply noted by name.

13 Thomas, *Story of Sandhurst*, 197 notes this addition to the curriculum, adding 'Such guidance would not have been thought necessary before the war.'

14 Carrington, *Reflect on Things Past*, 24, records the instruction given to him when he first reported to his Grenadier Guards Commanding Officer: 'I only want you to remember two things. On no account are you to marry until you are twenty-five and you are to hunt in Leicestershire at least two days a week.'

15 '. . . there was little sign of original thought, and the main mass of the candidates appear to be almost religiously Orthodox . . . and that many of the answers were such as to cause uneasiness whether the mental outlook of the Army as a whole is really showing the grasp of modern conditions that is required': comment by the examiner on the 'Strategy and Tactics' paper in the Staff College examination for 1935.

16 Bidwell, *Women's Royal Army Corps*, iii, iv. Women volunteers in the First Aid Nursing Yeomanry had of course been supporting a variety of military activities and operations since 1909. They were, however, at their own insistence an independent organisation and not part of the Army.

CHAPTER 12

THE OFFICER, 1940–45

The defeat of the 1939–40 British Expeditionary Force, an army so clearly outclassed, began a slow but on-going change in the nature of the British Army, a change that was to develop over the next forty to fifty years: essentially the progressive move away from the officer whose authority was based on class and the squirearchical tradition to a taut professionalism being seen, by the end of the century, as all that was needed from an officer. Regiments whose officers wished to retain a social cachet had now to start to measure up to the ever more testing professional standards required for 20th century military operations. These standards were increasingly expected not only by the NCOs on whom the Army's officers depended in all its operations, but also by the much better educated soldiers – few in the war were illiterate, virtually none after 1945. Further, some of the wartime and almost all the post-war operations carried a political dimension, in turn requiring ever-increasing professionalism.

The Army expanded to a 1945 peak of five armoured and nineteen infantry Divisions together with some forty independent brigades. This wartime expansion was based primarily on the pre-war Regular Divisions and the pre-war Territorial Army infantry Divisions together with new formations created by the 1939 doubling. These were supplemented by the creation of extra armoured

Divisions in which cavalry and tank regiments, mostly Regular, some Territorial, supplied the armour but whose infantry was drawn from a variety of sources. The elite 7th Armoured Division ('Desert Rats'), for example, had as its lorried infantry brigade three Surrey and London TA battalions from El Alamein to the Netherlands frontier – battalions that still retained many pre-war members.[1] The Guards Armoured Division was formed of war-raised Guards battalions in tank roles.

The Army's total divisional strength was much smaller than in the First World War. Among the chief reasons for this were the manpower demands, over one million, of the Royal Air Force, the continuing needs of the Royal Navy and within the Army, and because many campaigns and operations were some distance away from Britain, the larger numbers needed for logistic support together with the needs of the new specialist regiments and corps. These included the Parachute Regiment, the Royal Electrical and Mechanical Engineers and the Intelligence Corps which all survived into the post-war Army, and other regiments such as the Reconnaissance Regiment which did not.

At the outset, officers were drawn from the traditional sources, the school and university officers training corps. Applicants were invited to report to various centres, mostly university training corps centres. Selection followed a brief interview, heavily upper and middle class-based and exemplified in Evelyn Waugh's fictional conversation between an officer and a potential candidate: 'What makes the best officer?' with its answer 'The officer type.' The short interview procedure was replaced by regional Command selection board interviews, presided over by a Colonel, a procedure only a little less unsatisfactory. The needs of the Army for more officers and the general view that the retreat to Dunkirk had shown up serious shortcomings in officer selection and training then led to the establishment of War Office Selection Boards (WOSBs), in which practical leadership tests were included as well as interviews over three days, a psychiatrist being present as adviser, and a number of Officer Cadet Training Units (OCTUs) in different parts of the country, all resulting in much more open meritocratic selection, fewer failures in OCTUs and, in the long period 1940–44 when much of the Army was in Britain, more realistic training. Some experienced NCOs received commissions in the field. But to the end of the war front-line units rarely had more than three Regular officers on their strength; in the last year the officer shortage became so acute that Canadian and American officers were loaned to British battalions.

At the outbreak of war Woolwich was closed, never to reopen for officer training. Sandhurst became two tautly professional OCTUs, one for future infantry officers and one for future armoured regimental officers, the latter being run by a TA Yeomanry regiment. Both courses lasted sixteen weeks, the armoured course being followed by tank training at Bovington. Other OCTUs around the country trained future artillery and corps officers and a little later additional infantry officers. All those destined for Guards regiments, however, were sent to the Sandhurst OCTU until 1942 when this was moved to Mons Barracks at Aldershot, leaving only the armoured regiments OCTU at Sandhurst where it remained until the end of the war. Sandhurst also offered special short Young Officers, Liaison Officers and Training Officers courses, and some buildings were made over to house students on the short (three or four month) wartime Staff College courses.[2]

For many Regular officers the war offered opportunities of very rapid advancement, especially for the very able. The newly promoted Major L. Whistler of 1939 was a Major-General in 1945; the 1938 Lieutenant R.M.P. Carver became a Brigadier in 1944. Many a Captain finished the war as a Lieutenant-Colonel. Only a few wartime officers commanded combat infantry, armour or artillery regiments, though others with specialist qualifications became Brigadiers. At the end of the war, however, there were reversions in rank, sometimes painful.

In the 1940 campaign cases occurred of trained infantry soldiers cut off from their units and finding themselves mixed into logistics or ordnance units commanded by specialists in their duties but not trained for front-line fighting. Also on other occasions logistics units were ordered into an infantry front-line role for which again they and their officers were not trained. The lesson that was drawn, to affect all subsequent officer training, was that all officers (with the exception of the specific non-combatants such as doctors and Chaplains) in their training were to be taught the basics of how to lead an infantry platoon.

A second lesson drawn by many officers from the campaign was the need for officers and men alike to improve physical fitness, a return to the traditional British Army marching proficiency. Some officers found this uncomfortable.

The experience of officers and their men in combat varied greatly. In Norway and France the experience was chiefly one of sustained bombing and *blitzkrieg* followed by evacuation. Early success in East Africa and temporary success in North Africa were followed by a second dose of German *blitzkrieg* in Greece and Crete, with further evacuations. Reverses followed in North Africa; Hong Kong and Malaya saw humiliating defeat with officers captured by the Japanese suffering, at best special contempt and forced labour, at worst torture and death. In October 1942 successes reappeared with hard-fought but victorious campaigns in North Africa, Italy and north-west Europe, but although eventually brought to a victorious conclusion the Burma campaign was one of special hardship.

This work will describe the duties of ordinary regimental officers and the conditions under which they had to discharge these duties in the four most important campaigns – France and Belgium in 1940, North Africa, Burma and France and Belgium again in 1944–45. The experiences chosen cannot cover special forces such as parachute units or Chindits and will focus on the arm, or a unit in the area, that played a lead role in the four campaigns.

Numerous works narrate the story of the brief campaign in France and Belgium in 1939, though mostly from an overall operational view. The experiences of a junior officer are well detailed in a brief work, published during the war, written by Peter Hadley, a platoon commander in a Royal Sussex Regiment TA battalion. His experiences were typical of many units.[3] In early April the battalion landed in France and by a mixture of marching and uncomfortable railway journeys moved up to the Belgian border area for some final training before May 1940 unfolded. Routine duties for company officers included billeting arrangements in barns or empty houses, the maintenance of billeting records, when necessary latrine siting, foot inspections and blister pricking after marches, arrangement of sentry duties, pay parades, sports and games and the censoring of letters. Training included the practising of trench reliefs, marches and road runs, fieldcraft training in minor tactics, patrolling and use of compass, and the organisation of weapon training and field firing.

When the German onslaught opened, Hadley's battalion was moved forward into Belgium, his first duties being the guarding of a major railway junction and then preparation of his platoon sector in the first of many of his unit's defensive positions, with wiring, siting of weapon pits and arranging sentry duties followed on occasions by rearranging the positions to meet a superior's criticisms. As the unit came into contact with the advancing Germans Hadley led first a reconnaissance patrol of three and later a fighting patrol of ten. In several of the successive defensive positions the unit came under heavy and prolonged mortar and artillery fire; officers had to ensure their men were properly dug in. Stragglers from other units arrived, proclaiming in genuine error that they were 'all that was left of the . . .' These had to be reunited with their units; others not in error but in fear simply had to be ordered to return to the fight. On one occasion men from Hadley's own unit who had taken refuge in a cellar had to be given similar firm orders.

Officers had to overcome their own fatigue from strain, sleepless nights and long marches and to combat an all-pervading sense of isolation, of their unit being cut off from neighbours and left to fight all on its own. Throughout, officers also had to ensure weapons were always clean and ready and that essential stores and ammunition were to hand on the unit's few vehicles. Feet also had to be inspected, if conditions permitted, after long marches. For most of the brief campaign either rations or local food supplies were available, though in battle on some days men remained short of both food and water. Hadley's battalion was fortunate in that its defensive positions, although heavily bombarded, did not have to face a full tank and infantry assault. In these, other battalions were sometimes overrun, with officers and men alike being scattered, killed, taken prisoner or managing to escape in small scattered parties. In the final few days orders were issued to abandon all vehicles and the wounded, an order which Hadley tried to circumvent in respect of his own wounded men. After holding a covering position under continuous German bombardment and dive-bombing to which they had no weaponry capable of reply, the battalion, maintaining cohesion with difficulty, joined the straggling columns heading for Dunkirk. Officers as tired and as confused as the men ensured that all crouched beneath trees or dispersed into fields and ditches when German aircraft approached. In the last few miles, as the columns merged into vast crowds, officers ordered soldiers to hold hands to maintain unit and sub-unit cohesions, at the same time calling out the unit's name. Many regiments, however, became split up, only reuniting back in England. On the dunes and beaches staff officers ordered regimental officers to group their men in packets of fifty for embarkation, in their turn, in the assortment of ships. Officers and men had been without food for several days, were dehydrated, and were frequently subjected to German dive-bombing and machine-gunning air attacks. Occasionally officers had to intervene to prevent a stampede, but such incidents were the exception and, despite the scale of the defeat, Dunkirk can nevertheless justly be seen as a triumph for the British regimental officer. Except when units were totally overrun, discipline never seriously broke down and command and control were reasserted on the beaches.

The Army's next campaign, the war in the North African desert from July 1940 to the end of 1942, was one of very tough battles and operations, but also with periods in between of relative calm.[4] Armour, too often German, dominated the battlefields; spearhead British formations were built around armour. It was a war without hatred, British and Germans having a mutual respect for each other and, albeit from different perspectives, a poor opinion of the Italians who treated prisoners badly.

The terrain imposed its own conditions. Generally the ground was sand or gravel with a few small towns on the coast and low sandhills, rocky outcrops, wells, cairns and small funeral monuments forming the few landmarks inland. There the outcrops could form steep cliffs and deep gullies. It could be wet and muddy in winter, sweltering in summer but rarely unbearable, though occasionally in the worst heat men would collapse on to the floor of vehicles. The greatest impediments were the 45 mph *khamzeen* sandstorms occurring once or twice a month, stinging the skin and eyes, ruining uncooked food, tearing tents and bivouacs to shreds and turning oil on machinery green. Sometimes storms were charged with electricity, giving tank crews electric shocks and interfering with wireless communications. *Khamzeens* brought any fighting to a close; vehicles could pass within a few feet of each other without knowing of their presence.

The desert produced a range of medical problems, in particular skin sores, dysentery and jaundice but also its own particular variety of nervous stress. Flies were a constant nuisance and officers had to exercise supervision over latrine pits, the use of 'thunder box' latrines and burning of refuse.

The open spaces, except before Alamein with open flanks, suited the huntsman approach of many pre-war officers, especially those in the former horsed regiments. It was a paradise for the tactician, but with bases far in the rear a nightmare for the logistics officers who had to maintain supply by long columns of vehicles. The few maps, even those marking the Italian frontier forts, were inaccurate in detail; approach marches were ordered in terms of miles and degrees. In 1940 a simple sundial-type compass was used. Water was often more precious than fuel, with water that had been used for shaving being poured into radiators or recycled in filters.

In the first months of the desert war, when the Italians were the only opposition, the aims of regiments were to harass enemy communications, to prevent the Italians harassing their own and to cut the thick protective wire fences. These were armoured-car or light tank troop commander operations; to the troop commander with perhaps only three or four armoured fighting vehicles would fall the decision whether or not to attack a well-protected convoy, since the squadron commander could be a dozen miles away. The decision became more difficult after the arrival of the Germans.

The arrival of the Afrika Korps changed the campaign to one of a series of hard-fought battles in which, despite inferior numbers of men and tanks, the Germans scored spectacular successes until September 1942. For the tank troop or squadron commander peering through the slit in his tank's turret, battles were chaotic and confusing, columns of black smoke rising everywhere from burning vehicles, exploding ammunition and wrecked vehicles, tanks and guns all illuminated by the flashes of gunfire, tracer and Verey lights. Recognition as friend or foe, which was always difficult in desert dust clouds, often became impossible. A long-lasting weakness, ascribed by some to the regimental system, was the failure of proper well-coordinated infantry, armour and artillery cooperation. Armoured regiments preferred to strike in columns, tanks or armoured cars with some infantry but inadequate artillery, while the more defensively minded infantry sought security in 'boxes' akin to the squares of old, of one or two brigades. The Germans found the columns easier to knock out than the boxes, but until September 1942 had no insuperable difficulty with either. Column officers obviously had greater opportunities for individual initiative than regimental officers in a brigade box, but often, particularly when boxes were breached or more fortunately in a pursuit, squadron or troop officers found themselves fighting their own local battle. Success returned only when the Eighth Army had overwhelming superiority in tanks, guns, men and air superiority – and the command of General Montgomery.

In times of relative quiet, and at night when conditions so permitted, a regimental leaguer area would be set up. Tanks or armoured cars from three squadrons would be drawn up in double line facing outwards, the squadrons 150 yards apart and the tanks ten yards. Flank squadron tanks had their turrets turned outwards and to the rear, and machine-gun posts were set up at each corner of the leaguer. Between the left and centre squadrons the regimental headquarters and the attached infantry company would be sited, while between the centre and right squadrons would be the attached artillery battery, and anti-tank and anti-aircraft troops. Immediate resupply of the unit might be effected in the evening in two echelons, a B echelon commanded by a Major directing the forward move of supplies from their columns, and an A echelon commanded by a Subaltern then distributing these to the squadrons and other sub-units. Sometimes two troops might leaguer elsewhere in preparation for a dawn patrol to probe enemy positions or mount a raid. For the remainder reveille would provide tea, a cold meal of meat with onions or biscuits at midday, an afternoon of rest, a main evening meal at 7.30 p.m. and preparations for resupply with, for officers, perhaps a whisky thereafter. The usual daily ration was three cups of tea or water per man per day, and for all purposes a half-gallon of water – if it arrived.

Local morale depended on the supply, especially of tea. Generally the morale of officers and men rose or fell according to the tide of battle, falling to a very low point in mid-1942 when particularly among officers the reverses had induced 'a particular kind of scepticism, a kind of irony at one's own expense, a refusal to dramatise events when drama was inevitable'.[5] Conditions permitting, officers and men were allowed a week's leave every six to eight months. For the health of those soldiers who so needed, officers arranged controlled red light districts in Alexandria and Cairo where girls were regularly checked. Many officers found the cosmopolitan culture of Cairo provided much appreciated intellectual stimulus, while for some Shepheard's Hotel offered other distractions. The Army's venereal disease rate was high despite warnings given by officers, the issue of condoms and deductions of pay from men who contracted the disease.

The desert campaign created great spirit and enthusiasm but also a cult, especially among the cavalry regiment officers, displayed in cord slacks, desert boots and neckerchiefs. The cult and the habit of the column dash impeded formations, particularly the 7th Armoured Division, when regimental officers had to fight in very different terrain conditions in Italy and Normandy. A certain glamour and much public interest centred on the North African battles. In contrast little interest was shown in the long 1942–45 Burma campaign. Here one of the best accounts of infantry regimental soldiering and of the extremely difficult conditions in which officers had to lead men is provided by Lieutenant-Colonel Geoffrey White, who served in and later commanded the 2nd Battalion of the Dorsetshire Regiment throughout most of the Burma campaign.[6]

The campaign saw on occasions set-piece brigade- or two-brigade-sized attacks, but for the most part there was no clear front line and operations centred on the taking of particular areas or features known to be defended, usually very tenaciously in deep bunkers, by the Japanese. Attacks could range from different companies of a battalion tasked to take particular features or smaller platoon- and section-level assaults. Battalions were usually well supported by artillery and when terrain permitted very small numbers of tanks. Although much larger numbers of men were involved, the campaign resembled previous operations in Burma in being very much one for junior leaders, company, platoon and section commanders, who all in turn suffered heavy casualties.

As in earlier campaigns, the terrain presented a variety of difficult forms, mountains, hills, wet and reeking jungle, open plains and banana groves. An infantry patrol might survey a 1,000 yard area on a map and have to ascend or descend through 1,000 feet of undergrowth; on a longer march a patrol might have to climb 1,000 or 2,000 feet with full load. Even from a hilltop observation point all that might be seen was the tops of trees. On occasions officers had to lead their men on hands and knees, slithering in mud on steep slopes with their soldiers holding on to the water bottles of the men in front for cohesion. The climate added to the difficulties: although it was never really cold, temperatures could drop over 30°F between midday and midnight. Rain fell with tropical intensity, cover often being impossible or at least limited to stretched canvas or tree trunks; in favourable conditions transport delivered tents and bivouacs, in less favourable circumstances officers and men remained in wet clothing for long periods of time. Officers led patrols lasting two or three days in all weathers.

The conditions exacted a heavy sickness rate to add to battle casualties, with scrub typhus the most serious of the problems, but septic sores, fevers and heat exhaustion all added to the numbers. Officers had to ensure that NCOs and men maintained strict adherence to latrine sitings however tired soldiers might be, since infections carried by flies spread stomach disorders.

Company and battalion communication was a further problem. In dense jungle bugle calls were sometimes used, wireless often proving unreliable. All major supply, food, ammunition and when necessary water arrived by air drop. For much of their time the 2nd Dorsets' own mechanical transport was limited to ten jeeps (two with trailers), six 15 cwt trucks, a water carrier and four Bren gun carriers. Of vital importance was the battalion's Animal Transport Platoon, generally 100 mules and some ponies, together with bullocks and indigenous porters when needed.

At the outset tactics were defensive – 'boxes' as in North Africa. This soon changed to offensive defence, in the case of the 2nd Dorsets a special Guerrilla Platoon being formed to harass the Japanese and gather intelligence.

Movement was generally on foot, the longer marches preferably at night since in daytime dust was a serious hazard. In the monsoon seasons marching was often in very heavy rain. Fifteen minutes' rest was allowed in each hour of marching, with a 45-minute rest period every three hours. Officers gave priority to second-line stores for transportation in the few vehicles: blankets, bivouac tents, changes of uniform – sent on ahead to be ready for the arrival of the companies. Whenever feasible, attacks in hot weather would be mounted before 1000 hrs and arrangements made for the attacking sub-unit or units to leave their packs for later recovery.

The casualties that were suffered – after the Kohima battle the 2nd Dorsets were reduced to the equivalent of six under-strength platoons – imposed extra strains on officers and men alike, calling for more frequent routine guard and fatigue duties. Morale rose and fell with success, failure, casualties, the weather and fatigue, the examples set by officers and NCOs being all-important. In one rest period officers organised a pony and mule race meeting with trophies (fashioned out of empty tins and named after the Regiment's battle honours) for dressage and races. In another area the battalion built a temporary church dedicated to the patron saint of Dorsetshire. Of interest throughout is the noting of links maintained by the Battalion with its home county and in return the support they received from the county, and also the officers' knowledge of and respects paid to scenes of past service by the Regiment in Burma.[7] Overall, the campaign in Burma imposed a special strain on all who fought there, but particularly upon the officers. It was the Army's most testing experience in the Second World War.

A remarkable short work, *18 Platoon* by Sydney Jary, provides a full and detailed description of the duties and life of an infantry platoon commander in the final 1944–45 north-west Europe campaign, involving high-intensity fighting from Normandy into Germany.[8] In his preface Jary emphasises the two-way relationship, the influence that good NCOs and soldiers could have on their officers as well as officers' own influence on soldiers, and also the importance of the ability of regimental officers to choose good NCOs. Jary had to take over his platoon, one of the 4th Battalion, The Somerset Light Infantry, at the height of the Normandy fighting after it had very recently suffered a number of casualties. He immediately recognised a need for 'quiet firm and confident leadership', that either a lack of grip on himself, his men or the situation, or over-eager enthusiasm, or personal search for glory could let his platoon down, and that this would be reflected in the performance of the whole unit. He saw discipline and regimental pride as assets, but in real danger the young officer had to possess the hearts and minds of soldiers, who must trust his capabilities and him as a man. Soldiers would forgive one mistake but not if it was repeated. He was also acutely aware that rigid adherence to the dogmatic teaching of the Battle Schools would be fatal and, particularly in the sunken lane *bocage* country of Normandy, that imagination – was there an ambush in a *bocage* lane, a machine-gun post in a farm, a tank lurking in a village? – was essential. Jary was very fortunate in his NCOs who, after a brief cautious period of appraisal, trusted him as he trusted them. His relationship with his long-term company commander was not always harmonious, both having strong personalities. Interestingly he sets out why another company commander was a failure, that irritable officer's idea of command being supervisory and critical rather than having any concept of leading from the front. He had, apparently, been a schoolmaster in civilian life.

In battle itself Jary believed that, even as a platoon commander, he must always be proactive, seeking to dominate events, and not reactive. He found this most difficult and most frustrating in meticulously planned large-scale battles where, even if opportunity presented itself, personal initiative to exploit a local advantage was not possible.[9] He believed this was caused by over-reliance on tank and artillery support and served only to stultify individual resourcefulness. For this he blamed the Battle School teachers, regimental officers with memories of the Somme and later experience limited to Imperial security duties. Certainly Jary's platoon leader duties were, except for patrolling, in some contrast to those of Hadley in 1940 – participation in battalion and company attacks, the crossing of the Seine in storm boats, leading a platoon in single file to infiltrate an enemy position at night, clearing a village. Company attacks would take the form of two platoons advancing in extended line with bayonets, the third providing covering fire from the flank, the rear sections of the two forward platoons clearing buildings. 'Reading the battle' to dominate, Jary learnt that sustained momentum of advance, by-passing enemy machine-gun post screens, led the Germans to fear being outflanked and to withdraw.

In Holland in two different areas the battalion was twice contained by stubborn German defences and despite well-dug company positions suffered casualties from machine-gun, artillery and mortar fire. The cacophony of noise and autumnal weather further lowered morale. The temporary static conditions did, however, return to platoon commanders a measure of personal initiative in reconnaissance and patrol work to relieve the routine of 'stand to's and the organisation of feeding, two meals a day being doled out in individual mess tins. Jary, being last, was left with cold portions to add to the early morning discomfort he experienced in checking his platoon's positions, feeling dirty and with bootlaces cutting into swollen feet, with aching stomach and a foul-tasting mouth. The unit washed and shaved in water from puddles, so keeping clean and preventing lice. Slit trenches, food cans and newspapers served for latrine purposes.

By early December and with entry into Germany, Jary found the stress was beginning to tell with men and brother officers being killed, the privations and suffering of his platoon crouching in waterlogged slit trenches with cold food, and the dead of both sides decomposing on the battlefields, but with the still urgent need to remain confident and enthusiastic and to overcome exhaustion after a battle. Personal and regimental pride stiffened his morale, as did the moral as well as the physical support of their linked artillery unit officers. To relieve the stress, brief periods of leave in Belgium were granted, but January cold followed in which men in forward standing patrols suffered severely from exposure, and attacks had to be mounted on snow-covered ground. With few exceptions in these final weeks of the war, fighting for the battalion became very much a case of one or two companies against German companies, company commanders being much dependent on patrol reports. In one company attack Jary and his platoon advanced three miles in a morning; brushing aside German opposition, he commented that it was classic light infantry: 'I like to think Sir John Moore smiled on it.' After crossing the Rhine in Buffalo amphibious vehicles, the 4th Somersets became the infantry attached to an armoured column, an infantry company carried either on the tanks in *Kangaroo* armoured troop carriers or in vehicles being required to clear enemy artillery and machine-gun road blocks in small sharp battles. The battalion's final battle was one of night street-fighting in Bremen, platoons and sections clearing suburban houses.

Summing up, Jary admitting to an undistinguished school career, found that his unexpected ability to lead often frightened men into battle gave him a new-found confidence and trained him to think ahead and plan; but it also taught him that success can only be achieved with a reciprocal loyalty to subordinates. The views in this summary would be shared by many regimental officers, Regular and wartime.

In the course of the war the basic structure of infantry battalions was changed. Individual battalions received a sub-machine carbine, the unreliable Sten gun and a shoulder-fire Projector Infantry Anti-Tank (PIAT) weapon launching an armour-piercing grenade, all at company level. At battalion level anti-tank platoons were developed, being eventually equipped with 6 pdr. or 17 pdr. anti-tank guns. Several Infantry Training Centres, providing instruction for both officers and soldiers, were established and greatly improved efficiency, as did infantry battle-school courses run by divisions, artillery officers' courses and the senior regimental officers' course at Warminster. As already noted, some instruction was found to be too dogmatic and rigid in practice. Prior to the Normandy landings a combined operations training centre opened at Inverary in Scotland.

Tank officers' special armoured warfare training covered driving and maintenance, tank gunnery, radio, tactics and the command of the crew of the commander's own tank and the troop of three tanks. As successive models appeared – the *Matilda*, *Valentine*, *Crusader* and *Grant* tanks – officers had to relearn and train for each type, but success and superiority really only came with the arrival of the *Sherman* tank in the 7th Armoured Division.[10] The basic training in armoured OCTUs served only to perpetuate the armoured regiments' preference to try to fight its own operations rather than plan the all-arms battle; the lesson was long in the learning curve.

Royal Artillery officers fired a very wide variety of guns in the war. The work horse was the 25 pdr. field gun, but other battlefield weapons included 4.5-inch, 6-inch and later 8-inch howitzers, the 60 pdr. gun and on occasion still the old First World War updated

18 pdr. Anti-aircraft guns included the Bofors 40 mm, the 3-inch and 3.7-inch pieces; anti-tank weaponry included the 3.7-inch gun in an anti-tank role. Coastal artillery had perhaps the widest variety of guns, mainly naval 4.7-inch and 9.2-inch guns. In 1942 the *Priest* self-propelled gun appeared, providing a new dimension of tactical artillery support. Throughout the war aircraft spotting steadily developed in efficiency.

Royal Engineers found themselves with an ever-increasing variety of duties. In North Africa, Field Survey units had to lay out beacons fashioned from petrol drums. Their normal routine work of assault engineering, clearance of mines and of obstacles, demolitions, the laying of mines and bridge building became extended to specialised construction of roads, airfields, rail and water transport, oil pipelines and ports both small and large, the most important being participation in the vast artificial port of the Normandy landings. Specialist equipment ranged from bridge-laying and flail tanks to bulldozers and the enormously successful Bailey bridge.

Officers of the Royal Corps of Signals had to become very much more technically competent with more complex and (in the early years of the war) doubtfully reliable radio. There followed landline systems, theatre wireless systems and in the Far East very long-range radio. On the battlefield there were formation command networks, and at a more mundane level on occasions despatch riders, heliograph in some theatres, and even pigeons. Two (later reduced to one) special Royal Signals OCTUs were established to train officers. Intelligence Corps officers' battlefield duties included work with the Royal Signals in the often very hazardous 'Y' Service interception of enemy battlefield signals with also air photograph interpretation, questioning of prisoners of war, intelligence staff duties and field security.[11] Other officers served at Bletchley Park and in a variety of specialist duties ranging from topographical intelligence, colonial and port security, to work with the Special Operations Executive.

The wartime Glider Pilot Regiment and its successor the Army Air Corps took army officers into the air, not only in troop-carrying gliders but also in light aircraft. A few Regular officers opted for Special Forces – the Long Range Desert Groups, the Special Air Service Regiment and the Commandos (at the time Army as well as Royal Marines).

Combat staff work often suffered from the absence of pre-war experience in handling large formations and the rapid wartime promotion of young Regular officers into appointments for which they lacked sufficient experience and training. Logistic staff work was, however, often of very high quality, keeping combat units, far from even their forward bases and even further from Britain, supplied with food, water, ammunition and stores.

The expansion of the ATS, extending in 1943 to conscription of women and a peak 1943 total of over 200,000 of all ranks, greatly increased the number of women officers. At first these were poorly trained or totally untrained, selected for their willingness and social standing. Change followed with the opening in February 1941 of a women's OCTU, retraining courses for officers already serving and staff training, first at a special college and later in an ATS wing at the Staff College. In 1941 the ATS was placed under the Army Act and officers received commissions. The pre-war rank titles – Subalterns, Commanders and Controllers – were still retained but the badges of rank became the same as those of male officers.[12] A mild disciplinary code was set out, only women officers having the power to discipline women soldiers.

The officer–soldier relationship in the war was complex.[13] The conscript soldiers who came to fill most regiments, Regular and Territorial, were now better educated and brought up with radio and cinema. Many came from areas which had suffered economic hardship in the inter-war years, and some had been influenced by the class confrontation rhetoric of the political left, an influence that was to continue with press articles and with politically liberal educational material supplied by the Army Bureau of Current Affairs and soldiers' education schemes. The lack of military success in the first three years of the war served to increase the doubt, at times cynicism, of rank and file towards the officers, especially if duties were seen as pointless or simply designed to assert privilege or authority; certain officer privileges, particularly in respect of the use of transport for recreation, had to be withdrawn. The sharpest criticism of officers was levelled by soldier prisoners in Japanese camps where some officers appear to have secured privileges from their captors. Humour and soldiers' songs were sardonic. The majority of officers were wise enough to appreciate their soldiers' mood and take care to explain not only what had to be done but also why, in the terms of the social historian Morris Janowitz, an adjustment in the 'basis of authority and discipline towards more persuasive methods of control'.[14] Some wartime OCTU officers, however, held exaggerated ideas of their status and showed little concern for their men's welfare. It was therefore fortunate that in these years the Army was not faced with huge attrition battles comparable with those of 1914–18; units withdrawn from battle had much smaller percentages of casualties than in the First World War. The development of Army welfare services and perhaps above all the return, from October 1942, of military success in the Western War together with the personal charisma and style of Field-Marshal Montgomery restored the confidence of soldiers in themselves and in their officers. The Eastern War, with its initial catastrophes not relieved by any epic evacuation, was a different matter. The hardships of climate, terrain and disease, the long periods soldiers had to serve without home leave, the apparently irrelevant purpose of the campaign summed up by soldiers as 'who wants Burma anyway' and the 'Forgotten Army' feeling all created a resentful attitude, especially against officers in headquarter staffs believed to be enjoying the privileges of colonial society.[15] Certainly all approached the war with the belief that after the war

British society had to change, a view in some cases reinforced by their experience of inadequate officers.[16]

Apart from cases, mostly in France in 1940, when regiments were simply overrun by superior forces, there were only four cases of serious discipline breakdown, with officers losing control of their soldiers. Two were in battle, two on lines of communication. In 1940 soldiers of a Regular Army infantry battalion attacking a hill ridge on the Sudan–Ethiopia border panicked and fled, a rout apparently occasioned by Italian aircraft bombing soldiers on a bare rock hillside and the explosion of an ammunition dump.[17] Later in the same year, immediately prior to final collapse and surrender at Singapore, officers lost control of ill-trained men mostly just off troopships, who went on rampages. The lines of communication incidents were both the result of poor quality officer leadership. In 1942, 200 soldiers in transit in South Africa refused to board a transport ship, claiming the ship was insanitary and unsafe; thirty men were convicted of mutiny by a court-martial. In 1943, at the height of the Salerno landing battle, soldiers recovered from wounds, mainly Scottish, refused to join English regiments to which they had been hurriedly drafted, saying they would only return to combat duties in their original regiments where their loyalty and pride rested, other regiments being unacceptably inferior.[18]

Religious belief continued to play a part in the lives of officers and soldiers, though not to the same extent as in 1914–18. The mind-numbing enormity and huge casualties of trench warfare of that war had eroded the faith of many. Obligatory church parades were abolished, but substantial numbers continued to attend piled drums services in the field, and formation and unit Chaplains were appreciated.

It should also be noted that among the officers – and soldiers – serving in the Army were numbers from the Irish Free State, volunteers with a clearer realisation of the evil regimes they were fighting than their government in Dublin.

In conclusion the Second World War marked major changes in the recruitment of officers, their training, their relationship with soldiers and, by the end of the war, the public's perception of the officer.[19] In the early part of the war the Army, particularly officers, came under much public criticism for alleged injustices and out-of-date views. But the later military successes, the known aims of commanders and regimental officers to plan actions in which the lives of men would not be risked unnecessarily, soon restored much public confidence. The Army and its officers received the thanks of a grateful, if war-weary, nation.

NOTES

1   131 (Queens) Brigade, composed of the 1/5th, 1/6th and 1/7th Battalions of the Queen's Royal Regiment. Regular officers of the regiment served in the battalions.

2   Shepperd, *Sandhurst*, xi.

3   Peter Hadley, *Third Class to Dunkirk: A Worm's Eye View of the B.E.F. 1940* (London, Hollis and Carter, 1944).

4   Numerous works describe the North African fighting. This work, concerned with the conditions in which officers carried out their duties in battle and at other times, found three histories to be of special value. These are Dudley Clarke, *Eleventh at War* (London, Michael Joseph, 1952); J.A. Pitt-Rivers, *The Story of the Royal Dragoons* (London, William Clowes, n.d.); and Adrian Gilbert, *The Imperial War Museum Book of the Desert War, 1940–42* (London, Sidgwick and Jackson, 1992).

5   Pitt-Rivers, *Royal Dragoons*, 37.

6   Lieutenant-Colonel O.G.W. White, *Straight on for Tokyo* (Aldershot, Gale and Polden, 1948) and information given to me by a colleague and friend who served with the 2nd Dorsets, the late A.D. Pryke-Howard, in conversations in the early 1960s.

7   White, *Straight on for Tokyo*, 272, notes that an appeal for cigarettes made to the county in February 1945 resulted by the following May in the arrival in Burma of 131,000 cigarettes and 83 pounds of tobacco. Until these arrived soldiers had been making cigarettes from used tea leaves dipped in rum.

8 Sydney Jary, *18 Platoon* (Bristol, Sydney Jary, 1998). Cadets at Sandhurst in the turn of the century years were required to read this work. Also interesting as a contrast is Raleigh Trevelyan's account of life as a platoon commander in the Italian campaign on the Anzio beach-head. The strain of being contained in trenches on the beachhead by the Germans with frequent heavy artillery, grenade and machine-gun bombardments and many casualties, the fact that his NCOs were not of the same quality as those of Jary, and that Trevelyan himself was both a very sensitive and a very angry young man, give his account a bitter flavour, even including his period of convalescence after being wounded. Raleigh Trevelyan, *The Fortress: A Diary of Anzio and After* (London, Collins, 1956).

9 Jary's language describing this frustration is illuminating: 'To me the preparation for these battles assumed the demented proportions of a Kafka like nightmare ballet, in which the anonymous "they" ordained that "we" must perform a choreographed ritual *danse macabre*'. *18 Platoon*, 19.

10 The numbering is confusing; this division was essentially the second armoured division planned immediately prior to the outbreak of war.

11 The value of the 'Y' service in North Africa has not always been appreciated. General Montgomery's chief intelligence officer, 'Bill' Williams, told the author that in North Africa, if they did not already know from Y Service work material sent them from Bletchley, they considered that they had failed.

12 Bidwell, *The Women's Royal Army Corps*, iv–vii. Chief Controller, Senior Controller and Controller equated to Major-General, Brigadier and Colonel; Chief Commander, Senior Commander and Junior Commander to Lieutenant-Colonel, Major and Captain; Subaltern and Second Subaltern to Lieutenant and Second Lieutenant.

13 Jeremy A. Crang, 'The British Army as a social institution 1939–45', in Hew Strachan (Editor) *The British Army: Manpower and Society into the Twenty-first Century* (London, Cass, 2000) provides useful insights into the officers of the Second World War Army.

14 The brigade commander of 131 (Queens) Brigade of the 7th Armoured Division was generally greeted by boos when he visited the Bermondsey recruited 1/6th Queens – but he deliberately took no

offence and his orders were obeyed: Lieutenant-General Sir Lashmer Whistler, the brigade commander concerned, in conversation with the author in 1963; Morris Janowitz, *The Professional Soldier* (Glencoe, Illinois Free Press, 1960), 8–12, quoted in Patrick Mileham, 'Fifty years of British Army officership 1960–2010, Part I: Retrospective', in *Defence and Security Analysis*, Vol. 20, No. 1, 70, March 2004.

15 Barnett, *Britain and Her Army*, 464, quoting from Field-Marshal Slim's *Defeat into Victory*, notes how, when during the Burma campaign he asked a soldier what his particular duty was, he would receive a reply 'Four and Two' or 'Three and Ten' – the number of years and months the soldier had served in the Far East.

16 'It's our bloody turn now, your lot's out, our lot's in,' chorused soldiers at an immediate post-war garrison concert, their officers sitting in the front rows. *Coming Home*, BBC Radio 4, 12 May 2005. The phrase 'the officer class' was common currency of the political left at this time.

17 Anthony Mockler, *Haile Selassie's War* (Oxford University Press, 1984), 278. The event took place at Gallabat on 6th November 1940. The name of the regiment need not be recorded here; it later recovered its reputation.

18 Saul David, *Mutiny at Salerno: An Injustice Exposed* (London, Brassey's, 1994) describes this incident.

19 Wartime government-inspired films showed officers in a good light; most notable were those starring David Niven who had been a Sandhurst-trained Regular officer.

CHAPTER 13

THE OFFICER IN THE FIRST
POST-WAR YEARS

The first forty-five years after the ending of the Second World War found the British Army in the unusual situation of being the lead Service in peacetime, overtaking the Royal Navy, with a still substantial Army strength of 440,000 seven years after the end of the war. Initially there appeared no maritime threat, and when in the 1960s one appeared the United States Navy was considered to be the main safeguard, with the Royal Navy only in a supporting role. The Army, conversely, found itself with two demanding roles – initially the army of occupation in Germany that very quickly had to turn itself into Britain's contribution to the NATO force shielding Western Europe (an armoured force-driven role), and at the same time a counter-insurgency infantry-driven force engaged in military operations arising from withdrawal from Empire. A conflict fitting neither pattern was the Korean War of 1950–52, more akin to the Italian campaign of 1943–45 or even the 1914–18 Western Front.[1]

This chapter is concerned with events up to the early 1960s which were fought by an Army largely composed of conscript soldiers, led by officers of whom some were Regular and the juniors mostly from two-year National Service, a number of whom found military life enjoyable and later transferred to either better paid short-service or full Regular commissions.[2]

With the independence of India and the ever-increasing costs of recruiting, maintaining and retaining trained soldiers came, inevitably, massive reductions in the size of the Army. First to go were the Second Battalions of infantry regiments in the late 1940s, followed by amalgamations of a number of cavalry and infantry regiments, a process extending to the 1960s. Infantry amalgamations, with regiments being so closely associated with counties or regions, were viewed by officers with mixed feelings. To an ambitious minority the grouping of regiments and occasional cross-posting provided new career development opportunities; to the majority the changes were viewed with weary resignation as inevitable, while others saw the changes as the work of War Office 'rats [which] would hardly be too strong a term who were nibbling away at the infantry regimental tradition'.[3] In some cases the amalgamations and groupings preserved the elite status of the regiments concerned, for example the formation of the Royal Green Jackets; in other regiments amalgamations linked equals, in yet others regiments were ill-matched in style and the amalgamations were initially difficult. In two cases, one Scottish and one English, regiments opted for total disbandment. Some amalgamations created the 'big regiment' while others simply combined two, or in one case three, regiments; after the end of National Service depots became grouped, many in consequence being closed. For officers and senior NCOs who had devoted years of service to their regiments the process was often difficult, at times emotional, with cherished emblems, customs, regimental occasions and territorial links weakened or lost. Many officers left the Service. For the Royal Artillery, the Royal Engineers and the numerous service corps no painful cap-badge change was necessary, overall reductions simply being in the number of units.[4]

Following the independence of India, four of the ten Indian Army Gurkha regiments were transferred to the British Army, their officers now familiarising themselves with their soldiers' homeland at a recruiting centre in Nepal. The regiments were, however, never posted to Germany (nor, later, Northern Ireland) and officers' career prospects tended to suffer from the absence of these experiences.

For the first time in peacetime women officers and soldiers were included in the Army; after various interim arrangements the Women's Royal Army Corps was formally established in 1949 as a non-combatant corps under military law and with a stiff selection procedure for officers. The Corps' officers now had the same rank titles as male officers and the Corps School of Instruction included an Officers Training Wing and a Cadet Training Wing. Battalions and regiments until 1961 retained the same basic paper establishment, infantry battalions having four rifle companies, a support company with machine-gun, mortar and anti-tank platoons and a headquarters company. For different theatre roles there would be minor changes. From 1955 onwards the very different .762 mm self-loading rifle began to be issued, replacing the Lee Enfield, its machine gun version replacing both the Bren and the Vickers guns. In the artillery the 25 pdr. remained, supplemented by some regiments equipped with the new 105 mm pack howitzer.

Post-war commitments in Europe included minor roles in Trieste, Greece and Austria with a major and growing role in Germany. Trieste required a two-battalion garrison until 1954. In Greece support for the government against a Communist uprising involved initially a division, scaled down to a brigade in 1949, and finally one battalion prior to withdrawal in 1950. Neither of these commitments was pleasant, the units not being well received. The reverse was true for the brigade of occupation in Austria which extended a warm welcome to the Army until withdrawal in 1955, and gave officers an especially happy posting.

Germany was to prove the major strategic commitment, the occupation garrison and emergency food relief duties of 1945 having to change rapidly to a fighting force in face of the perceived Soviet menace. In 1947 a second British Army of the Rhine (BAOR) was established, with an infantry division, an armoured division and a parachute brigade; in 1951 a second armoured division and a Corps Headquarters arrived, with a third division in 1952 and a fourth a little later. There was to follow over the next forty years a succession of formation and deployment plan changes, controversy over whether the best controllable size of a fighting formation should be a division or a brigade, and an eventual overall reduction to three divisions.

For the regimental officers, military life in Germany in the 1950s was a monotonous cycle of training new batches of conscripts in ill-fitting battle-dress uniforms, ceremonial, exercises and field firing on a number of German ranges, and introduction to the possible conditions of nuclear warfare, officers reading Geiger counters, calculating plumes of radioactivity and adjusting to protection kit uncomfortable for all but especially difficult for anyone in command. Compensation for officers took the form of a useful overseas living allowance, many and varied sporting activities, and opportunities for tourism. In Berlin the Soviet threat, particularly during the 1948–49 blockade when the British element of the garrison was increased to a brigade, was real and actual. On two occasions battalions had to be deployed in fighting order to face a Soviet general's threat to areas in the British Occupied Zone.

The one big conventional, in 21st century terms symmetrical, conflict in this period was the Korean War of 1950–53. The conflict arising from North Korea's assault upon the South involved all arms of the Army but most essentially the infantry who suffered heavy casualties. The terrain posed particular problems for commanders, with groups of pudding-bowl shaped hills, some as high as 1,000 feet, paddy fields, swamps and poor roads and tracks; tanks could only be deployed in small numbers, if at all. The climate was severe, especially in winter, affecting not only men but equipment.

The first battalions to arrive were under strength and had to be reinforced by companies from other regiments; they possessed mortar and machine-gun platoons, anti-tank weaponry being left to the Americans. The Royal Artillery supported with 25 pdr. guns and 4.2-inch mortars; the tank regiments, only one at any time, possessed some of the new and highly successful *Centurion* tanks together with the older *Cromwells*. The early operations, defence of the Pusan area and then advance northwards, were straightforward battalion and company tasks, patrolling and ambushing with later attacks; in the advance infantrymen were mounted on tanks, carried in vehicles or marched. With the arrival of winter and the entry of the Chinese into the war, fighting became very much more testing for regimental officers. Swarms of Chinese in successive waves would mount attack after attack, on occasions as many as sixteen in a few hours, regardless of casualties. The attack would begin at night and be accompanied by the clamour of trumpets and yells. The Chinese, well armed with sub-machine carbines and light mortars, would seek to outflank units which were often obliged to hold too wide a frontage and, if newly arrived, in areas not adequately protected by wire and minefields. Ammunition supply was some-times inadequate, fighting culminating in bayonets or fists in the trenches. Companies, and at the Imjin a battalion, the 1st Gloucesters, were overrun. By the summer of 1951 the Chinese had been held, the capital, Seoul, had been retaken and the conflict had become static. Battalions manned a forward line with one or two companies, but behind this the other companies lived in shelters half dug, half wooden sided and roofed, eating in relative comfort and able to enjoy sports and concerts. Officers' Messes even held guest nights.

The return of colder weather saw further Chinese mass attacks now supported by heavy artillery bombardments. During these attacks officers and NCOs would try to maintain cohesion, direct fire, control ammunition supply and help the wounded. Units in defence engaged in active patrolling, success depending on accurate navigation among hills and minefields of the patrol commander, usually a Subaltern, with also periodic attacks on Chinese positions, sometimes charges up hills, sometimes into deep-dug Chinese tunnels and shelters. Fortunately in this winter, proper clothing and body protection tunics had arrived. This pattern of fighting continued until the July 1953 cease-fire.

In all phases the war was very much one for company and platoon commanders, who led with valour and skill, receiving many gallantry awards, a number of them posthumous.[5] Regimental pride was an all-important factor. Officer casualties were heavy; other battalions and units lost only slightly fewer killed. Some officers taken by the Chinese were tortured, and all were subjected to attempts at ideological brainwashing. In captivity, unless officers were separated from rank and file, they worked to restore morale among soldiers by giving them duties such as latrine digging, exercising to keep fit and developing a spirit of comradeship and optimism.[6]

Officers also faced an unusual difficulty in 1950 when units were reinforced by the recall of Second World War reservists, all five years older, uprooted from their civilian occupations, and until actual front-line deployment often unenthusiastic. The Commanding Officer of one battalion – before he was killed – had written some 400 letters concerned with individual soldiers' welfare.[7]

The 'Cold War' commitments were one side of the Army's work; the other side concerned the ending of Empire, to use the *post-hoc propter-hoc* term 'decolonisation'. Here, if not always so at the outset, the military came to be used not as an instrument for the retention of Imperial power but as a force to ensure withdrawal would be orderly and the successor regime acceptable to Britain, a policy generally successful but failing spectacularly in Palestine and Aden. The political issues and also the British command structures and policies varied greatly; this work is simply concerned with the roles of regimental officers in the different situations.

The immediate post-August 1945 scene required a British military intervention in the Netherlands East Indies where nationalists were holding hostage Britons and others who had been prisoners of the Japanese, their release being secured only after a pitched battle. The Indian sub-continent, particularly in the big cities, was in ferment, at first with nationalist mobs and mutinous sailors, later with the inter-communal conflict of hysterical crowds engaged in genocidal killing and looting. Infantry battalions had to try to hold factions apart, if necessary firing upon riot leaders, and later collecting corpses by the score or even hundreds for burial, a role that ended only with the independence of India and Pakistan in August 1947. The last years of British rule in Palestine saw a war-weary army, with units under strength, trying to cope with a problem lasting to this day. A well-armed Jewish uprising marked by vicious ferocity opened in October 1945. The ferocity was deliberately designed to provoke the Army into over-reaction, and officers had as a priority to maintain restraint amongst themselves and their soldiers. Violence steadily escalated with sabotage attacks on the railway, government offices, military barracks and groups of or individual soldiers. Officers led troops in crowd dispersal, raids, searches for individuals, arms, time bombs and booby traps, in the pursuit of gangs and in the big urban cordon and search operations. In Tel Aviv the operation involved eighteen regiments, an inner and outer cordon, house-to-house searches, screening and the provision of tents for women and children for four days, together with arrangements for food, the sick and refuse collection. In late 1947 the form of violence changed to being one principally of Jew against Arab; British efforts became limited to trying to secure life and prepare for evacuation, which was completed at the end of June 1948.

Earlier in 1948 the Communist-inspired insurrection in Malaya had opened, involving British units in a conflict to last nine years; at its height fourteen British battalions, an artillery regiment, two armoured-car regiments, eight Gurkha and four Malay battalions (both of the latter with British officers) had to be deployed. The terrain favoured the insurgents and gave battalions, now mostly National Service men led by many National Service platoon officers, special difficulty, with thick jungle or, on the slopes of the central mountain spine of the Malay peninsula, bamboo forests, numerous rivers and swamps requiring men to march thigh-deep in water. The jungle was dark for men on foot, and noisy from bird and animal life. Over a period of time it could have a depressing effect, especially during evening rain. The heat, producing body sores, the mosquitoes, leeches and hornets in the swamps all added further to discomfort.

The campaign was a challenge for company and platoon commanders.[8] At first companies would be sent to the edge of the jungle to protect plantations and, later, villages. The company commander would work closely with the local administrative and police officers and send patrols, usually led by a Subaltern, into the jungle to look for insurgent movement, supply routes or camps, and to prepare ambushes in which officers and men would have to lie perhaps for two days.[9] Patrols would be out for two, three or more days; at the outset these were of company size but quickly reduced with experience to twelve or fewer. Carrying stores and ammunition, these patrols would move silently, navigating by compass, cooking in the dark and, when not hiding up in an ambush, sleeping under a rigged mosquito net. Sometimes company-sized operations, cordons, sweeps or landings from the sea were mounted, supported by aircraft and artillery and leading to brisk engagements at insurgent camps. When the policy of villageisation was introduced battalions would cordon a large area to ensure all inhabitants, perhaps 30,000–40,000, would be obliged to live in a group of villages. They would build wire and ditch protections, man checkpoints and search workers in case they were carrying rice supplies for insurgents on their persons or on their bicycles. As the campaign developed units were deployed to deny any food supplies for the insurgents, and helicopters became available to lift detachments into the jungle for surprise attacks. Armoured cars guarded food convoys, and SAS teams were dropped into the jungle. Regiments served in Malaya on three-year tours, but there was constant turnover of personnel. The insurgents fought with determination; among the 359 British soldiers (plus a further 159 Gurkhas) killed were 70 officers.

Suppression of the largely Kikuyu ethnic Mau Mau uprising in Kenya from 1952 to 1956 was on a smaller scale, involving at its peak six British Army battalions and six battalions of King's African Rifles with British officers.[10] For battalion officers, as in Malaya, the immediate task was the security of settlers' farmsteads; this was followed by operations generally directed by company commanders working with the local police, administration officials and sometimes Royal Air Force officers. To begin with, these operations took the form of either cordons and searches of particular areas, or patrols, lying up from three to five days in silence, heavy rain and near-freezing temperatures and usually led by a Subaltern, in the dense, prickly undergrowth and bamboo forests of the Aberdare range. These were tasked either to hunt down a Mau Mau gang or to prepare ambushes on Mau Mau supply routes. Patrol leaders would slowly have to hack their way through the forest, navigating by compass and using maps not always clear on detail; whenever possible movement also had to be silent. The altitude could affect men, leaving them breathless and out of humour; wild animals, especially buffalo, rhinoceros and elephant, added to the hazards.

Later, when more troops were available, one or two battalion-sized sweeps into Kikuyuland and the Aberdares were made, detachments were deployed guarding the labour force building roads into the Aberdares, others were at work training a Kikuyu home guard organisation, and a number of officers were engaged in intelligence work. The last series of sweep operations in the Aberdares, on Mount Kenya and in the Rift Valley, were on even bigger scales, one involving nine battalions, aircraft and mortars. Thereafter battalions were given specific areas to clear and control on their own initiative. The capital, Nairobi, presented a particular problem, one battalion having to be kept in the city for urban patrolling and security; in April 1954 a massive cordon and search operation involving four British battalions and one King's African Rifles battalion was mounted. The four-year campaign cost the lives of five officers, one being a Lieutenant-Colonel ambushed by the battalion he commanded.[11]

The EOKA uprising in Cyprus from 1955 to 1959 presented regimental officers with new challenges and problems, the most difficult being the cold ferocity and determination of the guerrillas and the whipped up, venomous, often wild hatred displayed by urban crowds, women spitting and school children being used to throw stones or use catapults against troops. The Army's units, at their peak over twenty-five including artillery and armoured regiments in infantry roles, were committed to two different types of operations. In urban areas, in support of the police, units would be deployed in the traditional box pattern but with a police recorder by the side of the platoon commander, one soldier equipped with a tear gas projector and another with a coloured dye projector, to prove a deterrent when faced with almost hysterical women demonstrators. Troops wore steel helmets and face shields, used dustbin lids as personal shields and charged with batons. They were ordered to be courteous and fair. Officers generally succeeded in ensuring good behaviour despite the intense provocation, though on occasions, notably after the murder of a sergeant's wife, suspects were roughly handled. Curfews were imposed and had to be enforced, but soldiers were targets for grenade attacks, snipers and ambushes throughout.

Besides the control of street rioting, officers had to lead detachments of troops in sweeps, some of platoon or even section size, to pursue individuals or man a road block. Other sweeps were of company or battalion size, with several major sweeps into the Troodos mountains or suburbs of Nicosia involving several battalions supported by helicopters. The Troodos were natural guerrilla country, bitterly cold in winter, and at first when intelligence was insufficient the sweeps achieved meagre results; by 1958, however, control had been largely reasserted. In the streets troops became needed to keep rival Greek and Turkish rioters apart. Intelligence officers were increasingly involved in security, particularly the illegal entry of weapons, and the Royal Signals were occupied with the jamming of inflammatory broadcasts from Athens. Seven officers lost their lives in the five years of violence.

All these commitments were finished or greatly reduced by 1962, the end of National Service. The several Middle East commitments opened with the National Service army, but were to continue further into the 1960s in Aden, as described in Chapter 14.

Unrest and rioting in Egypt from 1945 onwards led to the withdrawal of British troops to the Canal Zone where in 1951 a guerrilla campaign of sniping, ambushing of trains and bombing required officers to deploy themselves and their men in guarding essential installations, protecting civilians and providing dock labour. These operations concluded with a company attack supported by tanks on an insurgent stronghold. Sixteen infantry battalions, seven artillery and two regiments of armour were involved. The 1956 Anglo-French Suez operation saw conventional British brigade-sized air and sea landing assaults on Port Said that met weak opposition. From 1956 onwards, two or three battalions supported by artillery were at work in support of local levies in the Aden hinterland areas engaged in low-level counter-insurgency, skirmishes, sweeps, surrounding of small rebel strongholds and mobile flag marches. The mountainous terrain, involving patrols climbing ridges on occasions over 2,000 feet high in intense heat, provided testing work for junior officers. The years also saw one- or two-unit level commitments of a minor nature in other areas of the Middle East – Aqaba from 1949 to 1957, Sharjah and Bahrain in 1955, Oman in 1957 and Kuwait in 1961.

Elsewhere, small-scale internal security duties involving British battalions arose in Hong Kong, Zanzibar, the Caribbean, British Guiana, the Bahamas and Jamaica. In British Honduras relief work after a hurricane provided one battalion with an unusual medical role, coping with 600 casualties and 4,500 inoculations per day for several days.[12]

From 1951 on, movement of infantry units was increasingly by transport aircraft, deputed officers being responsible for the 'chalk', the soldiers travelling in any one flight. At home, officers and men were deployed unloading perishable cargo from ships during a 1950 London dock strike, and were used again during a 1953 petrol strike.

In 1947 Sandhurst was reopened, under the new title of the Royal Military Academy, reflecting its new character as the heir of Woolwich as well as its own history, and the abolition of fees reflecting the post-war Labour government. Cadets entered straight after school, aged eighteen, and from the start the Army sought to mould their characters into concepts of integrity, loyalty and duty. No great store was set on academic abilities, ample opportunities being available for the more average boy who showed acceptance of the concepts. A very few, carefully selected, were sent to universities for Arts or Languages degrees after Sandhurst. Its military training became markedly more professional than before 1939; on commissioning cadets could join regiments on active service and hold their own.[13] The academic departments largely continued work that had come to a stop when the cadet left his school, with languages (including Russian), mathematics, science and contemporary affairs in proportion appropriate to a cadet's choice of arm, but in 1965 it was still possible for the majority of cadets to spend two years at the Academy with no mention of the word NATO in their academic studies. The atmosphere was inward-looking, at times backward-looking. Despite the Labour government's wish to encourage entry from the ranks, the Academy's style was set by pre-war officers and the high percentage of the privately educated Public School boys who were unashamedly favoured by elite regiments in the Academy's arcane choice of arm procedures;[14] it was also generally reflected in the selection of cadet Under Officers. Great emphasis was placed on sport. As late as 1967 cadets leaving the Academy to go into Camberley were required to wear brown trilby hats. Academic work laid much importance on study of the interwar years, seen to be a lesson in the dangers of being unprepared. The early 1960s, though, saw a few developments foreshadowing the later moves to professionalism and the desirability to recruit cadets from all backgrounds. From 1947 leadership began to be taught with battlefield precepts – discipline, courage, loyalty, pride and endurance drawing on examples from the past – it being assumed that all cadets were, or were acquiring, the character of a gentleman. In the early 1960s an academic, John Adair, introduced Academy's first conceptual professional studies of leadership with his three circles: the task, the team, the leader, a managerial approach not always appreciating the particular character qualities needed for battlefield leadership. Professor Boswell (a former Woolwich teacher) and Peter Young (a retired brigadier) launched the Academy's highly successful studies in military history. Another academic, Philip Warner, appreciating the increasing interface between military and political situations and the better level of education of soldiers who now expected clear direction rather than the authority of social class from their officers, introduced studies in communication, later to become a component of all Sandhurst courses. Successive remarkable Guards Warrant Officers and NCOs administered a much firmer discipline than that of the pre-war years and set cadets examples of professional soldiering. Equally important, both for the character development of the cadet and for his future responsibilities for ensuring volunteer soldiers remained content in their service, was the inspiration and momentum given to vacation adventure training by an exceptional commandant, Major-General John Mogg, in the mid-1960s. However, it was still possible for another commandant at the end of the 1960s to claim that Sandhurst was the last finishing school for gentlemen left in Europe, and officers firmly believed that their integrity and concept of service reflected all that was best in human nature, giving them a natural authority. The few cadets from working-class backgrounds quietly adjusted to their new lifestyle, and most cadets enjoyed the experience of growing up the Army way.

The Sandhurst course became extended from eighteen months to two years in 1959. It contrasted with the much shorter courses run for National Service, and later Short Service or Short (16 year) Regular Commission officer cadets. Admission to Sandhurst and the two (later only one) officer-cadet schools, Eaton Hall in Cheshire until 1958 and Mons in Aldershot, followed the passing of three days of practical and interviewed tests at the Regular Commissions Board (RCB), the eventual successor (without the psychiatrists) to the wartime and immediate post-war War Office Selection Boards (WOSBs).[15] While the tests were conducted with strict fairness, advantage inevitably lay with boys who had had the opportunity of exercising some form of authority, either as a prefect or games captain at schools, or during a period of service in the ranks; the latter was not a requirement for Sandhurst applicants except in the Brigade of Guards. The style of the RCB reflected its criteria – whether a candidate will 'fit in' as well as an assessment of his capabilities. Regular commission candidates were generally (there were exceptions) expected to have five School Certificate credits or later Higher Certificate of GCE A-level passes, though for short service the A-levels were not required. The practice grew up of cadets with only O-level passes going through the Mons course and then applying to convert to Regular commissions with their commanding officer's support; also in the 1960s, following the contemporary expansion of university education, an increasing number of graduates sought commissions but were unwilling to attend a two-year school-leaver-level Sandhurst course. Sandhurst numbers began to fall from their early 1960s peak of over 1,000 cadets; further change became inevitable.

The need for officers in an army now mechanised and armoured led to the opening of an Army Sixth Form College at Welbeck in Nottinghamshire. Seventy-five boys per year with promising school careers were taken for a two-year Higher Certificate (later a GCE A-level) course in science subjects, after which they progressed firstly to Sandhurst, a very few then moving on to Cambridge and the remainder to a degree course at the Royal Military College of Science at Shrivenham, near Swindon, after which they joined one of the technical corps. Welbeck boys generally came from a much wider social background than the rest of the Sandhurst entry and found some social discrimination.

Of increasing importance in the developing professionalism were courses offered by the Arms Schools, perhaps the most important being the School of Infantry at Warminster. Cadets leaving Sandhurst either immediately or very soon after attended Arms School courses; other courses for particular regimental appointments or tours of duty – jungle warfare, intelligence, anti-tank – followed in an officer's career in whose development the Annual Confidential Report played a key role. Specialisation in any subject other than that needed within the regiment was, however, seen as harmful to career development. An inadequate system for junior officers' education of periodic essays, and preparation for the competitive entry examination for the Staff College – one private institution ran a correspondence course – was thought quite sufficient for their further education. Entry was regulated by quotas from each branch of the Army; the eight examinations included three on tactics and one each on Administration and Morale, Military Law, Military History, Military Science and Current Affairs. The course itself, however, was strictly orthodox, concentrating on the teaching of staff procedures and providing little opportunity for original thinking. In sum the officer in the 1945–60 period was generally well trained but poorly educated for his profession.

Officers' mess life changed with the arrival and turnover of National Service officers, with the more stuffy practices of some regiments forgotten except by a very few. Many officers still saw command of their regiment as their military career aim; for the ambitious, entry to the Staff College was essential. Agreeable postings with the Territorial Army, in embassies and from the 1950s in NATO headquarters, provided variety. Lieutenant-Colonels not earmarked for promotion could 'soldier on' in a Major's duties on a special list and slightly reduced pay, but for many with the all-important boarding school allowances for their children, until they were fifty-five. Help was available in finding post-service jobs, many still working for the Army in administrative posts as Retired Officers. Short-service commissioning became increasingly popular, especially in the Guards and cavalry, where a Public School-educated young officer after three years' service was well placed for the City or for life as a country gentleman. Cross-rank friendships between officers and senior NCOs were often very close, but always within the conventions of the Army and regiment. Conscript soldiers accepted their call-up as part of life. In one or two Scottish regiments, however, grievances reached back home in Scotland with stones through the windows and other harassments for the families of unpopular officers and NCOs.

In general in these years the Army enjoyed public support but with the proviso that the nation wanted compulsory National Service ended as soon as possible. Criticism of all defence expenditure came from extremists of the political left who were often sympathetic to the Soviet Union, and there was periodic press and Parliamentary criticism over the Korean War and later Suez, together with alleged excesses in the counter-insurgency campaigns in Kenya, Cyprus and Aden. These, however, never amounted to any sustained anti-Army sentiments. Regiments returning from overseas received civic welcomes, crowds lining the streets on ceremonial occasions.

From 1955 to 1959 the post of Chief of the Imperial General Staff was held by General Sir Gerald Templer, one of the ablest officers produced in the long history of the Army. His vision and impetus was to have enormous impact on the post-National Service all-Regular Army in the decades that followed.

NOTES

1 A very full and detailed account of the Army's operations in this period on which, supplemented by individual regimental histories, this author has drawn is Gregory Blaxland, *The Regiments Depart* (London, William Kimber, 1971).

2 In 1947 legislation provided for a year's National Service; this was extended to eighteen months in 1948 and to two years in 1950. The last call-up took place in 1960.

3 Bernard Fergusson, *Wavell: Portrait of a Soldier* (London, Collins, 1961), 85. For a different view General Sir Brian Horrocks opined that one good commanding officer was worth 100 years of regimental tradition.

4 The 1950s disbandments and amalgamations reduced the infantry from eighty-five to sixty battalions, and armoured regiments from thirty to twenty-three. The Royal Artillery lost the most; as well as losing twenty field regiments it lost a further fourteen when its Anti-Aircraft Command was abolished.

5 Three officers were awarded the Victoria Cross, of which two were posthumous.

6 An interesting short account of such work appears in Tim Carew, *The Glorious Glosters* (London, Leo Cooper, 1970), 107–108. The Gloucester officer described here even threatened recalcitrants with extra drills after their release.

7 Blaxland, *Regiments Depart*, 178.

8 'The battalion was lucky in having some excellent company commanders and a very high level of junior officer. To an extent the quality of the

junior officers depended on the job being done; they learnt their trade in the rather independent role they were given as platoon commanders. Those who failed to produce the goods were quickly got rid of.' John Baynes, *The History of the Cameronians (Scottish Rifles)* (London, Cassell, 1971), iv, 75.

9 Aggett, *Bloody Eleventh*, III, 517, notes: '. . . the Battalion becomes a series of flying squads. Platoon relieves Platoon in a never ending procession of patrols and escorts.'

10 A study in particular concentrating on the standards of behaviour of the various security forces is Anthony Clayton, *Counter-Insurgency in Kenya* (Sunflower University Press, Kansas, 1984). The work records the excesses of one mentally unbalanced officer, but notes that the specific firm instructions of the Commander-in-Chief, General Sir George Erskine, on the standards he expected were followed by the Army, if not by other security forces.

11 Another was Major Earl Wavell, the son of the Second World War Field-Marshal.

12 Blaxland, *Regiments Depart* p. 369.

13 One cadet was commissioned at a December Sovereign's Parade. Early in the following year he earned a Military Cross leading his platoon in the Aden Radfan.

14 The September 1957 entry included 107 Public School boys, 29 Grammar or equivalent school boys, 37 from Welbeck College, a small number from schools in Ireland and Southern Rhodesia (some of the latter destined for the Federation's forces) and one entrant from the Army Apprentices College. Of the Public Schools, seven were from Eton, five from Harrow and nine from Wellington. *The Wishstream, Journal of the Royal Military Academy Sandhurst*, XII, spring 1958. A scholarship scheme by which the Army paid for the sixth-form years of boys at boarding schools served also to swell Public School numbers.

15 Eaton Hall trained cadets destined for the infantry and the Intelligence Corps; all other arms trained at Mons: *The Mons Officer Cadet School* (officially published, n.d.), 2–3.

CHAPTER 14

FROM ADEN TO BELFAST AND BASRA

The years from 1962 have seen very profound changes in the Army, not least in its officers, but at the same time with some features of the past reappearing, albeit in slightly different forms. Earlier centuries had seen the paradox of pleasure-seeking officers in peacetime transformed into courageous and resourceful battlefield leaders. The last decades of the 20th century saw officers more professional than ever before in the Army's history, but at the same time the decades saw a return to a more materialistic general approach and to personal lifestyles more 18th than 19th or 20th century.

Two sets of reasons created these circumstances, one military, the other social. On the military side, the major commitments – BAOR, Northern Ireland and peace-support operations – all required the highest standards of professionalism, now in new forms. In Germany, until the withdrawal of the Group of Soviet Forces in Eastern Germany, regiments had to be trained and prepared for deployment at forty-eight hours' notice, or even less. In Northern Ireland the Army had to contain one of the world's most sophisticated terrorist movements in full view of critical media and political figures. In peace support, in particular in former Yugoslavia, only well-trained and disciplined units could serve any useful role. In addition, the rapid developments in technology, in particular computers, in both training and operations, meant the learning of new skills for even the most junior officers.[1] And, finally, after the collapse of the Soviet Union political hopes centred, once again, on a peace dividend. In these circumstances no elite reputation, or even a royal Colonel-in-Chief, could necessarily secure a regiment found wanting.

Changes in wider society and social attitudes have made the Britain of 2007 very different from that of 1960. The 1960s culture of ending self-discipline and 'doing your own thing' and the 1980s 'enrich yourself' with no respect for authority were one side of the coin. The other was the rise in costs, as percentages of an officer's salary, of first-buy and later houses, furniture and school fees. A rapidly increasing percentage of officers were now graduates and were drawn from a much wider social base. Most of the graduates from the 1990s would have student loan repayments for themselves – and perhaps their partners – to pay as well.

After three years at a university (often preceded by a 'gap year'), one year at Sandhurst and some months at an Arms School, the Subaltern joining his – or her – regiment for the first time was now twenty-four or twenty-five years old and of necessity having to think in career terms. He or she might also find it difficult to adjust to, or even understand, the traditional ethos and moral standards of the Officers' Mess after uninhibited university life. But graduates wishing to make successful soldiering their career would have to learn and in some measure to adjust, the promotion stakes being highly competitive, and thereby make themselves truly professional. An officer who saw the Army as just a job was not likely to stand the pace for long, however frustrated he or she might feel about some aspects of the Army system.

In 1992, the Women's Royal Army Corps ceased to exist, its officers, nearly 200, being transferred and badged to every branch of the Army except the infantry and armoured regiments, though in these many women officers serve in non-combatant duties while remaining members of the Adjutant-General's Corps. In 2003 a woman officer successfully completed the extremely testing Special Forces selection course, the first woman to do so.[2]

The major operational commitment for the Army until 1991 was the three or four divisions of BAOR, the structure of the 1st British Corps changing from time to time. From the 1970s onwards, it was assessed that the Soviet Army's most likely strategy would be that of surprise. The endless round of exercises practised rapid deployment and a holding battle against a much superior force, perhaps resorting to nuclear weapons. Reputations and careers of Majors and regimental commanders could be made or broken near the inner German Border, the Sibesse Gap and the Einbeck Bowl, luck good or bad in the form of a visiting General playing an unforeseeable role. The exercises often degenerated into military gamesmanship; stores were in any case hopelessly inadequate for anything more than a few days' fighting. One feature both of the work of the Rhine Army and perceived as of growing importance in all other operations was intelligence, one of General Templer's priorities. The Intelligence Corps was expanded from 1957 to provide career Regular officers, selected from a variety of applicants to avoid cloning. The importance of intelligence gathering also became emphasised by all officers in front-line infantry and armoured units. Also of ever-increasing importance was army aviation; the Second World War Glider Pilot Regiment which had been disbanded in 1950 was reformed as a new Army Air Corps in 1957, providing very carefully selected young officers with an exciting helicopter role.

The first years of the 1960s saw some final decolonisation operations. The most difficult of these centred on Aden, for which as a prologue a sharp border conflict in the Radfan area north of Aden broke out in 1963. At its peak in 1964 the Radfan involved three British infantry units, the SAS, artillery and tanks, all in support of local forces. The actions were occasionally battalion-sized; more often company or platoon commanders' tasks involved picketing heights, sweeps and formal attacks on rebel strongholds. The Radfan suited the nationalist rebels' tactics – ambushes, mines and machine-gun sniping. The terrain – towering jagged ridges, at times so precipitous that one unit had to descend from one height by rope, together with the heat, necessitating a supply of two gallons of water per man per day – presented special challenges. Tracks and airstrips had to be built by the Engineers and air supply was often essential. Helicopters were used for the forward deployment of soldiers, four at a time in a shuttle on one operation. Conflict in the Radfan continued until British units were withdrawn from the area in June 1966, the rebels by this time being equipped with mortars and rocket-launchers.

In Aden itself and its immediate neighbourhood the violence from 1965 onwards was much more intense. Two brigades of troops with aircraft, artillery and armour had to be deployed. At first in 1965 infantry and armoured-car units had to face wild, hysterical crowds including women and children, rioting and sniping, to which they could only reply in self-defence; their main duties were guarding buildings and family quarters, picquets, checkpoints, swoops and searches, and enforcing curfews. In 1966, after the decision to withdraw was announced, virtually unmanageable difficulties arose. The local police and military mutinied; with great forbearance and control the Army succeeded in quelling the mutinies without making them ineffective as assets in controlling areas from which units were later to withdraw by stages. Two rival nationalist guerrilla organisations battled for control while ferocious attacks on the Army units and personnel continued. Observation posts were mounted on roofs of buildings but became the targets of snipers with rocket-launchers. Curfew patrols were shot at from house windows, morale fell and officers had some difficulty in restraining senior NCOs and men after killings of service personnel, especially following the deaths of twenty-two on one day in June 1967.[3] Operations changed from efforts to reassert control in particular areas to a carefully prepared area-by-area plan of extrication, reflecting great credit on the staff officers who prepared the plan and the regimental officers who carried it through.

At the same time, in the Far East, British and Commonwealth regiments were fighting a highly successful campaign defending the regions of the island of Borneo that did not wish to be part of Indonesia against Indonesian aggression. The first phase, from late 1962 to mid-1963, saw company and platoon-sized attacks and hostage rescue operations against rebels seeking to overthrow the Sultan's government in Brunei, tasks conducted in jungle and later in sweeps to catch fleeing rebels in mangrove swamps.

Companies or platoons were flown in to forward areas in light aircraft; thereafter movement would be by river craft or on foot through the jungle. Later in 1963 Indonesian 'volunteers' were sent in across the 950-mile long mountainous borders or landed from the sea. The campaign became increasingly intelligence-based, the Intelligence Corps and the SAS being notably successful in directing the security forces to areas penetrated by the Indonesians. Infantry company bases on hilltops in the border areas were built of sandbags and bamboo, protected by wire, spikes and overhead cover. Within these were sited mortars or light artillery; a few had helicopter landing pads. Bases were sometimes sited in pairs so as to provide mutually supporting fire. From them patrols and pursuit platoons or sections would set forth. At the end of 1963 Indonesian Regular troops were committed, requiring some fifteen battalions, artillery, armoured cars and engineers to contain.[4] Platoons would be dropped by helicopter in areas where Indonesians were reported, and patrol for one, two or even three weeks, living on one meal a day and resting in the dense jungle temporary base areas. Some patrols moved by small boats along the many rivers. Fighting was often brisk, the Indonesian Regulars being equipped with mortars, rocket-launchers and machine-guns;

mines were laid by both sides, and platoons would on occasions cross into Indonesian territory in pursuit of Indonesian detachments. Regimental officers' tasks also included an all-important 'hearts and minds' role, to retain the loyalty of local communities. Detachments from battalions would support Royal Army Medical Corps teams regularly visiting remote *kampong* settlements, often by helicopter. The campaign ended in 1966 following a military coup and change of regime in Indonesia. Minor colonial or post-colonial infantry unit duties also included security duties in Mauritius and Hong Kong, and the suppression of army mutinies in Kenya, Uganda and Tanganyika.

The year 1969 saw the return of British troops to the streets of Northern Ireland with the opening of 'The Troubles'. This work cannot be the place for a history of the events that followed, the changing aims and methods of different Republican groups, or events that did not directly concern the regimental officer and soldier on the ground. It can only be concerned with the changing duties of Regular battalions and those other units serving as infantry, many of which served many tours in the Province in the thirty years that followed. Space must also prevent concern, beyond brief mention, with the work of Special Forces, police or locally recruited Ulster Defence Regiment units, except to note that in the latter many Regular British Army officers from English and Scots units served as Commanding Officers.[5]

The first three years, 1969 to 1971, saw units deployed on the streets attempting to restore peace and order in face of taunting, spitting crowds, houses set alight and barricades seeking to create 'No-Go' areas. On often rainswept streets soldiers would have to shelter behind walls or vehicles against petrol bombs or barrages of missiles. House-to-house searches for weapons and curfews presented immediate problems for junior officers, who had to consider how far troops' presence and necessary actions, perhaps including breaking and entry, might in the event make matters worse, so leading to further violence or a riot. Riots had to be met by tear gas, rubber bullets and smoke grenades; riot leaders had to be seized and taken away for the police. For the infantry soldier life was one of endless stand-by, fatigue, poor feeding and poor accommodation in disused factories and other buildings converted into small fortresses.

In 1971 came the first deaths of soldiers with nail bombing becoming a major problem, poor intelligence making the results of mass arrests of little value. In Londonderry barricades were cleared under sniper fire, but Republicans threw bombs and missiles at troops and then retreated quickly into the Bogside estate. Pursuit incursions achieved little. The 'Yellow Card' system, a card giving each soldier precise instruction on when he might open fire, was first introduced and carefully explained by regimental officers. In Belfast company, platoon and NCO-led section patrols in Republican areas met hostile crowds, again with women spitting, yelling and banging dustbin lids. In January 1972, in an event in Londonderry that was to cause on-going controversy, a mass demonstration led to shooting in which thirteen civilians were killed, the unit concerned, a Parachute Regiment battalion, being convinced that its soldiers were being fired on. A spate of bombings and killings followed, some sectarian, some against the Army, whose strength had to be brought up to 22,000. Four infantry battalions, including armoured personnel carriers and armoured engineer units to break down barricades, were involved in an entry into the Republican areas of Londonderry; in Belfast eleven battalions were committed in a similar operation, so ending 'No-Go' areas. The year 1972 also saw the need for military measures on the border with the Irish Republic, from where Republicans were crossing and bringing weaponry, supplies and recruits. Pursuit into the Irish Republic was forbidden but the measures were to develop into a system of patrols, ambushes, Special Forces actions and the building of stockaded forts. To worsen the overall situation, Unionist paramilitary groups made their first appearance in Belfast.

Regimental officers and soldiers from 1972 onwards received special training before being sent on either long (two-year) garrison or short (three or four month) tours to Northern Ireland. Two special teams, one in Sussex and one in Germany, instructed officers in firm patrolling around crowds (and the dangers that could follow 'going in'), how incidents and ambushes could be baited and set up, how to anticipate escape routes, to keep in mind the need to move forward and retain the initiative if brought under fire, and to remember that they and their men might be watched every minute of the day. In return officers were to instruct soldiers to avoid any pattern in their lives but to look for any changes, however small, in the pattern of life around them.

The mid- and late 1970s saw the opening of a process of transferring much day-to-day law and order duties to the Royal Ulster Constabulary and the newly formed, locally recruited, non-Regular Ulster Defence Regiment. The British Regular units were deployed at times of crisis and on periodic street patrols in traditional style, with men on both sides of a street and the tail-end men covering their rear, but now also with new duties, particularly involving junior officers and NCOs, of intelligence gathering in Close Observation Patrols. In these, two or three men would lie hidden in attics or bricked up in houses for several days or more, equipped with binoculars and cameras watching for any slight changes in local life, and in particular the movement of suspects.[6] Attacks on the Army continued, the worst being the killing of eighteen soldiers at Warrenpoint in 1979. Checkpoints became dangerous, drivers being forced by terrorist groups to drive up to them in cars loaded with explosives. At flash points or after an incident battalions cordoned off areas, sometimes for several days. Women officers led small teams of women soldiers when searching female suspects.

By the 1980s the campaign had assumed set patterns. Republican groups partly funded in America acquired mortars, grenade launchers and heavy machine-guns, some from Libya. Bomb attacks were launched on Army personnel and bases in England and Germany as well as a ferocious bombing campaign against civilian and political targets in Britain. In Northern Ireland the Army establishment became set at three brigades, one in Belfast, one on the border and one in the centre-west, one battalion in each brigade now being on a 2½-year-long tour and the other two on six-month tours. The resident battalions furnished the Close Observation Patrols. The border became increasingly important; a system of watchtowers made of corrugated iron and scaffolding, concrete observation posts and two large main fortified forts all had to be built. Battalions on the border would rotate sub-units between watchtower duty, patrolling with patrols either on the move or in hides, or securing bases, those at the towers being in underground bunkers. All supply was by helicopter. Company officers made regular visits to the towers and led men out on the patrols. In the larger forts small Officers' Messes were possible, with hospitality in quiet times.

By the early 1990s it was clear that the Army had successfully thwarted Republican groups' aims to take over the Province or make it ungovernable, and had brought to a halt the most technologically advanced terrorist movement in history; cease-fires and the 'two steps forward, one step back' peace processes could commence.

For some regimental officers Northern Ireland was a real soldiering job with risks, involving the pitting of skills against a cunning and ruthless adversary and a stimulating change from the BAOR exercise army. For others it was a disturbing experience to see so much bigotry and hatred in a part of the United Kingdom. For most, perhaps it was simply 'Northern Ireland – again'. For the married it was separation and anxieties of relatives left behind at home. For a few there developed a real affection for the people at their best, but for others a revulsion against the so-evident local rackets and corruption. For almost all, Northern Ireland was frustration against the local authorities, police, politicians and for long the Irish

Republic *Garda Siochana*. Different battalions, or artillery units serving as infantry, had different styles but by the 1990s even the hardest, the Parachute battalions, had learnt the need to make their presence as uncontroversial as possible and to guard against the dangers of being brutalised by the situation. Soldiers and their officers nevertheless found the Yellow Card procedures difficult, especially as breaches resulted in civil court action.

Compared with Northern Ireland, the 1982 Falklands War was for officers the straightforward application of conventional infantry battalion battle tactics learnt at Sandhurst and the School of Infantry. The next series of operations, in the disintegrating Yugoslavia, required the development of special peace-keeping skills, some already practised earlier but now in unfamiliar terrain often without water, power or food supplies and working under an international mandate. The skills concerned maintaining or seeking to obtain consent, impartiality, legitimacy and transparency, negotiation, mediation and liaison, interpositioning and buffer zones. These had to be combined with the skills already learnt in Northern Ireland and elsewhere – minimum force and wherever possible non-lethal weapons, flexibility, rules of engagement, retention of the initiative and refusal to permit 'no go' areas, mine awareness and base security. Also to be included were any activities – public information, social, sporting or welfare – that helped relations with the local communities.[7] In Bosnia, officers led small detachments searching for missing persons and helping refugees. On some occasions officers had to steady young soldiers – and themselves – at sites of ethnic cruelties and revolting massacres, including those of women and children. Tactically Royal Engineers had to build roads and camp, and light tanks escorted military and humanitarian aid convoys. Troops were frequently under fire, some units for several weeks, but could generally only reply with direct rather than indirect fire. In the last of the former Yugoslav operations, in Kosovo, and also in Sierra Leone, a more 'muscular' style involving shoot-outs with rebels (frequently drug-crazed) was necessary to prevent killings and restore order. In the first Iraq war of 1991 and the second of 2003 officers had to supervise considerable prior preparation for their men and adjustment to equipment to fight in desert conditions; both wars were short and, in contrast to the Falklands or Yugoslavia, textbook all-arms operations involving tanks, self-propelled artillery and multiple rocket-launchers, helicopters and armoured personnel carrier infantry, all using up-to-date technology. The second war, however, immediately led into a delicate and dangerous peace-keeping role in the Basra area, together with welcome and constructive work in restoring the region's infrastructure. As 2004 progressed, however, units became increasingly involved in regimental officer-led wider anti-terrorist fighting, now extending to suicide terrorist attacks and roadside bombs. Equally dangerous and calling for the highest leadership and professional skills are the Army's brigade size anti-Taliban operations in Afghanistan, a major guerilla war.

The peace dividend thought to have been justified by the ending of the Cold War reduced the Army to an establishment of 110,000, with a further round of infantry and armoured regiment amalgamations.[8] Within many, but not all, regiments the traditional focus of county or regional loyalties was to change. Some, particularly in Scotland and Wales, still retained strong links to one or two counties and inherited traditional cohesion. In a new or recently amalgamated regiment pride came to focus more on recent achievements, in operations or on sports fields, a process to take time and requiring particular effort by regimental officers to achieve a similar unity of purpose.

Weapons technology, the need for flexibility and recruiting difficulties also all led to changes in the shape of units but in all, the command duties of Majors, Captains, Lieutenants and Second Lieutenants remained the same. Infantry battalions in all roles – armoured, air assault, parachute or light – were progressively scaled down to three rifle companies, with a manoeuvre support company including Milan anti-tank weapons, mortars and reconnaissance platoons and, in the light role, a machine-gun platoon. Armoured regiments retained four squadrons, each of four combat and one administrative troops. Divisional close support artillery regiments possessed four batteries, air defence regiments three and multiple rocket-launcher regiments two. In practice, battle groups combining sub-units of infantry, armour and artillery, usually commanded by the Lieutenant-Colonel from the regiment contributing the most, formed the battlefield operational unit. Royal Signals officers became involved in satellite communications and electronic warfare as well as battlefield and peace support communications. All these required considerable technical and logistic support.[9]

Changes in regimental life began in the mid-1960s. Pay parades, a valuable occasion for soldiers to meet officers, became replaced by bank account payments. In 1970 marriage allowance was replaced by a consolidated rate of pay for all, and housing (or an allowance) became payable to all married personnel irrespective of age.[10] Basic pay rates for officers are based on the salaries of equivalent grades in the Civil Service to which was added an 'X factor' of 10 per cent for male officers and 6 per cent for women to compensate for the risks of the profession and frequent moves. Women officers' pay was later raised to the level of male officers and periodic adjustments were made to meet rises in the cost of living index. Battledress finally disappeared in the 1960s, to be replaced by barrack order of shirt, pullover and trousers and combat kit in the field. Officers are nevertheless still required to buy Service Dress and in many regiments blue or green No. 1 Dress, a uniform allowance still being paid on commissioning, to the relief and profit of regimental tailors and outfitters, many now long established.

The very great social changes of the last decades of the 20th century are reflected in the attitudes and behaviour of many officers. Fewer now come from traditional military families, recruitment being much broader-based, and regional accents can be heard in most Messes. The proportion of graduate officers in combat as well as in technical regiments steadily increased. Many of these officers pay a purely professional regard to their regiment's traditions and history, unlike the total devotion and social commitment of their predecessors. They see the idea of an officer and a gentleman with particular class standards of behaviour as faintly archaic. The Army became increasingly hard-worked, Mess life suffering accordingly, many officers seeing the Mess as little more than a convenience and Mess social functions as tedious. Many among the unmarried preferred to live out in a flat. In London several of the military clubs were closed or combined. A junior staff officer working in the Ministry of Defence is now more likely at lunchtime to be seen jogging around Whitehall than with the suits, bowler hats and rolled umbrellas of the 1950s. As well as professionalism immense store is set on physical fitness. Messes now sell little alcohol at lunchtimes and often not much more in the evenings except at weekends and on special occasions, when too much may be consumed. Money, and the pressing need to save it for home, mortgages, families and cars, governs the lives of many, particularly if student loans also have to be repaid. However, a few regiments still try to keep up appearances with expensive lifestyles, horses, skiing, champagne parties, West End tailoring for officers' plain clothes and membership of the Guards and Cavalry Club.

Among other traditional values being challenged is that of personal morality, many young officers maintaining the free behaviour, at least until marriage, of previous university life and seeing nothing wrong in so doing. There are, however, taboos that still exist. A 1993 paper issued by the Adjutant General set out behaviour expected of officers, covering in particular drugs, bullying, racial or sexual harassment, same-sex relationships and relationships with service personnel who are not officers. Later, same-sex relationships became permissible provided they did not affect personal or unit efficiency; much, however, still depended on the attitudes of individual Commanding Officers to such relationships. Divorce is now accepted as a part of life, though in cases of divorce Commanding Officers have to certify that the divorce will cause no harm to good order and military discipline. The divorce rate is higher than in comparable civilian professions as a result of long periods of separation occasioned by many of the Army's commitments, frequent house moves and the inability of many wives, a number now professionally qualified after university education, to find fulfilment.[11] The arrival of women officers in regiments and Messes sometimes creates sexual tension, particularly if they are young and attractive.[12] These issues may not be only those of attraction but also of local jealousies involving male officers' suspicions of women 'playing their sex' and women who are given administrative rather than command duties becoming resentful.

Only a minority of officers are regular Christian church attenders, though the Officers Christian Union still flourishes. However, before an active service operation or even a major exercise, a surprising number attend services arranged by regimental or formation Chaplains, danger serving to concentrate minds. An underlying Christian pattern of thinking remains strong in respect of actual fighting. A very clear and representative example of this is the address given to his battalion immediately prior to the start of the Second Iraq War by the unit's commanding officer.[13] The address highlights all that the British Army stands for.

'Ethnic minorities', the term usually applied to people of a different skin complexion, are not yet well represented among the Army's officers, the cultural differences often being very great. The largest number are to be found in the medical corps, with others in the logistic corps but still relatively few in the combat regiments.

For Sandhurst, where numbers had been falling fast in the 1960s, 1971 ushered in a twenty-year period of change. A 1966 project to transform Sandhurst into a degree-awarding institution akin to West Point was turned down, a degree education for officers not being thought necessary at the time. In its first form the changes agreed provided for a narrowly professional, intensive two-term (twenty-five week) Standard Military Course, modelled on that of the short-service Mons Officer Cadet School and Second World War OCTUs, containing no academic content at all and with the previous emphasis on gentlemanly style reduced to a few brief sessions on military etiquette. Within this narrow professionalism, character formation was not seen as important. This course was for all Regular or short-service aspirants. Those who had been accepted for Regular commissions stayed on for a further twenty-one week, largely academic, Regular Careers Course covering War Studies, Military Technology, Political and Social Studies and Communication; all foreign language teaching was ended. Civilian university graduates in any discipline, hitherto regarded with suspicion by the Army except in the technical corps, were now to be sought to fill the ranks. Courses for graduates – sixteen weeks for those with military experience, twenty for others, both with little academic input – were accordingly started. The Regular Careers Course and graduate students at first wore the uniforms of the regiments into which they had been commissioned, but this was soon found (as in the 1870s) to be a serious mistake.[14] The whole hurried, joyless system led to criticisms from regimental Commanding Officers who found their young officers very inadequately trained. The non-graduate courses were all lengthened by three weeks, and the graduate courses by one week. In 1987, following further criticism, the non-graduate courses were lengthened to three terms with an academic input, and the Regular Careers Course system was ended. In 1992 a common course of a year for all graduates and non-graduates was initiated, ending the period of turbulence and returning some measure of enjoyment, style and character development back to cadet life. All cadets are expected to qualify as a unit expedition leader (UEL) during one of the two vacations, and the military training includes long exercises in the field and a counter-terrorist exercise in which Gurkha soldiers play the roles of a Northern Ireland hostile crowd with relish. Sport retains its traditional importance.[15]

A College for Women's Royal Army Corps officer-cadets was opened near Camberley in 1965, providing a twenty-one week course. The College became a constituent part of Sandhurst in 1981, the buildings being closed and the women cadets moved to the Sandhurst campus in 1984; the women's course was lengthened to twenty-eight weeks in 1996. Women cadets did not participate in the ceremonial Sandhurst 'Sovereign's Parades' until on one occasion the Queen enquired why. In 1992 women cadets entered the new common commissioning course for the same training in all aspects as the men in probably the best course run by the Academy in its long history.[16]

The changes ran parallel to changes in the cadets themselves. The non-graduate is only likely to be successful at the Regular Commissions Board if he or she has had either soldier service or been on some form of adventurous training after leaving school, raising the average age of non-graduates to nineteen or twenty. The number of graduate entrants steadily increased, by the turn of the century generally comprising some 55 to 65 per cent of each of the three intakes per year. The number of Public School entrants fell sharply in the 1970s but rose again slightly in the 1980s, though still forming a minority. The cadet companies are now from one intake only and strictly functional with no internal cadet hierarchy. With the Public School entrants forming only a small proportion, the old Public School trend-setting of the 'cadet government' Under Officers was ended. The Academy's style is now vocational and mature.

The academic work became of university standard in War and Political Studies, but also with practical communication training including facing the media in television interviews and peace-keeping negotiating skills. Overall the course is structured so as to provide for a first term of basic military training, a second term of basic officer training and a third term concentrating on character, values and leadership, an emphasis increasingly necessary in view of the changes in society and the wider basis of officer recruitment. In one respect, however, little has changed: the Guards and cavalry regiments still select almost (but not entirely) from Public School products, graduate or non-graduate.[17] These regiments also attract sons of officers of less stylish regiments, being unhappy with amalgamations or social changes.

On joining the unit the young officer continues the tradition of interviewing individually each soldier under his or her command at the first opportunity. Thereafter, in addition to Arms School and subsequent later specialist courses, junior officers receive a limited further general professional education. When the Regular Careers Course was ended a Junior Division Staff College Course for Captains was created, including War Studies and Defence Policy modules; this was replaced in 2003 by a programme of instruction given by Sandhurst lecturers at different garrisons and stations. The Staff College examination procedure ended in 1971 and was replaced by a new Staff Promotion Examination of three papers: International Affairs, War Studies, and Military Management and Administration. Staff training became tri-Service in 1996, a new College building for this Joint Service Command and Staff Course being built at Watchfield near Shrivenham. The course, which can now lead to a Master's degree, lasts for three terms, one term being single service. Original thought is now permitted, and often encouraged, to challenge military orthodoxy. The undergraduate engineering and science courses formerly offered for officers destined for the technical corps at the Royal Military College of Science have been terminated, the College becoming post-graduate only; young officers, including Welbeck boys and girls, are now sent to civilian universities before attending Sandhurst. Welbeck is to be replaced

by a new government Sixth Form College for candidates for all three
Services and the Civil Service.

Career development is taken seriously at both individual and ministry levels. Officers commissioned from Sandhurst are generally only
on a three-year contract. Those wishing to pursue a long Regular
career have to prove their quality at two stages, at the ages of 30–31
and 37–38. Generally officers know or are advised how far they are
likely to go up the ladder after staff training and can plan to stay
on or decide to leave. Although it may still be an asset to have
served in the Guards, Cavalry, Royal Green Jackets or Royal Horse
Artillery in the quest for senior rank, others of special ability,
not necessarily from major public schools, and particularly from
the Parachute Regiment or with SAS experience, are now well
represented at the top.[18] For the able but less ambitious there are
numerous training postings both at home and overseas, such as to
NATO staff, as military attaché and on exchange postings, that can
carry an officer to Lieutenant-Colonel or full Colonel. Successive
reductions, though, have led to a number of officers being made
redundant. Women officers often opt to leave the Service in their
thirties, so easing the promotion paths.

The officer–rank and file relationship in the last three decades
of the 20th century reflected the social changes. Gone, even in the
Guards, is any automatic old-fashioned respect for a social class
status, though where an officer is otherwise fully professional a
traditional background could sometimes, but not always, be an
asset. Regimental loyalty again has come to depend greatly on the
competence of officers, male and female, and their willingness to
become as fully involved as the rank and file in any work that is
dangerous or plain tedious. The newly commissioned young officer
is often regarded warily by his soldiers, equally often with good
reason, as Sandhurst cadets have virtually no contact with unit
soldiers. Regimental sports teams, even when including an officer,
may now be captained by an NCO.

The familiarity or distancing in day-to-day officer–NCO relationships do not now always fit into the former patterns. On active service, in the Falklands or Iraq, Arms School top-down patterns could still be followed with Battalion, Company and Platoon Formal O (Orders) groups in which commanders issued firm orders with no question of familiarity ever arising. Northern Ireland, however, posed a very different problem. Many of the surveillance tasks falling to an infantry battalion required only two or three men led by an NCO. Officers giving instructions for dangerous work had to adopt a much more informal style, accepting discussion, at times even negotiation.[19] After such close informality, regaining control in other circumstances could sometimes prove difficult. Similar issues had for some time affected officers in direct command of a tank, but here the officer and his crew of two might have had to live and work together perhaps for several days; the infantry officer has to send his men out in parties and cannot accompany them all. With the return to the all-volunteer Army and the late 20th century soldier, fresh attention has to be paid to the relationship. Units with both male and female personnel sometimes experience difficulty when women officers have to reprimand male soldiers, many still not taking kindly to such disciplining. On the sea voyage down to the Falklands officers found it necessary, in some units, to remind their soldiers, reared in exercise army training, that they were on their way to a war and that they were now going to have to shoot to kill – or be killed. In the long tense period between the arrival of regiments in Kuwait and the opening of the first Iraq War officers had to maintain efficiency, health and hygiene, and morale in remote desert conditions.[20]

A French general visiting a British regiment in the 1990s asked one soldier how long he planned to stay in the Army. The soldier's reply 'Just as long as I am enjoying it', summarises much of the everyday relationship between officers and rank and file; if soldiers are to be recruited and retained they must enjoy military life, and it falls on regimental officers to see that they do. For this reason young officers are required to have gained their UEL qualification at Sandhurst and in regiments to take soldiers, especially the unmarried, out on expeditions. Others may spend a period with recruiting teams.

Many of the social problems of late 20th century life appear in garrison towns – in both Britain and Germany. These can be especially difficult in Germany where wives, few of whom speak a word of German, have to be left behind when their husbands are on exercise, on a short tour in Northern Ireland or sent off to Iraq. Some very disturbed behaviour can result. In some German garrison towns the nearest school or hospital might be some distance away in another garrison town, and the houses occupied by families in both Britain and Germany are sometimes scattered rather than in a military estate, though the 'patch' is more common. Garrison towns and almost all regiments have a 'Families Officer', usually a late entry officer with soldier service; originally the Families Officer was concerned only with housing but many now assist with family or social difficulties. Regimental officers have to familiarise themselves with the various support systems: medical staff, Chaplains, the Soldiers', Sailors' and Airmen's Families Association staff, the Women's Royal Voluntary Service and the Help Information Volunteer Exchanges. Many officers' wives are still prepared to help with wives' clubs, but such help can sometimes be viewed as condescension and resented. By the turn of the century the wives of NCOs could be educated or qualified as well as or better than the wives of officers.[21] For this and other reasons a number of officers' wives are no longer willing to participate in unit wives' clubs. An increasing number of wives do not follow their husbands even when accommodation is available, preferring to stay in their mortgage-purchased home.

Initial basic training also reflects the profound changes in British society. While much of the day-to-day training of recruits is the work of Sergeants, officers in basic training units have overall responsibilities and share their Sergeants' concerns. Many recruits are the products of indifferent State Schools and the violence and sex-obsessed culture of the populist media. Physically many are unfit and overweight, their feet maladjusted for army boots, and with little understanding of discipline and hierarchy or the needs for them. Officers have to caution them firmly on the dangers of excessive drinking, managing pay and money matters, any form of drugs and Aids. Officers in training units, particularly since the bullying scandals revealed in the 1980s court-martials and, later, the deaths of young soldiers at Deepcut Barracks, have to be very closely concerned with the care and welfare of recruits. They have to be on the watch for barrack-room bullying, and when the trained soldier joins his regiment officers have to ensure that initiation rites are not excessive. There have been particular difficulties over the treatment sometimes given to soldiers from ethnic minorities. The spotting and selection of future NCOs remains one of the most important tasks of company and battalion – or their equivalents in other arms – officers. In mixed units officers of either sex have to be on the watch for tensions that may be present in the ranks affecting efficiency. From 1984 unit Commanding Officers became responsible for the management of their own budgets and also responsible for the monitoring of the career development of soldiers under their command.

The turn of the century saw wider theoretical questions concerning the role of officers. In addition to those already mentioned, there remain major anxieties. Prominent among these is overstretching resulting from continual political demands for the use of regiments for a variety of commitments, requiring the reinforcement of under-strength units by squadrons or companies from other regiments, and more importantly causing ever-lengthening periods of separation from wives, children and partners. Secondly, in the context of families, officers have the ever-rising costs of family life for men and women, made worse by the nature of Army service and increasingly forcing them to think in careerist terms, with all the attendant dangers to true professionalism. Related to this is an anxiety that state-of-the-art technology leads to civilian rather than military approaches to duties, particularly in the technical corps, and not only over hours of work.

Behind these day-to-day questions lie even more profound anxieties. There is the concern, already noted, as to whether the traditional relationships between officers and now often well-educated senior NCOs can operate as smoothly and efficiently as in the past, and also whether the on-going reductions of the traditional marks of social difference, such as common to all medal awards in the political interests of the classless society, and the greater familiarity between junior officers and all other ranks, are not going too far, perhaps devaluing the authority of officers.[22] Fears exist that within the Ministry of Defence there are interests seeking to finish all traditional features of officers' lives – regiments, messes, uniforms – in pursuit of social engineering or cost-cutting, with no understanding of their value for the motivation of all ranks at unit level. Related to this issue of authority is that of the tolerance or otherwise of negotiations or subsequent unauthorised adjustments by NCOs or soldiers to orders issued by an officer, questioning whether too rigid insistence on every aspect and detail of an order may not prove counter-productive. In both these issues the experience of service in Northern Ireland, with the work focus so different from the traditional unit and sub-unit loyalty, has presented problems with the chain of command. There is also concern over the quality and motivation of some recruits, young men carrying the school and teenage indiscipline and lack of respect evident particularly in some comprehensive schools on to become rogue elements in regiments, out of the control of officers and NCOs. Finally, changes in national law have limited the powers of courts-martial and have permitted military personnel with a grievance, perhaps over negligence, to bring cases against the Army or individual officers in civil courts.

Perhaps the most profound of all anxieties at the start of the century concerns the preservation of 'fighting spirit' among the one-third of the Army in which men or women may have to kill, face to face, another human being. The issue had appeared less relevant as, since the Falklands War, so much of the Army's operations have been peace-keeping in which fighting spirit is generally not needed and may even be an impediment, or brief operations not concluding with close-and-kill fighting, and with the increasing efficiency of long-range fire-power. The fact, however, remains that modern society perceives a common humanity and individual men and women place a higher value on life, their own as well as that of others. Further, the tensions that may be present in the minds of soldiers may be complicated in ways that cannot be foreseen by technology. Patrick Mileham describes the infantry soldier of the near future as a '. . . walking (or running) technologically communicating, locating, navigating, reporting, intelligence gathering, virtual reality observing, self-sustaining cyber-space robot – but still a human being'. He also notes the fall in soldier recruiting for close-combat units.[23]

Also worrying for officers of all ranks are the fluctuations in the view of the Army held by the general public. The 1960s saw much anti-military rhetoric among the younger generation of the time, making the transition to the all-volunteer Army the more difficult. Most State Schools and newly created universities refused to have anything to do with cadet forces, university training corps or any form of recruitment, claiming a moral high ground. The wider public was more sympathetic, a sympathy fostered by Army Public Relations activities. In the Northern Ireland campaign in the 1970s criticism of the Army's actions was generally limited to the practices of some of the Special Forces and the interrogation of Irish Republicans, together with a political rather than military cry of 'Troops Out' voiced by a minority of mainly left-leaning political figures, a cry critical of the Army's mission rather than its activities.

The Falklands War commanded general public support as did, later, the successive peace-keeping operations in Bosnia, Kosovo and Sierra Leone, and the brief First Iraq War campaign. All these operations gained public admiration for the professionalism shown. Less happily for the Army was that the public, in its disquiet and unease over the treatment and deaths of recruits, failed to appreciate the wider social problem and to see that the lack of proper supervision was a consequence of underfunding following cuts imposed by Whitehall, overstretching and the consequential shortage of the best quality officers and NCOs. Pressure groups, political and social, argued that the Army should be an instrument of social engineering, placing this perception of the needs and rights of women, ethnic minorities and the disabled over the Army's primary role of military efficiency. These groups made little impact except when the media reported cases of discrimination against or victimisation of minorities. In other matters, too, the general public led by the more populist media still seemed to expect a higher standard of moral behaviour from the Army, in particular its officers, than it expected from other sections of society, the press relishing occasional accounts of scandal.

The Second Iraq War of 2003 was to open up wider fractures. Initially the Army was thought to have conducted a very efficient military operation and then turned commendably to civil reconstruction, all despite the fact that a large percentage of the British public was opposed to the war. While this had no effect on the regiments in the field, the climate of opinion so created was unhappy.

Opposition to the war was a major contributory cause of the developing criticism of the Army that opened later in 2003. Relatives of men killed used the media to criticise openly the force command and unit regimental officers – in one case a soldier was killed because his unit did not have full supplies of protective clothing, in two other cases decisions taken by unit level officers led to the death of men. In the past, shortage of equipment and even battlefield tactical errors were seen as a regrettable but inevitable part of Army life; such nationwide media criticism of unit officers represents a new development and may come to affect battlefield decision-making in the future. The reverse also applies: unit officers may be placed in impossible situations following the running down of stores and equipment or purported savings in the costs of training.

Further, the traditional principle of combat immunity of soldiers is now no longer held to be justifiable, and officers and soldiers are now liable to court actions over incidents involving damage and death while peace-keeping. Thus is added the possibility of court-martial to the dangers officers and men face in operations if the relatives of people injured, abused or killed may prosecute under human rights legislation, arguing that the soldiers' action was not taken in a situation of danger and alleging war crimes.[24]

In 2004 and 2005 there followed a succession of widely publicised reports of brutality by infantry soldiers, involving beating, sexual humiliation and in one case a death, of Iraqi prisoners held for questioning, and the opening of fire on civilians in circumstances where it was alleged no real danger existed. Press criticism of the Army followed in quantity and the issues now affect all aspects of officer leadership in regiments. They bring to immediate fore the questions of whether NCOs knew of the abuses by soldiers, if so whether they told their officers, if the officers knew whether they took any action, and whether the present structures of officers and NCOs can control the small but dangerous rogue elements in some regiments responsible for the occasional outbursts of the dark side of soldiering. When these issues are added to those already noted concerning fighting spirit (and the abuse of prisoners may be evidence of fighting spirit suppressed but on the battlefield suddenly released in cathartic distorted form when adversaries are powerless to retaliate), it is clear that the duties and role of the 21st century Army officer will be very much more complex than at any time in the past. From the military point of view, if well-educated officers

and soldiers are to be ordered to place their lives at risk in conditions of danger with equipment limited by a Treasury budget and then
to fight battles televised by a critical or hostile media, there should
in return be a greater understanding among the public, its political
leadership and responsible media, of the physical and psychological
needs and problems facing the Army.[25] The relationship between
the general public and the Army and its officers will now have to
be two-way if there are to be volunteers willing to serve in any rank.

NOTES

1 In Bosnia, for example, in the 1990s, an infantry corporal fixed his
   position by satellite. By the Second Iraq War sub-unit commanders
   in an armoured vehicle were able to see the movements of all the unit's
   vehicles with the aid of the Blue Force tracker system. Even arms of
   the Army in which hitherto no great technological knowledge was
   needed now had to have officers abreast of technology.

2 The arguments around women officers – and personnel generally –
   are complex. In favour of women it is argued firstly on political grounds
   that much warfare is distant engagement in which women need not
   be involved and that in some special activities women are more
   efficient than men. Against this it is argued that gender differences
   will affect cohesion and bonding and that women are not as strong
   physically as men, fatigue more quickly and that efficiency will be affected
   if women become casualties. In the British Army the matter was decided
   as much by recruitment needs as anything else. For a summary see
   Pete Bracken, 'Women in the Army', in Strachan, *British Army*, vii.

3 One battalion commander was shot dead under circumstances never
   satisfactorily explained. Matters were also not helped by the actions
   of a Scots battalion, the Argyll and Sutherland Highlanders, that had
   suffered casualties. The battalion's Commanding Officer, knowing
   the battalion was on a list for disbandment, wanted to demonstrate
   the unit's value and exact a measure of revenge, by reoccupying one
   area, the Crater, in which was a police barracks. The action was well
   publicised and successful in that later it brought about the surrender
   of the mutineers in the barracks, but the style and publicity was impolitic.

Behind it, also, lay a personality clash between the Commanding Officer and the General Officer in Command, who was himself constrained by political directives.

4 At any one time there were four British, seven or eight British-officered Gurkha, and one or two Australian and New Zealand battalions, together with Malayan and locally recruited units.

5 A valuable account of the Army's duties in the first twelve years of the campaign appears in Desmond Hamill, *Pig in the Middle: The Army in Northern Ireland 1969–1981* (London, Methuen, 1985).

6 A mass of literature reflecting every point of view on Northern Ireland in these years has appeared. For a specific focus on the work of British Army regiments, of special use are Antony Beevor, *Inside the British Army* (London, Corgi, 1991), xvii, and Tony Geraghty, *The Irish War: The Military History of a Domestic Conflict* (London, Harper Collins, 1998), Parts 1, 2 and 3.

7 In April 2004 the Army signed arrangements for officers to follow peace-keeping studies at the University of Bradford, Department of Peace Studies.

8 This total does not include Gurkha personnel (nearly 3,000 in different units and sub-units) or the home service units of the Royal Irish Regiment.

9 The proportion of support service officers to front-line combat unit officers steadily increased. In the April 2004 Commissioning Parade at Sandhurst 61 cadets, nearly one-third of the total, were commissioned into Services (Adjutant-General's Corps, Royal Logistic Corps, Royal Electrical and Mechanical Engineers and Royal Army Medical Corps (non-medical officers)), against 165 into the infantry, armoured regiments, Army Air Corps, Royal Artillery, Royal Engineers, Royal Signals and Intelligence Corps. *The Times*, 28 April 2004.

10 It was, however, to be a little while before the Army accepted a two-way obligation – the provision of a house for a woman officer married to a civilian.

11 The commitments are not only those of operations but for units in Britain to help Territorial Army exercises at weekends.

12 Beevor, *Inside the British Army*, 448, records that in several regiments male Subaltern officers make a communal bet of a case of champagne for the first officer to 'score' with a newly joined woman officer. Wise women officers lock bedroom doors.

13 The text is set out in Appendix 1.

14 Officers who had short-service commissions at the time and who wished to convert were required to return to Sandhurst for the Regular Careers Course. This led to anomalies, including that of a Guards Major who did not take to being treated as a recently commissioned cadet with any great enthusiasm. Special arrangements then had to be made for 'Returning Officers', as they became called, attending this course.

15 This account of Sandhurst is based on the author's own experience as a civilian lecturer in the Academy from 1965 to 1993. Mileham describes the Sandhurst of the 1970s as a 'boot camp', only a slight exaggeration ('Fifty Years, I', 74). The decisions for these courses were made by senior officers who were either commissioned in Second World War OCTUs or who believed that the products of such short, purely professional courses supplemented by training in regiments would be satisfactory for the Army that they saw as having only a BAOR battlefield role. Events were to prove this incorrect both in the adequacy of the training and as a forecast of Army commitments.

16 It should be noted that Sandhurst also provides other short courses – a pre-Sandhurst selection course, a pre-university cadetship course, courses for non-combatant officers (medical officers, Chaplains, lawyers, etc.), the Territorial Army and Army Cadet Force officers, and, from 2003, a course for Warrant Officers and Sergeants who have been selected for commissions.

17 The April 2004 Commissioning Parade may be taken as an example. Of twenty-four cadets commissioned into the Guards and Cavalry, seventeen came from major public schools, two from schools in South Africa and the remaining five from less well-known fee-paying schools. *The Times*, 28 April 2004. In 2006 the Grenadier Guards accepted as an officer a cadet of African parentage. The cadet had, however, been to a Public School.

18 The question is examined in great detail in the context of the 1970s and 1980s by R.G.L. von Zugbach, *Power and Prestige in the British Army* (Avebury, Aldershot, 1988). Zugbach argued that whatever might be happening at regimental level, and give or take occasional token senior appointments, power at the top in the Army was being retained in the hands of socially well-placed officers from elite regiments who specifically ensure the exclusion of others from new social groups. Since Zugbach's writing, however, there have been several senior appointments that challenge his thesis, and those appointed from the traditional backgrounds have clearly been of outstanding ability to justify their selection.

19 Beevor, *Inside the British Army*, 115–116, notes: 'It has been known for a gung-ho Subaltern to ignore orders to keep away from a particularly dangerous area, only to be told by his soldiers that if he wants to go on then 'You can bloody well do it on your own . . . Sir'.

20 The British public, accustomed to seeing Household Regimental officers in splendid uniforms, were treated one evening to the televised spectacle of a young Guards officer making a very traditional foot inspection. Christmas cakes sent out to units were liberally spiced with brandy, and top-shelf magazines were folded into copies of *The Times*, precautions necessary in view of local religious beliefs.

21 The wider issues and the tensions created between the needs of the Army and the interests, expectations and hopes of wives of both officers and rank and file at the turn of the century are interestingly examined in Ruth Jolly, *Military Man Family Man* (London, Brasseys, 1987). Also useful is Charles Jessop's 'Transforming wives into spouses: changing Army attitudes', in Strachan, *The British Army*, vii.

22 It was considered necessary at Sandhurst that the cadets course include a 'Value and Standards' module, including a special study of qualities of Army superiors and subordinates.

23 A very rewarding longer discussion of the issues appears in 'Fighting spirit: has it a future?', by Patrick Mileham in Strachan, *British Army*, xvii.

24 Articles in *The Times*, 11 May 2004, by Veronica Cowan and Rosalind English discuss the issues. Concern was expressed by former Chiefs

of Staff in a debate in the House of Lords on 14 July 2005, Field-Marshal Lord Bramall pointing out that an inhibiting fear of later civil court action could lead officers to decide not to pursue a necessary military operation, thereby putting their own soldiers at risk. Another aspect of the difficulties that may face officers was highlighted in a well-publicised 2006–7 court-martial of a battalion commander, as a result of media and political pressure seeking an officer's scalp. Soldiers of the unit concerned grossly abused a prisoner and the commander was charged with failure to supervise his men. The colonel concerned, who had already been awarded the Distinguished Service Order and had been promoted for his leadership in Iraq, was acquitted; but much damage to the Army was done.

25 The point was very succinctly made in a letter from Brigadier Tom Foulkes to *The Times*, 9 March 2004: '. . . soldiers are not fools and their loyalty is not unlimited, don't ever take it for granted again'. The word 'soldier' here covers all ranks. A comparison can also be made between the concept of loyalty of the Guards Major who personally visited the homes or hospitals of all the men under his command who had been wounded in the Falklands War, and the very limited concern of political leaders for men wounded in Iraq in 2003–05.

CHAPTER 15

BRITISH OFFICERS OF IMPERIAL
REGIMENTS

A large number of British officers served for their whole careers or for short periods in regiments of the Empire, the vast majority of these in India. British Army Regular officers, as well as serving with their own regiments in India, served in formation command and staff appointments, and also in the artillery units in India. The combination of British regiments serving in India and the Indian Army was known collectively as 'The Army in India'.[1]

The forces, European regiments and regiments of Indians officered by Europeans, of the East India Company have already been mentioned in earlier chapters, together with the assumption of direct British Crown responsibility for India in 1858 and the subsequent absorption into the British Army of the Company's regular European infantry regiments. There still remained a quarter of a million Indian soldiers organised into three separate armies for Bengal, Madras and Bombay, together with a small number of frontier units that all passed to the British Crown. Each Army had a mix of Regular and irregular infantry and cavalry regiments, with different command hierarchies. The officers were now to receive British Crown Sovereign's commissions, no longer those of the Company. In 1895 the three armies, that of Bengal now including the frontier units, were brought together as one Indian Army. This Army was to last, and achieve world fame on battlefields in Europe and Africa as well as Asia, until 1947. These merit listing as being the campaigns and conditions in which British regimental officers had to make decisions and command: the late 19th century North-West Frontier Campaigns; in the First World War, France, Gallipoli, Iraq, Egypt and Palestine, East Africa; between the Wars the North-West Frontier, Iraq, Shanghai, Burma; and in the Second World War, East Africa, North Africa, Italy, Malaya and Burma. The experiences of officers were the same as those of British officers described in earlier chapters. The soldiers suffered more from the climates, especially in France in 1914.

Service in the Indian Army was a career independent from that of the British Army. If selected, cadets joined the Indian Army from Sandhurst, and served in and were promoted in Indian regiments; again, if selected, they attended the Indian Army Staff College at Quetta that was opened in 1907, and could rise to General rank in India.

At the outset Indian Army units were officered in a very different fashion to those in the British Army; as time passed successive administrative reforms were eventually to standardise on a more British pattern, though with certain distinctive features. Until a programme of training Indians as King's Commissioned Indian officers (KCIOs) was begun in the 1920s, regiments were officered by a small number of British officers together with a larger number of Indian Viceroy's Commissioned Officers (VCOs), Subedars and Resseldars equating to Captains, and Jemadars to Lieutenants.

In the late 19th century reorganisations, the Regular cavalry regiments of twenty-six European officers per regiment and the irregular regiments each with only three or four European officers were restructured to a common regular pattern of a British Lieutenant-Colonel in command, and three (later four) British officers in command of squadrons, within each of which were two troops commanded by a Resseldar assisted by a Jemadar. Regiments were sword or lance, with carbines or, from the early 1900s, rifles. After the First World War regiments were again reformed to a pattern of four sabre squadrons, each squadron of three troops supported by a light machine-gun troop.

The infantry regiments were similarly reformed. The pre-Mutiny Regular battalions had a British Lieutenant-Colonel and ten companies commanded by either a Captain or a Lieutenant each assisted by a British Subaltern, while irregular battalions had only three European officers, largely for supervision, a Major or Captain in command, a Second-in-Command and an Adjutant. After reorganisation battalions, now of eight companies, had six British officers, including the Quartermaster and medical officer, serving at the battalion headquarters with a further two, one for each 'wing' of four companies, the companies themselves being commanded by Subedars. Supervision was, however, found to be unsatisfactory and further European officers were added at different times, by 1914 resulting in a battalion being officered by fourteen British and sixteen Indian officers. The new structure provided for four companies with British Majors or Captains in command and British Subalterns under training. In 1922 the infantry battalions were grouped in 'big regiments' of four or five service and one training battalion. In Divisions one British and two Indian battalions continued to be brigaded together.

Until 1914 most cavalry and infantry regiments were still organised on the traditional *silladar* system by which, in return for an enhanced rate of pay, soldiers contracted to pay for and provide their own equipment (less weaponry), food, medical treatment and in the cavalry horses; these were all on hire purchase or sale from regiments to maintain uniformity. As a system it was cheap for the government, it kept crime to a minimum as discharged soldiers lost all, but it involved regimental officers in a vast amount of book-keeping. It made soldiers stakeholders in the regiment, appealing to their self-respect. The system, volunteer recruitment, the custom of holding durbars, at which officers sat listening to the opinions and concerns of soldiers, and the VCOs all illustrate the special relationship between the Indian Army soldier and his officers. The Indian Army was not a force of indigenous soldiers serving as mercenaries, rather it was a partnership between men of two very different continental cultures but each greatly respecting the other's military capabilities, enjoying the profession of soldiering and sharing senses of humour. In some regiments soldiers would formally obey but clearly not accept an officer until, in their eyes, he had proved himself as suitable and worthy of their comradeship.[2]

With only a few exceptions, the soldiers were recruited in the north of India where people were thought to be 'martial' and physically robust enough for duty in cold climates. In most regiments men were posted into single-caste or single-ethnicity squadrons or companies in which many soldiers were often related, forming a friendly competitive rivalry with other sub-units in the regiment, all a matter of honour.[3] Soldiers saw the Indian Army as an Indian, not a British Imperial, institution but with pride in allegiance to the King-Emperor and admiration for British officers, their leadership in battle and concern for soldiers' welfare at all times. In the cool seasons officers would lead out recruiting teams, in so doing learning about each individual recruit's home and family in a way more personal than in the British Army. Officers also always met former members of the regiment, keeping them well informed of regimental news and events. Until the era of Lord Kitchener as Commander-in-Chief of the Indian Army (1902–09) officers joining the Indian Army were initially posted to a Staff Corps, for three years until 1895, thereafter one. From the pool they were posted out to regiments. Many in practice stayed for several years with one regiment, senior officers often being given civil administration appointments. After the Kitchener reforms cadets at Sandhurst opting for the Indian Army, often with family connections and among the most promising, were sent on commissioning to India to serve with a British battalion for a year or more. In this period officers of the Indian regiments which they hoped to join would assess their suitability, and, if accepted, the young officer would make his career in that one regiment. He would be expected to learn at least one Indian language. Promotion in peacetime was by seniority: a Lieutenant would have to serve ten or eleven years before becoming a Captain and a further seven, eight or more before promotion to Major.

The Indian Army after Kitchener's thorough reorganisation and at the outbreak of the First World War was as large as the British Army. It comprised thirty-eight cavalry regiments, 130 infantry battalions, three engineer regiments and twelve mountain pack artillery batteries, all structured into nine divisions and five brigades, of which one was in Burma and another in Aden. The seventy British Army strength artillery batteries serving in India have already been noted. In the First World War ten more divisions were raised. The mistake was made of giving all wartime officers permanent commissions, creating a problem after the war. In the early 1920s the strength, including units in Burma, was reduced to twenty-one cavalry regiments, eighty-four regular, nineteen training, twenty Gurkha and nine pioneer battalions, and nineteen mountain batteries.[4] There were also, for the adventurous, the semi-regular North-West Frontier Scouts units, the most famous being the Khyber Rifles, to which officers could be attached for a tour of duty. In the 1930s the Indian Army was allowed its own artillery, though with British officers still in command of batteries.

In the Second World War, at its peak in 1944, the Indian Army, greatly expanded with new regiments and those of the princely states, fielded two armoured, eleven infantry, one airborne, three training and three garrison-holding divisions. The expansions in both wars posed serious problems. In the First World War some battalions had had very little experience with the Lee-Enfield rifle, in the case of one unit arriving in the Middle East none at all. In the Second World War only a very few cavalry regiments had received tanks as late as 1941; some cavalry regiments fought from lightly protected vehicles as motorised infantry. Some Second World War Divisions and units, hurriedly recruited (without the bonding of the pre-war Regulars) and inadequately trained, did not measure up to the world standard Indian Regular Divisions that matched, sometimes outmatched, the British Divisions in East and North Africa, Italy and Burma.[5] Some of the wartime Emergency Commission Officers (ECOs) were recruited locally from tea planters, the business community, or as boys straight from schools; others were recruited in Britain and trained in the same way as those for the British Army, either in Britain or at OCTUs in India. Many were excellent, but some others less so. Again in both wars, as in the British Army, the standards and experience of the pre-war Regular officers set the standards; in return Indian soldiers expected and ensured that these standards were maintained and often, in difficult times, also set good examples of frugality. The fact that the Indian Army was traditionally concerned with either internal security or the protection of the North-West Frontier, both home commitments, left it less well provided with support services. The three Engineers corps of the days of the Company were amalgamated in 1932 but until the outbreak of war still usually had a British Captain, sometimes with also a Lieutenant, in command of field companies; their expertise lay more in railways and signals than in mines or fortifications. The Indian Medical Service, the government medical department, was initially responsible for medical arrangements for all ranks, including officers; some but not all of its officers were European. Later an Indian Army Medical Corps with a number of British officers was raised. At the end of the 19th century a small number of nurses were sent out from Britain, forming the nucleus for the Queen Alexandra's Military Nursing Service for India who looked after British personnel and their families of both the British and Indian Armies.

By or during the Second World War the Indian Army included a Signal Corps, a Service Corps, an Ordnance Corps, an Electrical and Mechanical Engineers Corps and an Intelligence Corps. A number of wartime British officers served in these.

In an average peacetime year an officer of the Indian Army would have marched some 1,500 miles and climbed 80,000 feet over various hills. When regiments were not on active service on the Frontier, in Burma or elsewhere, or committed to internal security duties, the sporting and social life of a British officer in the Indian Army was full and varied. For local leave there was big-game hunting, shooting, fishing and mountaineering; a hunt, the 'Peshawar Vale', with hounds brought out from England, hunted jackal. The wealthier, mostly in cavalry regiments, played polo; the less well-off indulged in pig-sticking. Regimental cricket and hockey teams flourished. Mess life, modelled on that of the British Army, also flourished, with Colours and silverware, rites and customs, but also with the addition of big-game trophies around the walls and tiger-skin rugs on floors or walls. Dinners, balls, parties, the local club with its gymkhanas, tennis and in the evenings card games broke the monotony of training. As in the British Army a petty snobbery existed between the cavalry and the infantry, and between regiments of the same arm.[6]

Married officers lived in bungalows; the unmarried, perhaps four or five together, would share one bungalow while eating in the Mess. Servants attended to uniforms. Home leave, with journeys to and from Britain in the magnificent liners of the P & O Steamship Company, came round every four years. At the same time life in Imperial India was governed by strict rules of precedence, pecking order and conventions in which the military had its place, but not always at the top table, at district, provincial or gubernatorial dinner parties.

Within a general male culture, female company and the few chances of marriage continued to be provided by daughters of officers, businessmen and administrators and also girls working as teachers or nurses. Other officers took the opportunity of leave in

Britain to marry; shipboard romances also occurred during the long sea voyages. Any overt relationship with Indian women brought strong disapproval. Some officers sought covert comfort from Indian professional ladies; others befriended bored wives in hill stations whose husbands' absences on active service seemed to permit some relaxation of marriage vows. For officers' wives, with numerous servants to undertake all aspects of housework and children probably at school in Britain, life could easily slip into unreality, with gossip sharpening jealousy or desire.

The end of British rule in India meant that within a few months the careers of British officers of the Indian Army came to an end. A few were accepted, though not always made very welcome, in regiments and corps of the British Army. Most pre-war officers, now six years older, were content to retire on pension and start a new life elsewhere. The wartime Captains and Subalterns were not on Regular commissions and were young enough to embark on new careers.

A limited number of Regular officers of the British Army served on attachment to regiments raised in the Crown Colonies. Until 1939 Captains, Majors and Lieutenant-Colonels served in battalions and occasionally also in local artillery units; in the Second World War and afterwards in the National Service years Lieutenants were also eligible to apply to serve. The attachments were known affectionately as 'scallywag soldiering'. Wise battalion commanders realised that a young regimental officer would gain useful experience of responsibility and adaptability while serving with a colonial regiment, though others were sometimes reluctant to part with a good officer. Tours could be for up to six years in West Africa or four in East Africa. For the years of peace in the colonial period the battalions were little more than a *gendarmerie*, one or two per colony, available to support police at times of local unrest, but the regiments became active in the two World Wars. A number of smaller colony regiments were part-time, some being officered by local settlers. The most important, to which the large majority of British officers who opted for a colonial regiment tour of service were sent, were the two groups of African units, raised from earlier small units in which a few British officers had served. These regiments were, in West Africa, the West African Frontier Force formed in 1887 and made Royal in 1928, and, in East Africa, the King's African Rifles formed in 1902.[7] In the 1920s these were administered by two Colonels in the War Office, an indication of their relatively small significance.

Officers opted for African service for a variety of reasons – change and excitement, money either to earn and save or to pay off debts (pay was almost trebled, useful allowances were also payable, no income tax was deducted and pensions were enhanced); sport of all varieties, with equestrian events and polo, particularly in West Africa; and greater opportunities for command and decision-making. Promotion with home regiments while an officer served in Africa was secured. From the generally poor quality of officers, it would seem that before 1914 and occasionally thereafter they were sent on African service sometimes because their home Commanding Officers wanted to be rid of them. By the 1920s, however, the quality steadily improved and African battalions became well and efficiently officered. Officers were required to learn the local military *lingua franca*, in West Africa Hausa, in East Africa Swahili or Cinyanja. Their primary interests, however, remained the British Army and few made any serious effort to study local societies. Until 1945 officers, with the exception of Lieutenant-Colonels, were expected to be unmarried. Battalions were raised by territory but ethnicities were mixed in companies. Basic training of soldiers included hygiene, the importance of time, marching, rifle training, words of command and drill. Later field training was for forest or savannah conflicts. Rifles were issued to soldiers, but machine-guns and ammunition were kept in armouries.

In addition to infantry a small number of specialists, engineers, signals, Chaplains, medical and nursing officers, all served in Africa.

The only distinctive feature of officers' uniforms was a slouch hat, with appropriate regimental insignia.

Life was agreeable; in regiments Messes complete with regimental Colours and silverware were developed. Officers were automatically members of local white-only clubs. Tobacco and alcohol were duty free, drink unfortunately proving too great a temptation for some. All officers had a personal servant and there were generous local and home leave grants, varying a little by territory. From 1945 wives (except for National Service officers) were flown out and housed in bungalows and attended by servants. Many helped with welfare work in wives' clubs and clinics.

Until 1914 the use of African women seems to have been common, women even appearing in Messes.[8] After the First World War 'sleeping partners' were common and accepted in West Africa, but in East Africa such arrangements were frowned upon, and after 1945 all were ended – at least officially – in both regions. Many Second World War officers, a mixed bag it would appear from the number of courts-martial, also went with local women. These officers came from the same variety of backgrounds as officers in home formations and regiments, and were joined by Colonial Service officials, planters and settlers. A number had no real empathy with their soldiers, as occasional protests and disciplinary problems were to show.

West African troops fought to occupy the German West African colonies in 1914–16, and later joined East African troops in the German East Africa campaign. In the Second World War both West and East African troops fought against the Italians in East Africa, and two West African and one East African divisions participated in the Burma campaign. After the war East African battalions took part in the campaigns in Malaya and Kenya. Thousands of other African men, from every British territory, served in both wars in porter or labour units. Those in the East Africa campaign of 1914–18 were shockingly officered by locally recruited white officers, over 40,000 dying of neglect, hunger and disease. The Second

World War units were well organised and the men cared for. In Kenya (as with the colony's settler population) a tendency to 'larger than life' behaviour occasionally manifested itself. Adjutants who were heavily in debt were disciplining officers who were only slightly less heavily indebted; or the officer in charge of courts-martial was himself court-martialled.[9]

Soldiers in both regions were drawn from 'martial races', remote peasant societies where men saw service as Crown protection of their way of life with useful remittances home from pay. Ceremonies, music and drill appeared to be a new, almost magical, ritual providing security. The officers were generally well regarded, particularly if they entered into sports and dances and possessed a sense of humour.[10]

Until the late 1950s, the relationship was paternalistic. Soldiers' wives, and other women, lived in barrack lines. In consequence officers became much more involved in soldiers' domestic affairs than in Britain. In West Africa, they were assisted by an official 'lines manager', the wife of a senior NCO. In West Africa also, officers learnt to respect, if not to understand, what appeared to be magic practices. Discipline was more severe than in British regiments; offered the choice of fines, confinement to barracks or 'six for arse' with a cane, almost invariably the soldier's preference was for the third. Although officially forbidden, flogging with a hide whip was still administered at least until 1945. Standing orders for one King's African Rifles battalion published in 1930 directed that no soldier might beat his wife without his company commander's permission.[11] In Nigeria in one battalion the Commanding Officer personally vetted the women chosen by soldiers for marriage.

As the colonial era drew to a close in the early 1950s in West Africa, a programme of training African officers was begun which enabled the phasing-out of British officers to be effected smoothly. In East Africa the process was delayed, with very few officers at independence.[12] In consequence, to African rank and file it appeared that nothing had changed in the armies. Further, British officers had begun to lose touch with their soldiers who saw their past services no longer appreciated by new political elites but in whose hands their futures were going to lie.[13] These frustrations led to the January 1964 mutinies in Tanganyika, Uganda and Kenya which had to be suppressed by British forces; the results were profound in each territory. British officers served on in the Kenyan Army for several years but left Uganda and Tanzania. It is, however, appropriate to conclude by noting that former officers and personnel of the King's African Rifles and other East African units now living in Britain launched a charity to help old African veterans in need. This, the *Askari Appeal*, had raised £250,000 by 2005.

NOTES

1 The most important work on the Indian Army remains Philip Mason, *A Matter of Honour* (London, Jonathan Cape, 1974) but also useful are Heathcote, *Indian Army*, and Ian Sumner, *The Indian Army 1914–1947* (Oxford, Botley, 2001).

2 John Clay, *John Masters: A Regimental Life* (London, Michael Joseph, 2001).

3 In the 1919–39 period the only infantry regiments to experience breakdowns in discipline were two, both composed of one single ethnicity; poor officering was also responsible.

4 These totals do not include the forces, of varying and mostly second- or third-line quality, maintained by the rulers of the larger princely states, in total sixteen regiments of cavalry, forty-six infantry battalions and seven artillery batteries. British officers advised but did not serve with these units. Regiments from the princely states served in several theatres in the First World War.

5 The Commander-in-Chief Middle East, 1941–42, General Sir Claude Auchinleck, was said on one occasion to have remarked that properly trained and properly led the British soldier could be every bit as good as the Indian. John Masters, *The Road Past Mandalay* (London, Michael Joseph, 1961) provides a good account of a British officer serving with the Indian Army in the Burma campaign.

6 The Queen Victoria's Own Guides Cavalry Frontier Force, and Skinner's Horse (with their distinctive yellow tunic coats) headed the cavalry in status, the Frontier Force Rifles, the Frontier Force Regiment and the Punjab and Gurkha regiments the infantry.

7 Regimental histories of both regiments setting out their notable achievements in both World Wars exist, but the special studies of officers here are taken from the material submitted by former officers to the Oxford Colonial Records Project which is more useful in the context of this work. The studies were subsequently published in Anthony Clayton and David Killingray, *Khaki and Blue: Military and Police in British Colonial Africa* (Athens, Ohio, Ohio University, 1989).

8 Colonel Richard Meinertzhagen in respect of East Africa and the future Marshal of the RAF, Lord Trenchard, in West Africa were both scandalised by the wine, women and gambling in Messes they joined. John Lord, *Duty, Honour, Empire: The Life and Times of Colonel Richard Meinertzhagen* (London, Hutchinson, 1972), 185; Andrew Boyle, *Trenchard* (London, Collins, 1962), 73, 81–82.

9 General colonial wisdom attributed larger-than-life behaviour to the altitude. More likely was the example around them of societies apparently uninhibited by the constraints of metropolitan social life.

10 Sport included football and athletics. The KAR had its own game, Karamoja, in which teams of any number tried to carry a football to an opponent's goal but had to drop the ball when touched. In mild saturnalia officers were expected to join in dances – for ten minutes.

11 *Standing Orders of the 6th Battalion, The King's African Rifles, 1930* (Dar es Salaam, Government Printer, 1930), 38. The order was amended a little later, but another order sanctioned corporal punishment for soldier offences, the Commanding Officer's permission being necessary.

12 A programme of commissioning senior warrant officers as 'effendis', modelled on the former Indian Army VCOs, had some palliative success – and one conspicuous failure, Idi Amin.

13 Timothy H. Parsons, *The 1964 Army Mutinies and the Making of Modern East Africa* (Westport, Connecticut, Praeger, 2003), ii, iii, provides interesting detail.

CHAPTER 16

THE OFFICERS OF THE SUPPORT SERVICES

This chapter aims to summarise the history, over the centuries, of officers serving in the Army's Support Services. These fall into two broad categories, combatant and non-combatant, the former covering ordnance and logistics and certain specialist technical and administrative personnel, the latter authorised to fight only in self-defence and including medical, dental, nurses and veterinary officers and Chaplains. Space unfortunately prevents recording the important and essential work of officers of both categories in all the Army's various campaigns; only a few illustrative examples can be given. In the campaigns, Support Service officers, combatant and non-combatant, shared most of the hardships and risks of the front-line units. In many, especially in the three medical corps, life and death decisions had to be made in conditions of the greatest difficulty and danger. Despite all this, for long Support Service officers were regarded as second-class citizens by most officers in the combat arms, a view based as much on the slightly lower social origins of the Support Service officers as on their roles.

A Board of Ordnance was first established in 1683 concerned with what would now be called procurement, its officials being civilians.[1] In 1792 an Ordnance Field Train was formed to provide field supply for the Artillery and Engineers, its officers remaining civilians although they wore uniform. The Field Train served in all the campaigns between 1792 and 1815 but was run down to cadre strength after Waterloo and proved totally inadequate in the Crimean War. A Military Stores Department was created in 1859, its officers receiving commissions and being trained at Woolwich; for rank and file a Military Store Staff Corps was formed six years later. The Military Store Department was later renamed the Ordnance Store Department and from 1881 began to recruit officers from other units. The Ordnance Store Companies including rank and file became Ordnance Store Corps in 1889, but their officers did not hold combatant commissions. In 1896 the Department, the Store Companies and other branches including clothing were amalgamated into an Army Ordnance Department and Corps.

As has already been noted, provision of stores and food to troops in the field lay for long in the hands of private finance initiative contractors supervised by Commissaries, mostly civilian Treasury officials.[2] These officials under Wellington were given a relative military rank, the Commissary-General that of Brigadier-General at the top, down to clerks who were given the rank of Ensign at the bottom; eighty-seven Commissaries and 255 clerks were at work in the Peninsula. Their status, despite the relative ranking, however, remained that of civilians, all military officers taking precedence. Attempts were made to run an organised proper military transport corps with the short-lived Corps of Waggoners of 1794–96, the Royal Waggon Corps of 1799–1802 and the Royal Waggon Train of 1802–33; many of their officers, particularly after 1815, were veterans on half-pay following reductions in line regiments. In a further defence reduction, reminiscent of the unfortunate 'no spare capacity' policies of 160 years later, the Waggon Train was disbanded in 1833 with inevitably disastrous consequences.

The Crimean War was also to show up the total inadequacy of the existing Commissariat system and a Land Transport Corps was formed in January 1855 and was at work in the Crimea by the spring. By March 1856 the Corps in the Crimea comprised seven regiments each of two battalions divided into three squadrons. In each regiment one battalion was concerned with ammunition and ambulances, the second with stores and supplies. The best of the 48 officers were NCOs promoted from cavalry and infantry regiments; others, less satisfactory, were officers transferred from East India Company regiments, many of whom had to be replaced.[3] After the Crimean War a Commissariat Staff Corps officered by uniformed civilians was formed for supply, and the Military Train of serving Army officers and soldiers in six battalions was established. For transport each of the Train battalions had twenty-seven officers and was divided into four troops commanded by a Captain and a Lieutenant; most of the officers came from the cavalry. In 1869 an Army Service Corps was established to replace both; while rank and file were soldiers, the officers were technically still civilians in a 'Control Department'; they were recruited from regiments holding the rank of Captain until promotion to Acting Controller, then Assistant Controller and on to Deputy Controllers. Later in 1875 the Control Department was changed into a Commissariat and Transport Department whose officers initially held Commissariat Controller titles until 1880 when these were changed to military rank and the officers were expected to have Staff College or staff experience. Eventually in 1888 a sensible rationalisation created a new Army Service Corps in which officers could make a lifetime career with pay and promotion on the Royal Engineers pattern and with specialist training, and in the words of Fortescue '... take their rightful place as brother-soldiers and not be treated as mere clerks and servants'.[4]

The duties of Army Service Corps officers were varied. In operations in Sudan in 1896–98 officers organised camel train supply columns, each column of some 1,400 animals. In the South African War ASC officers and companies organised railway, ox and mule supply columns, the latter using wagons often in need of maintenance. Officers of the Ordnance Department and Corps improvised field stores with the greatest difficulty. In 1900–08 all ASC officers were required to take mechanical transport training. The First World War saw a massive expansion of the Corps, from 500 officers in 1915 to 12,000 in 1918, and a slow but progressive shift away from horse transport to motor transport. Each Division had a Headquarters and four Horse Transport companies, and a Divisional Supply Column of three-ton lorries. Other officers were responsible for supply units, movement of stores by rail, base and field supply depots, bakeries, fuel tankers, coal supplies, ambulance drivers and heavy gun towing drivers, and in the Middle East for mule and camel drivers. Ordnance officers maintained a Base Ordnance Depot at Le Havre, together with subsidiary depots, ammunition dumps and artillery workshops. In the inter-war period the ASC, now the Royal Army Service Corps, completed the process of conversion from horse to motor transport. For officers, in view of difficulties in attracting Sandhurst cadets, it recruited a number of university graduates, many with engineering degrees. These attended a Junior Officers course at Aldershot and were attached for nine months to an infantry battalion; other supply and transport courses for Captains and Majors were also organised. The Ordnance Department Officers and Corps were amalgamated to form the Royal Army Ordnance Corps (RAOC) in 1918.

The RASC served everywhere in the Second World War, officers' command tasks ranging from Supply Reserve and Base Supply Depots on the various fronts to Divisional Supply columns, usually of three companies (Baggage, Supply and Ammunition), general transport companies, tank transport companies, amphibious transport companies, mule transport organisation, petrol units, water supply units, air drop companies and motorboat companies. The RAOC also served in all theatres, its officers being responsible for Base and Forward Ordnance and Ammunition Depots, maintenance units for stores and ammunition, laundry and bath units, industrial gas units and Ordnance beach detachments. Officers and soldiers of both corps often found themselves used as infantry at times of crisis. In the post-1945 operations, officers learnt further new skills of air despatch and hovercraft operations. RAOC officers – and also some Royal Engineers Officers – developed much-admired skills first learnt in the Second World War in the fields of explosives and delayed action bombs, five specialist officers losing their lives in Northern Ireland. In 1965 the RASC became the Royal Corps of Transport, absorbing the few remaining Royal Engineers transport duties but losing its stores responsibilities to the Royal Army Ordnance Corps. The latter decision was reversed in 1993 with the formation of the Royal Logistic Corps, responsible for both transport and stores and the largest corps in the Army.

The RLC also incorporated three further small corps – the Royal Pioneer Corps formed in 1939 with officer responsibilities for the recruitment of civilian labour for military purposes, the Army Catering Corps formed from the RASC in 1941, and the Royal Engineers Postal and Courier Service, responsible for army mail.

Another large corps is the Royal Electrical and Mechanical Engineers (REME) formed in 1942 from personnel of the RASC and RAOC. It is a corps with a high ratio of officers to soldiers, and with the vast majority of the officers being graduates. The role of the corps is that of recovering, repairing and maintaining vehicles of all types, helicopters and electronic equipments. Recovery of vehicles may include recovery while battle is still in progress. A REME detachment commanded by a young officer is attached to every armoured regiment, every armoured personnel carrier infantry regiment and every helicopter squadron. More senior officers command armoured workshops and base workshops.

In 1992 an Adjutant-General's Corps (AGC) was formed to embody services whose work is chiefly concerned with personnel rather than equipment. The oldest components of the AGC that retain their name within the AGC are the police and provost branches, with their long history. Provost duties from the

Restoration monarchy onwards were carried out by officials and later by NCOs.[5] In the late 19th century the senior Provost-Marshal was granted a commission as a Captain or Major, but the Military Mounted Police, formed in 1855, and the later Military Foot Police of 1882 were officered by men from regiments, as was the Military Prison Staff Corps, later the Military Provost Staff Corps. In 1926 a Corps of Military Police was formed, but as late as the 1950s the very small numbers of officers remained officers seconded from other regiments.[6]

Duties for military police officers in peacetime have included disciplinary issues, investigation of crime, policing of garrison towns and off-limit areas, drugs and some ceremonial. In the second half of the 20th century the corps had particular surveillance responsibilities in Northern Ireland and Berlin. In symmetrical conventional war, duties include custody of prisoners, surveillance of civilians, traffic control and freeing roads of refugees, provision of bodyguards and escorts for senior personnel, and the return of deserters and battle-stressed stragglers to their unit.

After the Second World War National Service officers were used for what was known from 1946 as the Royal Military Police. In 1954 direct commissioning of officers into the corps was sanctioned, with the first Sandhurst cadet commissioned in the following year. By the end of the decade Regular officers of all ranks were serving in the corps and from 1992 women officers were commissioned direct from Sandhurst into the corps.

Of the other Corps incorporated into the AGC the oldest was the Royal Army Pay Corps. This has its origins in an officers-only Pay Sub-Department of the Control Department. An other-ranks Army Pay Corps was created in 1893, the two being amalgamated in 1929 to form the Royal Army Pay Corps. The present-day officers of this branch of the AGC are concerned with information technology as well as pay. Also formed in 1920 was the Army Education Corps, after 1946 becoming Royal (RAEC). The officers of this branch of the AGC are routinely concerned with officers' and soldiers' education, now including Open University and other tertiary and national vocational education qualifications, language training and the administration of Army schools in garrison centres overseas; in war (and major exercises) officers may be required to be meteorological staff officers. The Army Legal Corps was formed as the Army Legal Services Staff list in 1948; its officers are trained lawyers and now have legal advice on Rules of Engagement as well as court-martial processes among their duties. Officers and women of the Women's Royal Army Corps, as already noted, were either transferred to other corps or regiments if appropriately qualified or remained within the AGC mainstream.

The most important of the non-combatant corps is the Royal Army Medical Corps (RAMC). Medicine in the Army had a lamentable history until the years after the Crimean War. Although surgeons served with units from the Restoration Army, for long their status equated with that of the drummers and fifers, despite their having Regular Commissions.[7] Conditions had changed but little by the time of the Peninsula War where many regimental surgeons, albeit often of good will, lacked any proper professional medical training. But the war was to initiate a few small changes, some officers appreciating the need to separate sick from wounded, and a growing recognition that evacuation of the wounded, often many thousands, could not be left to regimental bandsmen.

The suffering and scandals of the Crimean War at last brought reform, though its speed was slow. An other-ranks Medical Staff Corps, later to become an Army Hospital Corps (with, from 1860, an Army Medical School), was formed for battlefield stretcher-bearer and field hospital duties, and an Army Medical Department of officer doctors. Men from both these bodies served in the various Victorian colonial campaigns together. A system of 'movable and stationary field hospitals' with Department doctors, Hospital Corps bearers and Transport Corps ambulances was set up for divisions, with, further back, hospital ships and base general hospitals. In 1898 the two bodies were merged to form the Royal Army Medical Corps. The merger, intended to form a proper battlefield and hospital service for the Army, was formed too late to prevent or cope with the appalling disease and death rate of the Boer War.

The shortcomings led to further reform; by 1913 the RAMC had a strength of thirty-five companies in Britain and overseas, and over 1,000 serving Regular officers, but poor rates of pay led to recruiting difficulties throughout the century. Many doctors held Irish qualifications; if their skills did not always match those of doctors trained in Britain they established a lasting tradition of care and good humour. The First World War saw massive expansion and a system of treating wounded in a chain from the unit's own doctor and Regimental Aid Post to Advanced and then Main Dressing Stations, a Casualty Clearing Station and then on to Base Hospitals.[8] The officers of the Corps came to develop world-class expertise in the treatment of shock, blood loss, bacteriology of wound infections and reconstructive surgery, and, less spectacular but vital, hygiene in trench warfare. Officers and men of the RAMC won numerous bravery awards, notable among them the only two men ever to receive a bar to their Victoria Cross, Lieutenant A. Martin Leake and Captain Noel Chavasse.[9]

Both the First World War and even more the Second World War were to bring the skills of specialists in almost every medical field available to the wounded; blood from Field Transfusion Units saved scores of lives, and Head Injury and Field Surgery Units coped with complex cases. The evacuation of casualties by air, in small aircraft and Dakotas, was first developed in the Burma campaign. Medical officers accompanied glider assaults, parachute drops and beach landings; others had to cope with the problems of the dead and survivors in Nazi concentration or Japanese prisoner-of-war camps. In the postwar years medical officers served with the Army in every campaign and developed, by means of helicopter and aircraft, ever more swift procedures for the evacuation of casualties to the treatment they needed, generally on tri-service arrangements. The first helicopter example appears to have been the lifting of a wounded Royal Marine to a Casualty Clearing Station on an aircraft carrier during the 1956 Suez operation; by the time of the Falklands War such procedures were routine and exceedingly efficient.[10] The campaign in Northern Ireland was to give officers of the Corps a special expertise in the treatment of burns. After the end of the Cold War it was decided to close almost all military hospitals in Britain and for Armed Service doctors to staff or assist in the staffing of wards in certain National Health Service hospitals, run in partnership with the Ministry of Defence. From the 1960s on, the RAMC included women medical officers and a number of doctors from ethnic minorities.

Provision of nursing staff before the Crimean War was as haphazard as the provision of doctors; women certainly tended the sick in the 18th century wars, but they were untrained and were drawn from camp followers. Little had changed by the outbreak of the Crimean War, during and after which Florence Nightingale was to achieve so much. The three major military hospitals that were built in the 1860s and 1870s engaged civilian nurses and it was not until 1881 that an Army Nursing Service came into being, preference for recruits for training being the widows or daughters of officers.[11] From the outset it is clear that these Nursing Sisters, on qualification, were accepted as having officer status, though this was not formally approved until 1904. In the South African War, the Sisters worked in hospitals and trains, their work being recognised by the creation of a special Order, the Royal Red Cross.[12] More importantly, as a result of the experiences of the war, in 1902 was formed the Queen Alexandra's Imperial Military Nursing Service (the 'QAs'). The Service was to perform devoted work in every theatre and campaign in the two World Wars, both in its own nursing and in the supervision of reservists and wartime volunteers.

Their status, however, remained anomalous. After the institution of the Military Cross for officers and the Military Medal for soldiers in 1915, Sisters were awarded the Medal, but not being commissioned although of officer status they were not eligible for the Cross. In 1926 they were granted equivalent ranks with Army officers but with the rank titles of Principal Matron (Lieutenant-Colonel), Matron (Major), Sisters (Captains), and Staff Nurses (Subalterns). In the major military hospitals in Britain and overseas (over 250 QAs were serving in India in the 1930s), QA messes presided over by the Matron provided a social life in peacetime. In war QA nurses often worked in forward area battlefield conditions – in the siege of Tobruk, on the Normandy beaches, in bamboo and grass-thatched wards in Burma.

After the Second World War, in 1948, the Service became the Queen Alexandra's Royal Army Nursing Corps, but only in 1959 were Sisters given Regular Army officer ranks. QA NCOs who qualified as State Registered Nurses became eligible for Commissions. QAs participated in many of the post-1945 conflicts, from Korea to service on board ship in the Falklands War and the Iraq wars. Many now work and complete their training in Ministry of Defence wards in civilian hospitals. The Corps is now no longer women only, male nurses serving in all ranks. Following the 1983 changes in the qualifications of nurses, Registered General Nurses must have one year's post-registration experience to be eligible for a commission. Further postgraduate training is also provided.

The remaining small corps should not be overlooked. The most important is probably the Army Dental Corps formed in 1921, becoming Royal in 1926 and actually leading the way, in the Second World War, of gazetting women officers with full military rank.[13] Present-day dental officers have a war role as anaesthetists. Next should follow the Royal Veterinary Department formed in 1858, becoming an all-ranks corps in 1900, a vital component of the Army in the age of the horse and in practice the REME of the day. In 1910 the corps totalled six Colonels, five Lieutenant-Colonels, twenty-five Majors, eighty-two Captains and fifty Lieutenants, but it is now reduced to a Colonel, four Lieutenant-Colonels, sixteen Majors, four Captains and one Lieutenant. The Small Arms School Corps and the Army Physical Training Corps, whose titles are self-explanatory, are officered entirely by promoted Warrant Officers and NCOs.

The inclusion of Chaplains in regiments from the Restoration onwards has already been noted, though the arrangements for them were never properly formalised. Chaplains' commissions were sold by Colonels, Chaplains sold them on to deputies and many were absent from their duties; apparently in 1796 no fewer than 340 were 'on leave'. In that year the first Chaplain-General was appointed, his duties also extending for some reason to the establishment of telegraphy.[14] The purchasing of Chaplains' commissions was abolished and a Chaplains Department established. Nine Chaplains were present at Waterloo, ranked as Majors. The 1818 *Army List* is the first to note a Chaplains Department, a Chaplain-General, twenty-six Chaplains on full pay and six on half pay. In 1827 the first Presbyterian and in 1836 the first Roman Catholic Chaplains were authorised. In 1859 Chaplains were graded in a system lasting to the present day with the Chaplain-General ranking as a Major-General, a Chaplain First Class as a Colonel, a Chaplain Second Class as a Lieutenant-Colonel, a Chaplain Third Class as a Major and a Chaplain Fourth Class as a Captain. Progressively in the second half of the 19th century Wesleyans in 1881 and Jews in 1892 were appointed Chaplains; in the 20th century Baptists and Congregationalists were accepted. Chaplains are usually posted to garrison stations, schools and hospitals, sometimes to single units. Regular Army Chaplains are normally expected to have served at least three years in their respective order. Until 1945 Sunday church parades were obligatory, it being argued *inter alia* that attendance secured freedom of worship against any intrusion by other duties! During weekdays 'Padre's Hour' was included in unit training programmes.

The duties of Chaplains in war, from the Crimean War to the present day, have been the arrangement of Divine Service, comfort for the wounded and sick, the burial of the dead and letters to their relatives. Professionally, they were seen as an important factor in the maintenance of morale. In peacetime Chaplains teach in schools, marry, baptise and conduct funeral services for Army families, and may also have the task of breaking news of injury or death to relatives. At the outbreak of the First World War the Army Chaplains' Department totalled 117; on Armistice Day in 1918 the number had risen to 3,474; one serving Chaplain, the Rev. T. Bayley Hardy, was awarded the Victoria Cross. An interesting recent analysis of the work of Chaplains in Western Front trench warfare came to several particular conclusions.[15] In respect of soldiers the study noted that recruits were often ignorant of or hostile to Christianity and unable to see its value, and found the horrors of the war inconsistent with a belief in a just God. The Chaplains themselves, however, came to see an unexpected 'unconscious' Christianity that had been stifled by ignorance and poverty but was evident in the self-sacrificing spirit of soldiers, a reversal of traditional Victorian views of human nature being dominated by sin. The response of Chaplains to their soldiers' views was to assert that God suffered along with man to redeem human free-will, and also in practical terms to press for social change and the removal of class barriers, a pressure to which the senior officers and the Church responded only conservatively.

In 1919 the Chaplains Department became Royal with a peacetime strength fixed in 1929 of 140, of which 100 were Anglican Communion. A similar massive expansion followed in the Second World War, Chaplains participating in training, successes and reverses with all units in every theatre, ninety-six losing their lives. Some stayed with one combat unit throughout the war; the Rev. G. Claxton, for example, served with the 2nd Dorsets in France in 1940 and throughout the Burma campaign, being held in the highest regard by all ranks.

In the post-1945 years the Royal Army Chaplains Department, realising that more soldiers entering the Army had little or no idea of the Christian faith, embarked on a variety of Christian character and leadership training programmes, study weekends and work in Army Apprentices and Junior Leaders schools as well as station or unit parochial duties. Chaplains, along with all other non-combatant officers, attend a short introductory course at Sandhurst after their selection. In 2004 it was announced that Muslim, Buddhist and Sikh civilian clerics would be appointed to work for all three Services.

NOTES

1 Brigadier A.M. Fernyhough, *A Short History of the RAOC* (RAOC, 1980), sets out the history of the Corps and its predecessors.

2 Graeme Crew, *The Royal Army Service Corps* (London, Leo Cooper, 1970), sets out the history of the Corps and its predecessors.

3 Fortescue, *RASC*, I, 156. These officers 'had accepted commissions in the hope that they had found an easy place for which habits of laziness and luxury in India thoroughly fitted them'.

4 Fortescue, *RASC*, I, 214.

5 It should be noted that minor police duties in regiments are carried out by the units' own Regimental Police under a Provost Sergeant responsible to the Adjutant.

6 G.D. Sheffield, *The Redcaps: A History of the Royal Military Police and its Antecedents from the Middle Ages to the Gulf War* (London, Brassey's, 1994), provides a comprehensive history. Also useful in respect of the First World War is Sheffield's chapter 'The operational role of British Military Police in the Western Front 1914–18', in Griffith, *British Fighting Methods*, iv, 70–86.

7 Redmond McLaughlin, *The Royal Army Medical Corps* (London, Leo Cooper, 1972), provides a useful short history. A fuller, more detailed account is that of Dr John S.G. Blair, *Centenary History of the Royal Army Medical Corps, 1898–1998* (Edinburgh, Scottish Academic Press, 2001).

8 A valuable account of the work of the RAMC on the Western Front is provided by Geoffrey Noon, 'The treatment of casualties in the Great War', in Griffith, *British Fighting Methods* v, 87–112.

9 The totals were seven Victoria Crosses together with the two bars, 499 Distinguished Service Orders and twenty-five bars, and 1,484 Military Crosses and 184 bars. Similar totals went to the non-commissioned ranks, notably among stretcher-bearers.

10 Rick Jolly, *The Red and Green Life Machine: A Diary of the Falklands Field Hospital* (London, Century, 1983), provides a most interesting account.

11 Juliet Piggott, *Queen Alexandra's Royal Army Nursing Corps* (London, Leo Cooper, 1975), provides a full account.

12 The Order was amended in 1931 to provide for Second Class Associates, with the First Class remaining as Members.

13 *The Army List 1945* notes sixteen women Lieutenants, three recorded as 'Mrs.' and the remainder as 'Miss'.

14 The Rev. P. Middleton Brumwell, *The Army Chaplain* (London, A. & C. Black, 1943) and Brigadier the Rt Hon. Sir John Smyth, *In This Sign Conquer* (London, Mowbray, 1968) provide accounts of the evolution of the Royal Army Chaplains Department.

15 'British Army Chaplains of World War I: reactions to service at the Front', by J.L. Iremonger, *Seaford House (Royal College of Defence Studies) Papers*, 2003.

CHAPTER 17

CONCLUSION

At the start of the 21st century the profession of military officer is yet again in a process of theoretical evolution, but at the same time, at the level of the young Lieutenant or Captain in the regimental Mess, several old traditional practical and personal questions still remain. This conclusion will seek to summarise both.

Overall, the profession has come full circle. Until the 1950s strength and integrity of character was seen as the prime requirement. Character, however, was seen by critics outside the Army as associated with class. Officer recruitment was accordingly opened to wider society and it was thought that professionalism in training would meet the Army's needs. The late 20th century social changes in Britain and the new and very different operational requirements have shown that professional knowledge is not enough. If an officer's authority is to be accepted he or she has to be respected as an individual whose personal behaviour and integrity set an example. Sandhurst training now sets out to develop character and leadership as much as purely military skill, with emphasis on duty and trust, and officers always being seen to do their best, putting their soldiers before themselves and exercising judgement, moderation and fairness.

Sandhurst training is followed up by a paper for officers, *Values and Standards of the British Army*, signed by the Chief of the General

Staff and first published in 2000. The paper's main themes are commitment, self-sacrifice and trust. The behaviour of individual officers and soldiers is to be judged on a 'Service Test', whether or not the behaviour affects military efficiency. Commanders at all levels are instructed on adherence to the law, discrimination and harassment, bullying, drug and alcohol abuse, and debt. In respect of social conduct, firm instruction covers issues such as unwelcome sexual attention, behaviour that damages personal relationships or causes offence, and any taking of sexual advantage. *Values and Standards* is perhaps the most important statement of British military conduct for 200 years, since the days of Sir John Moore. A 1914 Old Contemptible officer would have found the necessity for much of the paper, and the social need for it, difficult to believe, but the main themes are timeless.

Some of the other purely military issues arising from day-to-day problems in the last years of the 20th century have already been described. Several are still the subjects of on-going study by staff officers above regimental level, but the impact on regimental officers is already evident.[1] First and most important is the need for officers to be much better and more widely educated; 'ours not to reason why' must now be forgotten amid the changing and complex conditions in which relatively junior regimental officers may have to make decisions. The wider purposes as well as the task of a mission have to be understood. It is argued they should consider any sensitive issue within two related frames: firstly, the consequence of their decision upon superiors at least two ranks higher than themselves and, secondly, their decision within the prescribed Army doctrine, detailed in numerous training manuals, for whatever type of operation in which they are engaged – open war whether symmetric or asymmetric, humanitarian, peace support, coalition, alliance or power projection.[2]

Training for this must balance the need to think and inform upwards while retaining room for original independent thinking, flexibility and scepticism. Officers will then have to think much more clearly not only on the means needed to fight, but also how best to apply knowledge and understanding to specific practices, and their own ability to motivate subordinates to carry out their duties, if necessary at risk to both their lives. The old 'practical chap with common sense' approach to difficult decisions is at best obsolete if not dangerous. Education is also essential to ensure that officers, as they rise in their careers, can work, express themselves or argue their case with civil servants and political figures, officers of the other services and of other nations' forces. For study and teaching in these fields a 'Defence Academy' umbrella organisation was estab- lished in 2002 incorporating the Royal College of Defence Studies, courses at different levels at the Joint Services Command and Staff College and the Royal Military College of Science, and the Conflict Studies Research Centre. Further, despite all the suspicions that the words 'administration' and 'management' may arouse, officers now have to accept that the tools of management are relevant. The pill in a number of fields is sweetened by the more military-sounding word 'sustainability' – the need to ensure that front-line troops will continue, for so long as is necessary, to receive what they need for operations. In the complexities of weapons development and procurement, a large number of officers can make careers in five specific 'fields of employment' – Defence Policy, Technical (acquisition/information systems), Combat, Logistics and Human Resources.[3]

Other fields in which officers are now being trained to think include awareness of the legal issues mentioned in Chapter 14 that can range from claims for compensation or of grievance, respons- ibilities in 'defence diplomacy' such as working within Partnership for Peace programmes and likely roles in wider national human- itarian work, rebuilding national infrastructures after a conflict such as that of Iraq and security, in particular at times of terrorist actions or threats.

A bricks and mortar issue is linked to these questions of training and character development. The upkeep of the Royal Military Academy at Sandhurst is exceedingly costly, the 19th century and 1960s buildings requiring almost continuous maintenance. Savings, ever popular at a political level, could come from a move to a smaller-scale institution on land that is less valuable. But such a saving would lose the very great impact on character formation made by the historic buildings and their traditions.

Finally, the officer, man or woman, remains an individual member of the human race, not just one more in a study group considering a technological development or military social behaviour. The general public still expects that he or she will maintain particular standards, but as an individual he or she will have their own personal characteristics – virtues, weaknesses, foibles, perhaps human relationship problems. And it is these day-to-day issues within the life of the individual regimental officer that also need to be remembered in any conclusion: to have its proper value this work must end by returning focus on the man or woman officer, him or herself.

Individual officers, throughout the centuries, obviously have much in common with each other, their brother and sister officers in the profession and regiment. But each, nevertheless, remains an individual with his or her own need to adjust their personality to the demands of the Army. Generally officers are self-assured, robust, cheerful and social, but years of service can change personalities, particularly before the late 20th century when service in hot climates together with customary lunchtime gin served to shorten tempers. At any time authority and power can corrupt, resulting in intolerance or abuse. Some officers may be very patient, cool and even imperturbable under stress; others may have tempers of varying length. Some may be self-indulgent in food, drink, the opposite sex or gambling, up to a point understood by soldiers but beyond this point held in contempt. Others may be austere, often more respected than understood by the majority of the rank and file. Many are adventurous, but others prefer routine. Some may be Christian, with firm beliefs and views on private morality not shared by all their fellows, among whom now may be Muslims, Sikhs or Hindus, who themselves have their own philosophies of life. Some may be snobbish, others not so or resentful of those who are. Some, particularly among the clever, may be ambitious careerists, always ready with the bright question or comment to attract attention at study days or conferences, and not a few prepared to push their own careers at the expense of others. In contrast, many officers are still devoted to their regiment, its welfare and its reputation, willing to take on the more tedious chores of Mess and regimental life with little thought to their own advancement. A wise regiment will seek both types of officer, the clever but also the steadier number. Regiments that have set out to recruit only the clever have found before long that they have created difficulties for themselves. Unpleasant, strong-minded personality clashes can erupt in the best-run and hitherto happiest of Officers' Messes – and quite ferciously further up the chain of command. Luck, too, can play a joker's part: sometimes officers performing well in the right place at the right time can find themselves unexpectedly on a fast track leading to senior rank. Occasionally on active service officers may face moral dilemmas – whether their Whitehall political or senior military commanders are issuing directions or orders that appear doubtfully legal or oppressive, or are not supported with the necessary equipment, or are unnecessarily jeopardising the lives of men under their command, or even whether the campaign as a whole is justifiable.

The apparent wealth suggested by the stars, crowns or scarlet gorgets can nowadays mask daunting personal problems of money – the need to keep up appearances within the style of the regiment and yet have sufficient left over to repay a student loan or to pay for a mortgage on a first-time buy house or flat, to preserve some quality of private or family life, or simply to pay the monthly mess bill.

A few officers, in particular those at middle or senior level, may know that they have a health problem, usually diabetes, arthritis, asthma or a minor heart condition. Some try to conceal this for a while. Although in many cases the Army will try to help with suitable postings, careers and family financial planning may be affected. This author served in the headquarters of a very senior General on a major exercise. The General, always courteous, himself knew what came to be common knowledge not long after, that he was suffering from advanced testicular cancer. Another well-known 20th century military personality laboured all his career under the knowledge that he was impotent. Most difficult of all perhaps are the feelings of gay or lesbian officers. Personal dilemmas and tragedies affect self-confidence.

Perhaps, especially in the present and last centuries, most important for the officer of either sex has been and is the relationship with his or her partner. The problems of overseas posting in the Imperial and British Army of the Rhine eras have been noted earlier. The difficulties now are 'Will the girlfriend like and adjust to the Army?'; after the wedding with officers mounting a church-door guard with swords, 'Will she join in readily with the military social circle and regimental responsibilities?'; 'Will she adjust to eight house moves in fourteen years?'; 'What do we do about the children's schooling (particularly if there are any educational problems)?'; 'What do I do, she says she won't go to Germany yet again?'; 'She has just got this very good job in Farnham and now we are told to leave Aldershot for two years in Cyprus'; 'I have just got back from Bosnia and have been told it's Iraq next week'; 'We have had perhaps 140 days together in the last 365'.[4]

For the young officer first joining his or her regiment there may be moments of self-doubt on first meeting their platoon of thirty soldiers and a very experienced, possibly bushy moustached platoon or troop sergeant. 'Am I up to this?'; 'Are they going to respect me?'; 'I know at Sandhurst they said they would, but will it work for me?'.

For officers of Captain or Major rank there are the questions: 'Why did he get that good posting, what does he have that I don't?' or 'It's just because I'm a woman, I suppose'. Later there may be further questions: 'Where does this get me when it all ends?'; 'If I don't get promotion, where will we be?'. Such questions are only a little easier for the graduate officer unless his or her degree carries a marketable professional qualification such as engineering.

Lastly, most officers experience fear in the ultimate test, combat. For many both before and during a battle there is the question 'Can I conceal this fear and keep the confidence of my men?'.

So behind the glitter of the officers' mess-kit, the Mess silver and the drinks handed round by the Mess staff have laid and do still lie frustrations, perhaps jealousies or bitterness together with all the personal anxieties of the ordinary human being. Some of these feelings are, of course, to be found in many other professions but rarely in such acute forms. The Army officer is under pressure from two sets of compelling loyalties – the vertical one of the chain of command, but also, and vitally important, the horizontal one of pride in a regiment and the respect of regimental peers. It is to the particular credit of the character of British officers that these personal individual human problems are so often subsumed or reconciled in the interests of the service. For them, it is not just a job.

NOTES

1 The issues are considered in 'Fifty years of British Army officership 1960–2010, Part II: Prospective', by Patrick Mileham, in *Defence and Security Analysis*, Vol. 20, No. 2, 179–199, June 2004.

2 The military terminology can confuse the more general reader but does serve to illustrate the needs: 'command, control, communications, computers, intelligence, interoperability . . . digitised battlespace . . . weapon platforms', etc.

3 Mileham, 'Fifty years, II', 188. These fields fall into six 'Working Environments': Field Forces, Ministry of Defence, Alliances, Defence

Procurement/Defence Logistics Organisation, International and Training Establishments.

4 The wife of a Lieutenant-Colonel well described the anguish and marital friction on learning that her husband was to be posted to a war zone, Iraq, for a year. In their almost sixteen years of marriage she had moved house thirteen times, eleven of them arising from Army postings, four of which were abroad. Alice Harrison, 'What if he doesn't come back?', *The Times T2*, 11th June 2004, 4–5. The article drew a spirited reply in the form of a letter to *The Times* dated 17th June 2004 from the wife of a retired senior officer: 'Instead of complaining she should buckle down to the task of supporting her husband morally and emotionally, and make plans now to care for his soldiers' wives who do not enjoy the same benefits and privileges accorded to a senior officer's wife.'

ADDRESS GIVEN BY LIEUTENANT-COLONEL TIM COLLINS TO HIS BATTALION OF THE ROYAL IRISH REGIMENT ON THE DAY BEFORE THE OPENING OF THE 2003 IRAQ WAR

We go to liberate, not to conquer.
We will not fly our flags in their country.
We are entering Iraq to free a people and the only flag which will be flown in that ancient land is their own.
Show respect for them.

There are some who are alive at this moment who will not be alive shortly.
Those who do not wish to go on that journey, we will not send.
As for the others, I expect you to rock their world.
Wipe them out if that is what they choose.
But if you are ferocious in battle remember to be magnanimous in victory.

Iraq is steeped in history.
It is the site of the Garden of Eden, of the Great Flood and the birthplace of Abraham.
Tread lightly there.

You will see things that no man could pay to see
and you will have to go a long way to find a more decent, generous and upright people than the Iraqis.
You will be embarrassed by their hospitality even though they have nothing.

Don't treat them as refugees for they are in their own country.
Their children will be poor, in years to come they will know that the light
of liberation in their lives was brought by you.

If there are casualties of war then remember that when they woke up and
got dressed in the morning they did not plan to die this day.
Allow them dignity in death.
Bury them properly and mark their graves.

It is my foremost intention to bring every single one of you out alive.
But there may be people among us who will not see the end of this
campaign.
We will put them in their sleeping bags and send them back.
There will be no time for sorrow.

The enemy should be in no doubt that we are his nemesis and that we
are bringing about his rightful destruction.
There are many regional commanders who have stains on their souls and
they are stoking the fires of hell for Saddam.
He and his forces will be destroyed by this coalition for what they have
done.
As they die they will know their deeds have brought them to this place.
Show them no pity.

It is a big step to take another human life.
It is not to be done lightly.
I know of men who have taken life needlessly in other conflicts.
I can assure you they live with the mark of Cain upon them.

If someone surrenders to you then remember they have that right in
International law and ensure that one day they go home to their family.
The ones who wish to fight, well, we aim to please.

If you harm the regiment or its history by over-enthusiasm in killing or
in cowardice, know it is your family who will suffer.
You will be shunned unless your conduct is of the highest – for your deeds
will follow you down through history.
We will bring shame on neither our uniform nor our nation.

(On Saddam's chemical and biological weapons)
It is not a question of if, it's a question of when.
We know he has already devolved the decision to lower commanders, and
that means he has already taken the decision himself.
If we survive the first strike we will survive the attack.

As for ourselves, let's bring everyone home and leave Iraq a better place
for us having been there.

Our business now is north.

THE MAINTENANCE OF TRADITION IN THE BRITISH ARMY OF 2004–05

The names of armoured and infantry regiments in service in 2004 are printed in bold type; their predecessors' 1946 names, and earlier numbers in the case of infantry regiments, follow.

The Life Guards: 1st and 2nd Life Guards.

The Blues and Royals (Royal Horse Guards and 1st Dragoons): The Royal Horse Guards (the Blues); The Royal Dragoons (1st Dragoons). These two regiments combined to form, for service, the Household Cavalry Regiment and the Household Cavalry Mounted Regiment.

1st The Queen's Dragoon Guards: 1st King's Dragoon Guards; The Queen's Bays (2nd Dragoon Guards).

The Royal Scots Dragoon Guards (Carabiniers and Greys): 3rd Carabiniers (Prince of Wales's Dragoon Guards); The Royal Scots Greys (2nd Dragoons).

The Royal Dragoon Guards: The 4th/7th Dragoon Guards; The 5th Royal Inniskilling Dragoon Guards.

The Queen's Royal Hussars (The Queen's Own and Royal Irish): 3rd The King's Own Hussars; 4th The Queen's Own Hussars; 7th The Queen's Own Hussars; 8th The King's Royal Irish Hussars.

9th/12th Royal Lancers (Prince of Wales's): 9th Queen's Royal Lancers; 12th Royal Lancers (Prince of Wales's).

The King's Royal Hussars: 10th Royal Hussars; 11th Hussars (Prince of Wales's Own); 14th/20th King's Hussars.

The Light Dragoons: 13th/18th Royal Hussars (Queen Mary's Own); 15th/19th The King's Royal Hussars.

The Queen's Royal Lancers: 16th/5th The Queen's Royal Lancers; 17th/21st Lancers.

The Royal Tank Regiment.

Grenadier Guards.

Coldstream Guards.

Scots Guards.

Irish Guards.

Welsh Guards.

The Royal Scots (The Royal Regiment): 1st Foot.

The Princess of Wales's Royal Regiment (Queen's and Royal Hampshires): The Queen's Royal Regiment (West Surrey) (2nd Foot); The Buffs (Royal East Kent Regiment) (3rd Foot); the East Surrey Regiment (31st and 70th Foot); The Royal Sussex Regiment (35th and 107th Foot); The Royal Hampshire Regiment (37th and 67th Foot); The Queen's Own Royal West Kent Regiment (50th and 97th Foot); The Middlesex Regiment (57th and 77th Foot).

The King's Own Royal Border Regiment: The King's Own Royal Regiment (Lancaster) (4th Foot); The Border Regiment (34th and 55th Foot).

The Royal Regiment of Fusiliers: The Royal Northumberland Fusiliers (5th Foot); The Royal Warwickshire Regiment (6th Foot); The Royal Fusiliers (City of London Regiment) (7th Foot); The Lancashire Fusiliers (20th Foot).

The King's Regiment: The King's Regiment (Liverpool) (8th Foot); The Manchester Regiment (63rd and 96th Foot).

The Royal Anglian Regiment: The Royal Norfolk Regiment (9th Foot); The Royal Lincolnshire Regiment (10th Foot); The Suffolk Regiment (12th Foot); The Bedfordshire and Hertfordshire Regiment (16th Foot); The Royal Leicestershire Regiment (17th Foot); The Essex Regiment (44th and 56th Foot); The Northamptonshire Regiment (48th and 58th Foot).

The Devonshire and Dorset Regiment: The Devonshire Regiment (11th Foot); The Dorset Regiment (39th and 54th Foot).

The Light Infantry: The Somerset Light Infantry (Prince Albert's) (13th Foot); The Duke of Cornwall's Light Infantry (32nd Foot); The King's Own Yorkshire Light Infantry (51st and 105th Foot); The King's Shropshire Light Infantry (53rd and 85th Foot); The Durham Light Infantry (68th and 106th Foot).

The Prince of Wales's Own Regiment of Yorkshire: The West Yorkshire Regiment (The Prince of Wales's Own) (14th Foot); The East Yorkshire Regiment (The Duke of York's Own) (15th Foot).

The Green Howards (Alexandra, Princess of Wales's Own) Yorkshire Regiment: 19th Foot.

The Royal Highland Fusiliers (Princess Margaret's Own) Glasgow and Ayrshire Regiment: The Royal Scots Fusiliers (21st Foot); The Highland Light Infantry (71st and 74th Foot).

The Cheshire Regiment: 22nd Foot.

The Royal Welch Fusiliers: 23rd Foot.

The Royal Regiment of Wales: The South Wales Borderers (24th Foot); The Welch Regiment (41st and 69th Foot).

The King's Own Scottish Borderers: 25th Foot.

The Royal Irish Regiment (27th, Inniskilling, 83rd, 87th and UDR): The Royal Inniskilling Fusiliers (27th and 108th Foot); The Royal Ulster Rifles (83rd and 86th Foot); The Royal Irish Fusiliers (87th and 89th Foot).

The Royal Gloucestershire, Berkshire and Wiltshire Regiment: The Gloucestershire Regiment (28th and 61st Foot); The Royal Berkshire Regiment (Princess Charlotte of Wales's) (49th and 63rd Foot); The Wiltshire Regiment (Duke of Edinburgh's) (62nd and 99th Foot).

The Worcestershire and Sherwood Foresters Regiment (29th and 45th Foot): The Worcestershire Regiment (29th and 36th Foot); The Sherwood Foresters (Nottinghamshire and Derbyshire Regiment) (45th and 95th Foot).

The Queen's Lancashire Regiment: The East Lancashire Regiment (30th and 59th Foot); The South Lancashire Regiment (Prince of Wales's Volunteers) (40th and 82nd Foot); The Loyal Regiment (North Lancashire) (47th and 81st Foot).

The Duke of Wellington's Regiment: (33rd and 76th Foot).

The Staffordshire Regiment (the Prince of Wales's): The South Staffordshire Regiment (38th and 80th Foot); The North Staffordshire Regiment (The Prince of Wales's) (64th and 98th Foot).

The Black Watch, The Royal Highland Regiment: 42nd and 73rd Foot.

The Royal Green Jackets: The Oxfordshire and Buckinghamshire Light Infantry (43rd and 52nd Foot); The King's Royal Rifle Corps (60th Foot); The Rifle Brigade (95th Foot).

The Highlanders (Seaforth, Cameron and Gordon): The Seaforth Highlanders (Ross-shire Buffs, The Duke of Albany's) (72nd and 78th Foot); The Queen's Own Cameron Highlanders (79th Foot); The Gordon Highlanders (75th and 92nd Foot).
The Argyll and Sutherland Highlanders (Princess Louise's): 91st and 93rd Foot.
The Parachute Regiment.
The Royal Gurkha Rifles: The 2nd King Edward VII's Own Gurkha Rifles (The Sirmoor Rifles); The 6th Gurkha Rifles; The 7th Gurkha Rifles; The 10th Princess Mary's Own Gurkha Rifles. All these regiments were, in 1946, on the Indian Army establishment.

In 1922 five Irish regiments were disbanded: The Royal Irish Regiment (18th Foot); The Connaught Rangers (88th and 94th Foot); The Prince of Wales's Leinster Regiment (Royal Canadians) (100th and 109th Foot); The Royal Munster Fusiliers (101st and 104th Foot); and The Royal Dublin Fusiliers (102nd and 103rd Foot). In 1968 the Cameronians (Scottish Rifles) (26th and 90th Foot) and the York and Lancaster Regiment (65th and 84th Foot) were also disbanded.

Within the **Royal Regiment of Artillery** three regiments and the King's Troop, for traditional reasons wearing a different cap-badge, are styled Royal Horse Artillery. In the majority of regiments an historical tradition is maintained by the names of individual batteries. In the different Corps links with forebears are also perpetuated, notably the **Royal Engineers** with the Royal Artificers and the Royal Sappers and Miners, the **Royal Logistic Corps** with the Royal Waggon Train and the Land Transport Corps, the **Royal Army Medical Corps** with the Medical Staff Corps, and the **Intelligence Corps** with the Field Intelligence Department. Similar traditions are maintained in Territorial Army units.

RESTRUCTURING

In December 2004 plans to restructure the infantry, over a four-year period, were announced. The Guards regiments, the Parachute Regiment, the Royal Irish Regiment and the Royal Gurkha Rifles were exempted from the plans. The new format for the line infantry of regiments of five or six battalions is intended to produce greater flexibility and stability for officers and men while preserving a measure of tradition. The format maintains the existing Division groupings for basic training and administration. Within these Divisions battalions are being formed into large regiments as follows:

Scottish Division

The Royal Scottish Borderers, 1st Battalion, The Royal Regiment of Scotland.
The Royal Highland Fusiliers, 2nd Battalion, The Royal Regiment of Scotland.
The Black Watch, 3rd Battalion, The Royal Regiment of Scotland.
The Highlanders, 4th Battalion The Royal Regiment of Scotland.
The Argyll and Sutherland Highlanders, 5th Battalion, The Royal Regiment of Scotland.

Queen's Division

The existing three regiments, each of two battalions, the Princess of Wales' Royal Regiment, the Royal Regiment of Fusiliers and the Royal Anglian Regiment remain unchanged.

King's Division

A new regiment called the Duke of Lancaster's Regiment and formed from the King's Regiment, the King's Own Royal Border Regiment and the Queen's Lancashire Regiment; and a new Yorkshire Regiment, formed from the Prince of Wales's Own Regiment of Yorkshire, the Green Howards and the Duke of Wellington's Regiment.

Prince of Wales Division

A three-battalion Mercian Regiment to be formed from the Cheshire Regiment, the Worcestershire and Sherwood Foresters Regiment and the Staffordshire Regiment; and a two-battalion Royal Welsh Regiment formed from the Royal Welch Fusiliers and the Royal Regiment of Wales.

Light Division

A new five-battalion regiment, called the Rifles; the 1st Battalion from the Devonshire and Dorset Regiment and the Royal Gloucestershire, Berkshire and Wiltshire Regiment; the 2nd and 3rd Battalions from the Light Infantry, and the 3rd and 4th Battalions from the Royal Green Jackets.

The Scottish battalions have been permitted to retain traditional names before that of the new large regiment. Regiments will have a common cap badge and all ranks may be cross-posted to different battalions to meet particular needs or the career development of individuals.

Each unit will be trained for a specific role, thereby avoiding the constant movement and retraining of battalions and providing individuals with less frequent moves.

It may, in some cases, take time before the new large regiments provide individual members with the personal motivation and sense of identity so important for morale, efficiency and recruiting.

INCOME, PAY AND EXPENDITURE

Some notes on pay, expenses, cost of living and comparability with other occupations or professions are necessary. They have, of course, to be set against the facts that until the mid-20th century most, though by no means all, officers had private sources of income in property or business, that until the 19th century corrupt practices enabled many officers to supplement their pay in a variety of ways, including investment of the profits of a sale of their last appointment, and that from the 18th century onwards a variety of official allowances for certain skills, for service overseas and, subject to age, for marriage and the education of children were payable.

Some rates of pay and costs of the purchase of first and later commissions have been noted in the chronological chapters. To these outgoings must be added others difficult to assess: until the mid-19th century residence charges, the cost and upkeep of expensive uniforms, the payment for servants, the costs of horses and sports equipment, the social lifestyle in vogue in particular regiments which could extend to London club memberships, expensive civilian clothes, matters of personal appearance such as wigs, high-quality wines and hospitality. Besides these 'regimental' outgoings there might be the costs of family life. Notes can only throw shafts of light on particular areas; no overall balance sheets are possible.

The value of the pound sterling has of course declined over the centuries. Readers may need to be reminded that until the introduction of decimal coinage, twelve pennies (d) equalled one shilling (s), and twenty shillings equalled one pound.

As already noted, in the reign of Charles II an Ensign was paid £54 per annum, a Lieutenant £73, a Captain £146, a Major if commanding a company £237 and a Lieutenant-Colonel if commanding a company £273; these rates were increased a little towards the end of Charles II's reign. They were not always actually paid. In comparison, large landed estates could bring their owners huge profits, and even smaller estates could provide more comfortable lifestyles. The average income of the 600 knights has been estimated at £650, of the 3,000 esquires at £450, and of the 12,000 gentlemen at £280. A solicitor on first appointment might start at £10 per annum, rising to £70, but in later life the law could bring a successful practitioner an income of several thousand pounds. A vicar's income (with a free house) might be £50 per annum, a curate's £20, a schoolmaster's £30. The Provost of Eton earned £75 with free housing and food. A boy could be given primary day school education for as little as £2 per year; boarding Public Schools such as Winchester or Westminster varied between £20 and £40 per year. On more mundane but essential items a horse could cost £30 to £70, a beagle £30.

In the 18th century medium-sized estates generally brought in an income of £2,000–£4,000, smaller ones £200–£1,000. Bishops of smaller dioceses received £300 per year, but bishops of large dioceses owning land as much as £3,000. A four-bedroomed house might cost £200–£300, a cottage as little as £40. Rent in a fashionable London town house could be as much as £300 per year. Visits to a doctor could cost a guinea (£1 1s 0d), a smart suit £15, a wig £5.

Officers' pay remained unchanged until 1797 and by the 1830s it had risen only slowly, a Lieutenant now receiving £118 per annum, almost all of which for several years would have had to be spent on uniform and horses on first commissioning. The full uniform cost for a Cavalry Cornet in a very expensive regiment was well over £300. A Captain was now paid £211, a Major £270–£292 and a Lieutenant-Colonel £320–£365; to these rates could be added interest earned from the profits of the sale of their previous commission. The lowly Cornet would, however, find that from his 5s 3d per day (£95 per annum) he would have to spend 2s 6d or more for his food. These rates remained unchanged until the end of the century. In addition, an officer was still expected to own his own horse, costing at least £100; in the cavalry officers might have two horses, and polo ponies as well. A polo saddle cost £6 and a pig-stick lance 12s 6d.

A successful barrister would be earning £5,000 per annum, a doctor £1,000–£2,000, a school headmaster £500–£1,000. The minimum income acceptable for the status of a gentleman was considered to be £300–£400, from which rent, national and local taxes, payment for a servant and food had to be paid. The first motor-cars at the end of the century cost £100–£200.

By the Edwardian decade, from an income of £700 a business or professional man might have to pay out £100 in rent and taxes, £104 for food for himself and his family, £42 for two maids, £20 for coal and light, £25 for insurance, £26 for laundry and £100–£150 per child for school fees.

In 1914, on new rates fixed at the end of the 19th century, a newly commissioned Second Lieutenant was paid in the region of £182 per annum, a Lieutenant £200 and a Captain £273. Basic food commodities continued to be supplied to Officers' Messes, but almost all Messes improved the fare supplied, some expensively, others less so, and charged officers for the extra messing. The pay rates were slightly reduced in the 1920s but increased in the late 1930s, again only marginally. From these rates extra-duty pay for an officer's servant and perhaps also for a groom had to be deducted, as well as the monthly Mess bill.

For comparability, a Civil Service Assistant Principal, almost always a graduate fresh from university, in the 1930s would be starting on an incremental scale at £275. Doctors earned rather more as did most business executives, the clergy significantly less.

Income tax by 1939 had risen to a rate of 5s 9d in the pound, in effect costing a single person on £300 per year £12 2s 6d; at £500 a single person would be paying £56 12s 6d and a man married with two children £8 6s 6d; at £800 a single person would be paying £122 12s 6d, the married man with two children £67 12s 6d.

Typical life insurance premiums – for a payment of £100 plus profits on death – were £1 6s 4d for a man aged 20, £2 6s 8d for a man aged 30, £3 3s 8d for a man aged 40, and £3 15s 8d for a man aged 45.

Medical treatment for officers, soldiers and their families was of course provided by the RAMC. If an officer chose to go to a civilian general practitioner the doctor's fees would be generally based on the rental value of the patient's property. Doctors charged 5s–15s for a day visit, double at night, plus the cost of travel. Consultants charged as much as three guineas (£3 3s 0d) for a consultation.

Preparatory School fees averaged £8 per term for a day boy, with lunch £12 and with full board £24. Public School fees varied: Eton charged £245 per year, Wellington £125–£175 and King's School, Bruton £94–£114.

A new small car could cost as little as £350, family cars £500–£700. House prices of course varied, but a pleasant five- or six-bedroom house outside London could be bought for less than £3,500, with smaller or less attractive houses even less.

London Clubs such as Whites or the Guards charged an entry fee of £15 and an annual subscription of £20; some had greatly reduced charges for country members. Day-to-day costs included all newspapers at 1d per day except *The Times* at 2d. Petrol costs varied but averaged 1s 6d per gallon. A pint of beer or a tot of gin or whisky cost 6d or 7d.

Prices steadily rose in the Second World War years and the 1950s, and small adjustments were made to rates of pay, and rather later, pensions. In the 1960s, as noted in Chapter 14, pay rates and pensions were consolidated on the basis of comparability with Civil Service grades plus an addition to recognise the risks of the profession and the frequent house moves. At the same time charges were introduced for residence in barracks and married quarters, and also food except when on operations or field exercises. Various allowances continued to be payable – boarding school allowances for children, overseas allowances for postings outside the United Kingdom, separation allowances, uniform allowances on first commissioning with a small annual upkeep allowance, and a number of allowances reflecting special qualifications. Fewer officers, in most regiments only the Commanding Officer, were allowed a batman, though for a while in some units and training schools several officers might share the services of a servant, who of course had to be paid.

Following consolidation, by 1974 a Second Lieutenant's pay was £6,000, a Captain's pay £9,700 and that of a Major £13,000. In the 1970s to the 1990s periodic reviews of pay rates were made, giving increases that largely but not entirely reflected increases in the cost of living and overall amounting to some reduction in real income. By the start of the 21st century average starting rates of pay had risen to £18,125 for a Second Lieutenant, £21,970 for a Lieutenant, £27,783 for a Captain, £34,967 for a Major, and £49,369 for a Lieutenant-Colonel. Detail would fill a volume but the 1930s costs noted earlier of insurance, school fees, motor cars, social facilities and especially house purchase had all inflated in much greater proportion by 2000, a situation that of course applies to all other professions.

Sources: John Burnett, *A History of the Cost of Living* (Harmondsworth, Penguin, 1969); regimental histories; *Whitaker's Almanack 1939*; the author's septuagenarian memory.

OFFICERS TRAINING CORPS

Officers Training Corps, at school and at university level, have provided a substantial number of Regular officers for the Army, and an even larger number for the Territorial Army and the two World War armies. Some school Corps can boast a very proud record; the Eton College Corps, for example, has produced thirty-six Victoria Cross and two George Cross winners, including naval and air force recipients.

The earliest school corps were part of the late 1850s Rifle Volunteer movement. The first to form was at Rossall School in 1860 followed in the same year by Eton, with Felsted, Harrow, Marlborough, Rugby, Cheltenham and Winchester a few months later, and over subsequent years many more. One attraction for boys was shooting, a trophy presented by Lord Ashburton in 1861 being hotly contested and still contested to this day. In the early years the school corps had an anomalous unrecognised status, and it was not until 1868 that corps could become affiliated to the local Rifle Volunteers. Eton, probably leading the field, had a corps of over 300 boys organised into eight companies, part of the 1st Buckinghamshire Rifle Volunteers. Entry was limited to boys in the fifth and sixth forms, parades were held on Friday afternoons, extra musketry instruction was available on Mondays, there was an annual Field Day, some masters served as officers and an annual subscription of 10s 6d had to be paid. At first weaponry was limited to muzzle-loading rifles; in 1885 the Martin Henry rifle was issued, to be replaced in 1890 with the Lee Metford, and later by the Lee Enfield. The first Army Sergeant to be posted to the Eton Corps arrived in 1871; attending the school chapel, he was mistaken for a General by the Provost. The College soon possessed an Orderly Room and an Armoury. In 1908 the corps became the Eton College Officer Training Corps, part of a national OTC.

Following the Second South African War and the perceived need for more officers in the event of a major war, the Officers Training Corps was formally established in 1908 with a senior division for universities and a junior division for schools. At schools, in order to provide the necessary two years' service before a boy could attempt the Certificate A, a certificate of very basic military training, the entry age was lowered to fourteen. Many more schools established their own corps. By 1911 there were 153 schools with OTC contingents of varying sizes; the number rose to 183 by 1939, offering training in weaponry, map-reading and minor tactics. The larger schools raised bugle and drum bands. Recently retired Army Sergeants were employed by schools, who received a War Office grant for training. Major public school products went to the more elite regiments, boys from the minor schools to the less fashionable.

During the Second World War the title of all school corps was changed from OTC to Junior Training Corps; boys over seventeen served in local Home Guard units. After the war, school corps, now reduced in total numbers, were restyled Combined Cadet Force, many incorporating naval and air contingents. The military training became better structured with, in many corps, a programme providing for an initial first term's work on drill and weapon training with a 36-hour field exercise all leading to an Army Proficiency Certificate, the examiners being Regular officers and NCOs. Later training included orienteering, signals, assault courses and a variety of specialist courses including parachuting. There was usually a week-long corps camp in the summer. Schoolmasters continued to provide corps officers, special training courses for them being provided at the Army Cadet Training Centre at Frimley. Girls in mixed and some girls-only schools became eligible to join, and corps were established in several single-sex girls' schools. From 1957 a minimum age of 15 years and ten months became required.

Attendance and membership have in theory always been voluntary. Peer-group pressure generally ensured a very high percentage at least until 1945, but since then there have been fluctuations, and unenthusiastic boys or girls in many schools have had alternative social service or other options from which to choose. Nevertheless, the school corps remains an important feature of life in many Public Schools, other private sector schools and surviving Grammar Schools. University and other tertiary education corps followed a slightly different pattern, at the outset individual students joining local Volunteers, Oxford and Cambridge being the first. Before long universities were producing companies for Volunteer units. In Scotland, where students were generally poorer, only a few individual students could afford to join the expensively uniformed local units, with one or two St Andrews students, for example, joining the Fife Mounted Riflemen. Later in 1883 two professors raised an undergraduate battery with the assistance of a retired RHA sergeant and a small grant from the university. The Cambridge University contingent to its local Volunteer Corps in the Second South Africa War was sufficiently large to be awarded its own Battle Honour, the only University Training Corps to possess one.

With the formal formation of the Officers Training Corps university contingents expanded. Officers were recently retired Regulars or Territorial Force, the larger corps commanded by a Lieutenant-Colonel, the smaller by a Major, assisted by a serving Regular officer as adjutant. Corps members were expected to pass Certificate A and later a Certificate B, which equated with the Territorial Force Lieutenant to Captain promotion examination. A basic uniform was now issued, and training regularised, extending in Scotland in 1913 to a 'brigade camp' with contingents from Edinburgh, Glasgow and Durham, and Lee Enfield rifles were provided for training. The formal aim of the OTC was to train officers for the Special Reserve and the TF, but from the start it was hoped a few members might opt for Regular commissions. Past and present university OTC members flocked to serve in the Territorial and New Armies of the First World War and universities encouraged, in some cases coerced, undergraduates to join their corps. By 1918 there were twenty-one contingents, to increase only a little to twenty-two by 1939.

In the inter-war years standards of training rose, untrained Territorial Army officers being sent on occasions to university OTCs to prepare for a much tougher Certificate B. Inspections were testing and cadets who were inefficient were fined. Some corps opened specialist sub-units, in particular medical. In September 1939, as in 1914, members of OTCs came forward to serve, and were commissioned, but later in the year politics intervened, the 'O' was dropped from the title of the corps, and even men with Certificate B were ordered to serve in the ranks, all in the interests of 'democratisation'. After Dunkirk more sensible decisions provided for Certificate B holders to proceed straight to OCTUs and Certificate A holders to an infantry training unit for two months' preparation; corps were also again renamed Senior Training Corps. In 1941 and until 1944 service in the corps was made obligatory for all male undergraduates. Expulsion from a corps for a disciplinary offence meant expulsion from the university. Corps became part of the local Home Guard units and several specialist sub-units were formed in different corps.

In 1947–48 eighteen Senior Training Corps were reconstituted as part of the Territorial Army, members receiving pay, bounty and uniform with cadres of Regular officers and NCOs. The main aim was provision of basic training to deferred undergraduates, so enabling them to be commissioned more quickly in National Service, after passing a WOSB proceeding straight to Mons or Eaton Hall. Training standards were set and inspections were testing. Women's sub-units were formed in most UTCs. In 1955, to attract more undergraduates, the title of University OTC was restored and cadets who passed WOSB and Certificate B became eligible for Territorial Army commissions.

The ending of National Service led to a fall in numbers in most corps, and reductions in permitted establishments. Later in the 1960s the government even seriously considered disbandment. However, the perceived need for the Armed Forces to keep a presence on university campuses for general goodwill, and in particular recruiting possible Regular and TA officers, ensured survival. The existing University OTCs' catchment areas were extended to cover students at the new universities created from the 1960s to the 1990s, and numbers increased with the greater numbers entering all universities, in particular those men and women on the variety of university cadetships and bursaries for Regular officers developed in the 1970s and 1980s. The recipients were expected to serve in, and be under the watchful eye of, University OTCs. At the turn of the century there were nineteen University OTCs, thirteen in England, four in Scotland and one each in Wales and Northern Ireland.

INDEX